Teaching Primary Art

Teaching Primary Art

Jean Edwards

PEARSON

Harlow, England • London • New York • Boston • San Francisco • Toronto • Sydney
Auckland • Singapore • Hong Kong • Tokyo • Seoul • Taipei • New Delhi
Cape Town • São Paulo • Mexico City • Madrid • Amsterdam • Munich • Paris • Milan

PEARSON EDUCATION LIMITED
Edinburgh Gate
Harlow CM20 2JE
United Kingdom
Tel: +44 (0)1279 623623
Web: www.pearson.com/uk

First published 2013 (print and electronic)

ISBN: 978-1-4058-9941-3 (print)
　　　978-1-4058-9943-7 (pdf)
　　　978-0-273-78012-0 (eText)

British Library Cataloguing-in-Publication Data
A catalogue record for the print edition is available from the British Library

Library of Congress Cataloging-in-Publication Data
Edwards, Jean, 1963–
　　Teaching primary art / Jean Edwards. – 1st [edition].
　　　　pages cm
　　ISBN 978-1-4058-9941-3 (pbk.)
　　1.　Art-Study and teaching (Elementary)–Great Britain–Textbooks.　I.　Title.
　　LB1591.5.G7E39 2013
　　372.5'20941–dc23
　　　　　　　　　　　　　　　　　　　　　　　　　2012043805

10 9 8 7 6 5 4 3 2 1
16 15 14 13 12

Print edition typeset in 9.5/12.5 pt ITC Giovanni Std by 71
Print edition printed and bound in England by Ashford Colour Press

NOTE THAT ANY PAGE CROSS REFERENCES REFER TO THE PRINT EDITION

To the many children, teachers and artists I have been inspired by and learnt from over the years

Contents

Companion Website

For open-access **student resources** specifically written to complement this textbook and support your learning, please visit **www.pearsoned.co.uk/edwards**

Preface

This is a book to support those engaged in learning to teach art or support learning art in primary schools. It is a basic practical handbook to support students on undergraduate and postgraduate teacher training courses. It will also be useful for teaching assistants who support individuals and groups within art lessons and Higher Level Teaching Assistants (HLTAs) who cover art lessons for teachers' preparation, planning and assessment (PPA) time. Newly qualified teachers just starting out on teaching art to their class and those returning to teaching will also find it helpful.

I believe that it is vital that everyone who is involved in learning and teaching in art is focused on inspiring children and giving them opportunities to look at and experience a variety of art as well as make their own art that is individual and personal to them. In my own experience as a class teacher, art co-ordinator and more recently as a university lecturer I have found that children and adults can gain enormous pleasure, excitement and insight from being immersed in art. As a teacher your own confident and enthusiastic approach will motivate children and allow them to have a positive experience of art that will stay with them into adulthood.

The book is organised in two sections. The first section explores areas that underpin teaching and learning of art including: why we teach art; the art curriculum; planning and assessment; the work of artists; and teaching and support strategies. The second section explores the practical aspects of art: drawing, painting, making prints, making collage, working in three dimensions and making decorating textiles. Connections are made to the use of digital media in finding out about and making art and links are made to learning in other subjects.

I hope that in reading and using this book you will be equipped to support and teach art with your pupils with greater confidence and enthusiasm. You can then go on to devise your own art experiences, activities and events returning this book as a manual to support your subject knowledge and going beyond it to the many other useful texts that support more experienced and confident teachers.

How to use this book

The features and layout of this book are designed to guide you towards developing your subject knowledge and approach to learning and teaching in the classroom. Some of them ask you to observe, make or research in order to connect your own learning to experience in school. Others support you by indicating resources and reading that will help you consolidate and develop your approach. You should consider this book to be a reference text or manual that you can return to regularly as you plan and teach art in the primary classroom.

Practical tasks

The practical tasks are designed to support your own investigation and reflection. For students these tasks can be undertaken on placement in school. For those working in schools the tasks can be related directly to finding out more about policy and practice in order to develop your understanding of art in your workplace. The charts and pro forma used are provided electronically on the supporting website so that they can be printed out and annotated.

Case studies

The case studies are stories from practice that provide examples to illustrate the points discussed in the text. Some of them relate to student study and others to classroom experience. These case studies aim to help you build your understanding of subject knowledge and practical art in school. They can guide you to look for more examples when you are on placement or exploring art around your school.

Find out more

The 'find out more' suggestions point you in the direction of further resources to support your own subject knowledge or your teaching in the classroom. The links are also available on the website for ease of use.

Connect and extend

The 'connect and extend' suggestions encourage you to use academic literature to investigate further. These are especially useful for students who may be working on assignments at university. They indicate reports, research and academic journal articles of interest and that underpin subject knowledge and practice in art education.

Links to material on the website

Throughout the book there are links to material available on the associated website. These include the practical task materials; links to resources such as images and websites and examples to support your teaching.

Next steps

At the end of each chapter there are some suggested next steps to help you go further with your learning as your experience develops.

Guided tour

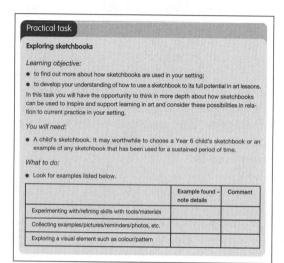

Practical tasks in each chapter are designed to support your own investigation and reflection. The charts and pro forma used are provided electronically on the supporting website so that they can be printed out and annotated.

Case studies are stories from practice that provide examples to illustrate the points discussed in the text. These case studies aim to help you build your understanding of subject knowledge and practical art in school, as well as to help spark your own.

Case Study

A teaching assistant creates a 'looking for pattern' trail for her R Year children to explore in order to develop their observation skills and ability to recognise patterns in their environment. She uses the digital camera to take close-up photos of ten patterns that she finds around the inside and outside areas. These include the pattern on a piece of fabric, bricks on a wall, a pattern carved into a wooden bench, and some markings on a flower. She has deliberately included patterns from nature and the built environment. Each pattern is printed out, strengthened by sticking it onto a 10 cm square card and laminated. She takes the children in groups of five on a walk around the setting to look for the patterns – each child holds two cards. She has planned out a route and places to stop and look as well as some clues if they are required. As the patterns are found each is talked about and labelled with a note of where they were.

Later, children will be asked to find and photograph a pattern that they have found to add to the collection. They will use the computer to make a label saying what the pattern is and where they found it.

Find out more

Explore online to find the following resources and save them to your favourites:

- Google Art Project – images of art from many galleries and museums and galleries around the world.
- BBC Your paintings – a searchable database of paintings available to see in the UK and resources to use in education
  LINK ON WEBSITE
- National Art and Craft Directory – an illustrated directory of artists and makers working now that can be searched by name, media and various other terms
- Engage – The national association for gallery art and education professionals, promoting access to and understanding of the visual arts through gallery education.
  LINK ON WEBSITE

These are all useful website for exploring works of art to use in the classroom and finding places to visit.

Find out more suggestions point you in the direction of further resources to support your own subject knowledge or your teaching in the classroom. The links are also available on the website for ease of use.

Connect and extend suggestions encourage you to use academic literature to investigate further. These are especially useful if you are working on an assignment at university. They indicate reports, research and academic journal articles of interest that underpin subject knowledge and practice in art education.

Connect and extend

Read the section entitled 'Focusing on key subject skills: drawing' (pp. 51–6) in the OFSTED (2012) report 'Making a mark: art, craft and design education'.

Think about how in the primary years we can build on the positive start that children experience in their early years and consider your role in giving the children you teach a positive experience of drawing that will support their enthusiasm and learning in this important area of art education.

Link

LINK
The photocopier can also be a useful tool in teaching: making copies of children's drawings so several next steps can be tried or resizing them to make them larger so additional detail can be added to help preserve an original whilst developing and experimenting.
You can also use digital photography to make supporting resources for teaching. This could include prompts and exemplifications to remind children of teaching points as well

Throughout the book there are **links** to material available on the associated website. These include the practical task materials, links to resources such as images and websites, and examples to support your teaching.

At the end of each chapter there are some suggested **next steps** to help you go further with your learning as your experience develops.

Next steps

- Look at the long term plan to identify the techniques and processes that will be taught in the year you are working. Have you used these before? If not, have a go at them yourself so you can anticipate how to teach/support.
- Check that medium term plans and resources are available in time for you teach/support effectively.
- Look for plans available from galleries and organisations that could help to develop and enliven your planning.

Further reading and **Web resources** are included at the end of each chapter directing you to specific references and links, directly related to material in that chapter.

Further reading

Cox, M., Cooke, G. and Friffin, D. (2009) 'Teaching children to draw in the infants school'. In Herne, S., Cox, S. and Watts, R. (eds) *Readings in Primary Art Education*. London: Intellect Books, pp. 153–68.

Fenwick, L. (2007) 'Investigating pattern'. *STart*, Vol. 24, pp. 24–27.

Fenwick, L. (2007) 'Drawing development'. *STart*, Vol. 25, pp. 22–25.

Hope, G. (2008) *Thinking and Learning through Drawing*. London: Sage.

Hughes, S. (2002) *A Life Drawing: Recollections of an Illustrator*. London: Random House.

Lee, G. (2009) 'Illustration: more than just a complement to text'. *STart*, 33. pp. 10–11.

Turk, K. (2007) 'Livening up life drawing'. *STart*, Vol. 25, pp. 12–14.

Watts, R. (2010) 'Responding to children's drawing'. *Education 3-13*, Vol. 38 No. 2, pp. 137–53.

Web resources

Examples of drawing in artists' sketchbooks: *http://www.accessart.org.uk/sketchbook/*

Henry Moore shelter drawings: *http://www.bbc.co.uk/learningzone/clips/henry-moore-s-underground-shelter-drawings-from-world-war-ii/11626.html*

Van Gogh's drawings: *http://www.vggallery.com/drawings/main_az.htm*

Shirley Hughes: *http://www.art-of-illustration.co.uk/shirleyhughes/*

Raymond Briggs: *http://www.guardian.co.uk/books/audioslideshow/2010/sep/21/raymond-briggs*

Simon's Cat – line drawn animations: *http://www.simonscat.com/*

British Museum: *http://www.britishmuseum.org/explore/highlights/highlights_search_results.aspx?searchText=drawings*

Publisher's Acknowledgements

Edwards Jean - Teaching Primary Art - 1st Ed.

We are grateful to the following for permission to reproduce copyright material:

Figures

Figure 6.2 supplied by Pauline Wood

Tables

Table in Chapter 1 from Primary-age children's attitudes to art, art making and art education, *The International Journal of Education Through Art*, (Gibson, R. 2008), © Intellect Ltd.

Cartoons

Speech bubble cartoons supplied by David Barrow and the text supplied by the author. Chapter 10 cartoon of children looking at sculpture supplied by David Barrow

In some instances we have been unable to trace the owners of copyright material, and we would appreciate any information that would enable us to do so.

Chapter 1

An introduction to art in the primary school

Introduction

Art makes a unique contribution to our lives and it is vital that when we are preparing to work in schools we are ready to give children the positive and inspiring learning opportunities they need to engage and enthuse them. This chapter will encourage you to think more deeply about your own experience of art and the particular contribution of art to learning. In this chapter the following areas will be explored:

● Your experience of art so far

● What is art in school?

● Why do we teach art in school?

● The role of adults

As someone planning to or already working in a primary school you must be prepared to teach all the subjects that are part of the curriculum. Whilst it is a challenge to maintain a genuine personal interest in all of these subjects it is important that you have the appropriate subject knowledge to support your planning and teaching, as well as the understanding of teaching strategies to support learning in art. You will probably find that your enthusiasm for teaching and seeing children learn will inspire you to enjoy and value some of the subjects you found less exciting as a child yourself. Often when we begin to explore a subject from the perspective of teaching it to a class of children we perceive it differently and understand more fully its potential for learning.

Your experience of art so far

Your own feelings and approach to art in education will be informed by the experiences you have had as a pupil and as an adult. It is important for you to reflect on these, considering their implications, so that you can support and teach children effectively. As your role in school develops in relation to teaching across the curriculum and teaching specific subjects your subject knowledge and pedagogical understanding will support you as a teacher of art. You will develop your understanding of the particular significance of the role of the adult in relation to the art curriculum and the teaching of art.

Your education

Your own art education will vary depending on when and where you went to school and how far you pursued art as a subject in school and beyond. It is important that you reflect on it so that you understand how it relates to your current understanding.

Practical task

Your own art education

Learning objective:

- to explore the impact your own art education has had on you.

You will need:

- the below pro forma (available online).

What to do:

- consider the questions listed below.
- make some notes about each one.

Questions	Your thoughts
Your education	
As a child did you like art?	
Did you make art or craft outside school?	
What was your art education at primary school like?	
What was your art education at secondary school like?	
Did you go on to gain any qualifications in art at secondary school and beyond?	

Guidance notes

- *Your interest in art at home:* You may have enjoyed art, making things and drawing at home regardless of what was happening in art lessons at school. This may have been related to your family's attitudes and interests and your own personal enthusiasm and motivation. Children often engage in art activities at home entirely without relating it to what they are learning at school – this is something to consider in relation to the children you teach.

- *Your primary education:* Your experience of art in the primary years may have influenced your subsequent interest and enthusiasm for art. It may be that in some areas of art you feel that your own learning has progressed little beyond this stage and perhaps the teaching you experienced left you at the early stages with no clear idea how to develop. This may have led you to put your enthusiasm and commitment into other areas of learning in the curriculum until now, when as part of your work in school you are supporting or leading learning in art lessons. If your own experience at primary school was positive and inspiring you will understand how important it is to ensure that the children you work with also have this experience. If your own experience in primary school was indifferent or negative your aspiration will be to make sure that you do not replicate this for the children whose education you are now responsible for.

- *Your secondary education:* At the secondary stage you might have been given opportunities to use unfamiliar media and use new techniques – I remember, from my own art education, learning photography and screen-printing. You will have been taught by specialists in the subject and have had the opportunity to work on longer and more personal projects to develop your own art. Your experience of art beyond primary school will perhaps be the point at which you gave up study of art in school. If this is the case it will be vital that you develop your understanding and knowledge of art with a focus on how to teach and support of children primary age.

- *Your qualifications:* If you went further with your education in art you may have worked on GCSE, A level, NVQ or even a degree in art or an art related subject. If this is the case your experience of further study will be a valuable resource to draw upon in your role as a student and subsequently teacher or as a teaching assistant in a primary school. It may later lead you into becoming art co-ordinator and supporting other staff.

In the task above you began to consider your own education and its implications for your role as a student, teacher or teaching assistant. In addition to this you may have had experience since leaving education that contributes to your understanding and view of art. Perhaps you now participate in making in areas that could be considered art, design or craft if a media or process has caught your attention and interest since leaving formal education. It could be an activity that you pursue as a break from studying or work, or that has developed from your life. If you are a parent, playing with your own children and supporting them in their own education may have led you to an interest in art and craft.

Your current awareness of art

Although your own experience prior to training to become or being employed as a teacher is significant, you are nevertheless likely to be planning and teaching art in the primary school regardless of it. A minority of schools may have a specialist teacher for art; some schools may have informal arrangements between staff to share out the teaching of some subjects in order to use strengths and interests; but in most schools you must be prepared to teach art to your class.

As an adult you might not be involved in art or craft at all, or perhaps you have a personal interest in it. Perhaps you belong to a group or class in your chosen art or craft activity or have attended a class or workshop as one off either yourself or alongside your own children. Increasingly, making things and using recyclable materials is a popular interest and can lead into art-related activity. Any enthusiasm that you have in art or art-related areas will be something you can draw on to support children's learning in your role in schools. Many galleries, museums and country parks put on workshops and classes that you can join in order to broaden your knowledge and experience, and these are often free or quite inexpensive.

Another aspect of our experience of art is that of looking at the work of artists, craftspeople and designers. This also important in relation to learning and teaching in the primary art curriculum.

Practical task

Viewing art

Learning objective:

● to explore your awareness of art and artists as a viewer.

You will need:

● the pro forma below.

What to do:

Annotate the headings with the names of artists, craftspeople or designers or their work that you are familiar with.

Art, craft or design in my home/garden   Exhibitions I have visited/heard about

Me as a viewer of art

TV programmes about art/artists that
I have watched

My favourite artists/pieces of art I can name

Art I've noticed in my locality

Guidance notes

- *Art, craft and design in your home/garden:* If you look around your home and garden you might be able to identify pieces of art, craft and design that you have chosen or been given and that hold a personal meaning for you. You might have a painting or print on the wall, a woven basket or clay pot on a shelf or table; a particular fabric design on your curtains and cushions. There may be items that have not considered to be art but were made or designed by artists, craftspeople or designers or by your own children in art lessons at school.

- *Visiting exhibitions/art in the locality:* We are surrounded by examples of art and exhibitions of the work of artists locally, regionally and nationally. Many are free to visit, both temporary and permanent. Even if you don't actively seek them out you may well come across sculptures in the local park or town square or exhibitions in your local gallery or museum. Start making a more conscious effort to look at these when you encounter them.

- *TV programmes about art/artists:* As well as encountering art in the locality there are many television programmes about art or that share art-related stories. When a big national exhibition opens there may be news stories, small items on magazine programmes and whole programmes about the artist and the exhibition. All of these serve to alert you to exhibitions of significance that could be worth seeking out to follow your own interest or broaden your knowledge and understanding as well as giving you ideas for teaching and learning.

- *Favourite artists/artists/works of art I can name:* You were probably able to name some artists as you read this because they have a high profile in the media if they have a current exhibition. You might also have been able to list some artists that you remember learning about at school. If you identified some art that you have in your home you might know who made it and might even seek their work out and collect it. In later chapters developing this aspect your subject knowledge will be considered more fully.

In the practical task above you were encouraged to consider your awareness of art and artists around you at the moment. Whilst being able to name or list artists and their work is no test of your interest or knowledge, your general awareness of the range of artists and people working in art, craft and design has implications for the children that you teach. If your knowledge of artists, craftspeople and designers is fairly narrow this can restrict the choices available to you to use in the classroom. This can make it more challenging for you to inspire children and introduce them to an interesting and diverse range of art, craft and design.

What is art in schools?

From your education and experience so far you might have a view or working definition of what art is. From visiting schools on placement or from working in a school you might have had that view expanded, developed and changed by the children, teachers and art that you encounter. Giving some thought to what art is, what art in school is and being able to identify when children are learning in art will be important for your success and effectiveness as a teacher of art. It is possible for children to be engaged in art-like activities that do not truly give them the opportunity to build on their skills, knowledge and understanding in art.

If you look the word 'art' up in the dictionary the definition is 'the expression of creative skill in a visual form such as painting or sculpture' (Soanes and Hawker, 2008, p. 470), whilst 'craft' is defined as 'an activity involving skill in making things by hand' (p. 227) and 'design' as 'a plan or drawing produced to show the appearance and workings of something before it is made' (p. 268). There is much discussion of how 'art' can be defined and what art is and what it is not. This definition has changed over time and is still changing as contemporary artists continue to create art and share it with audiences.

Currently in primary schools the curriculum includes exploration and learning to make art through drawing, painting, using printmaking, collage, textiles and in three dimensions along with using digital media to create art. Typically drawing is an ongoing thread that runs through and underpins most art so that children have opportunities to develop their drawing skills and apply them to making art in other media. In addition to learning to make art children in primary schools also look at and experience the work of artists, craftspeople and designers, from the past and the present, and from other places and cultures, working in a variety of media. Older primary age children begin to consider the reasons why art is made and what motivates and inspires artists. There is opportunity to learn about how artists might seek to provoke the viewer, night alert the viewer to injustice or protest about an issue. Often looking at art can help children look at the familiar and see it differently.

In some primary schools art as a subject can be identified on the timetable and in planning as a discrete subject. In other primary schools meaningful links between two or three subjects will be made where this will enhance and enrich learning in these subjects. This can make it less clear where and when art learning is happening. This may be called 'linked learning' or the 'creative curriculum'. It is important when planning in this way that we keep a firm grasp on learning and teaching in art and ensure that it does not become merely a medium for illustrating learning in other subjects.

Practical task

Learning objective:

- To identify when learning in art is taking place

In this practical task you will think about the need to be clear when children are developing their skills, knowledge and understanding in art rather than using them to illustrate within another subject. As cross curricular work becomes more common it is vital that you have a clear idea about how learning in each of the linked subjects is being developed.

You will need:

- the pro forma below.

What to do:

- Consider the activities listed below and decide whether they will support learning of knowledge, skills or understanding in art. Indicate using these symbols:
- √ – supports learning of knowledge, skills or understanding in art
- ? – could support learning of knowledge, skills or understanding in art depending on the emphasis or approach
- X – does not support learning of knowledge, skills or understanding in art

Activity		√	?	X	If ? or X how could it be changed so it is more focused on learning in art?
1	Children are making a Christmas card following the model demonstrated by their teacher				
2	Children are collecting different shades of blue and sticking them in their sketchpads				
3	Children are drawing an accurate picture of a flower and naming each feature with a label				
4	Children are making notes about a favourite sculpture from the local environment				
5	Children are making patterns to demonstrate their understanding of symmetry				
6	Children are role playing the relationships between people in one of LS Lowry's paintings				
7	Children are talking about what may have inspired artists to make their work, giving examples they have found				
8	Children are drawing a diagram of the construction of a Roman road				
9	Children are making thumb pots and coil pots to explore form and explore the properties of clay				
10	Children are working on a collaborative weaving based on their response to spring				

Questions to consider

- *Activities that develop knowledge, skills and understanding of art, craft, design:* It is likely that you identified activities 2, 4, 7, 9 and 10 as those firmly focused on learning in art. Exploring a visual element such as colour and learning or using a skill such as making pots from clay and weaving are activities that fall within art. Talking about art and artists are also activities that are based firmly within the art curriculum although they have links to speaking and listening as they provide the context for the use of speaking and listening skills taught in the English curriculum. Activity 7 may also have links to developing children's spiritual and cultural understanding.

- *Activities that may develop knowledge, skills and understanding of art, craft, design depending on the emphasis or approach:* Activity 5 (exploring symmetry) could be based on learning about pattern, a visual element, and how pattern is used in different cultures in art or it could be related to the mathematical understanding of how symmetry works and different types of symmetry. The skills, knowledge and understanding related to symmetry could be learned in either mathematics or art and applied in either subject. Activity 6 could be based on learning about an artist and how his or her life and experiences influenced their art or it could be focused on using imagination, expression and dialogue to develop language and speaking and listening skills in English. This activity could contribute to learning in both English and Art.

- *Activities that do not develop knowledge, skills and understanding of art, craft, design:* Activity 1, where following the teacher's model is likely to lead to similar or identical outcomes, is unlikely to lead to any new learning in art. It may provide a limited opportunity to consolidate skills such as cutting or sticking. Activities 3 and 8 are examples of drawing being used within a curriculum area rather than in art. The drawings are being made to illustrate particular features or aspects such as the botanical structure of a flower or the composition of a Roman road rather than developing children's use of line, tone or shape.

In this practical task you have begun to think about when learning in art is taking place and when something that looks on the surface like art may actually be more related to learning in another subject. Whilst applying skills, knowledge and understanding from the art curriculum to other learning experiences is a good idea, we must not lose focus on the subject itself within the linked learning unit. It is important to be clear in both thinking and planning about whether the learning experiences will support discrete learning in art; whether they are connected to another subject and support learning in both subjects; whether they provide opportunities to learn in one subject and use and apply in another; or whether they are merely illustrative. In further chapters the possibilities of linking art with other subjects will be explored more fully.

As well as making art and looking at art, being involved in learning experiences in art can make many other contributions to children's education. These will be explored more fully in the next section.

Why do we teach art in schools?

Art has been part of the curriculum in primary schools for many years. It is only since the late 1980s, on the introduction of a statutory national curriculum, that the content in terms of knowledge, skills and understanding has been outlined by a programme of study. The most recent document has been in place since 1999 and is currently under review. Given the contribution that art makes to the education of children, and subsequently its significance in the lives of adults, art will always be part of the curriculum in primary schools. It is important that schools and all the people working in them have a clear understanding of the contribution art makes to the education of the child. Exploring why art is taught in schools and the contribution it makes to learning will underpin your thinking and planning so that you ensure that children have the experiences they need in your classroom.

Find out more

Look at the school aims, vision or ethos. These may be displayed in the entrance hall and shared in more detail a school handbook or policy document. Consider how learning in art will provide a context for meeting these aims.

Look at the beginning of the school's art policy. What is the school's vision for the specific contribution art makes to a child's education?

If you are a student look in the information about art in your course – what does it say about why you are learning to teach art?

Personal development and lifelong learning

The art curriculum and learning experiences in art allow children to explore their own creativity in practical ways as well as learn about how others have followed their own creative impulses and ideas. There are many opportunities to engage with spiritual, moral, social and cultural (SMSC) development in the art curriculum. Personal qualities that are important in all learning can be applied, developed and strengthened in art. In all of these areas there are implications for children's learning not only in their primary years but for their future as adult citizens and lifelong learners.

Creativity

Giving children opportunities to be creative is something that most, if not all, schools aim for as part of their curriculum and their vision for the children they are educating. NACCCE (1999) defined creativity as 'imaginative activity fashioned so as to produce outcomes that are both original and of value' (p. 31) and stated that 'all people are capable of creative achievement in some areas of activity, providing the conditions are right and they have acquired the relevant skills and knowledge' (p. 30). Hickman (2010) goes on to say that whilst it is challenging to define the concept of creativity 'we are able to identify two observable phenomena, namely creative behaviour and the objects which arise as a result of creative action' (p. 117). The art curriculum can provide many opportunities for children to work creatively, although of course many other subjects and areas of learning can also do this and there are ways of planning and delivering the art curriculum in a way that does not offer or encourage creative thought and activity.

If we look more closely at NAACE (1999, pp. 32–4) definition and how it was explained in the report we can consider some implications for the art curriculum and planning and teaching art. 'Imaginative' in this context is taken to mean 'providing an alternative to the expected, the conventional or the routine'. 'Purposeful' is defined as 'actively engaged in making or producing something in a deliberate way'. 'Original' is related to what is original for the individual and their peer group rather than being completely original and unique. Finally 'of value' encourages us to think about being evaluative during and after the creative activity applying judgement and critical thinking.

When you are planning, teaching and supporting learning in art, it is important that you consider these aspects of creativity so that children have opportunities to respond creatively. If you, as the adult, have a distinct and closed outcome in mind towards which you are guiding and directing children, it is unlikely that they will be able to be imaginative or original. Although you will have a learning outcome and some learning objectives for children's skills and use of media and processes, these will need to be balanced with some flexibility and opportunity for choice. Planning time to stop, look, talk and think about the art children are making is important – during as well as after the art is made, along with scaffolding critical thinking so that this is supportive and useful. In addition to this, giving children opportunities to share their art with viewers in school and beyond is also a part of valuing their work.

Case Study

A class of Year 1 children are being introduced to painting with watercolours. Their teacher demonstrates how to dampen the tablets of colour to soften them; how to use thick soft brushes to apply washes and thinner brushes to add detail. The children explore what they can do with the paints, applying them to thick paper. After the class have experimented their teacher lays the paintings out on the tables and asks the children to look at them and notice the different effects that have been created. She asks some children to identify an area on a painting so that the artist can explain how they achieved it. Children are interested in how the colours merge if the paper was damp or are clear and distinct if the paper was dry; the marks that have been made by different-sized brushes; and the idea that a wash can be applied and then painted onto wet or dry to avoid a white background.

At the start of the next lesson the teacher then demonstrates or asks the children to demonstrate some of these ways of working with watercolours. In this next lesson children try out some of the suggested methods and build on their experience of using watercolours. Alongside this during the week the teacher shows them examples of paintings using watercolour on the IWB (interactive white board).

After these experimental and then more guided experiences children paint a watercolour. They have freedom to paint whatever they want from observation, experience or imagination and can use any of the painting techniques that they have tried. They can choose the size and shape of paper to paint onto. The teacher encourages them to be creative, follow their own ideas and inspiration whilst supporting those who are more hesitant with reminders of the range of paintings they have seen made by other artists. Children are encouraged not to copy but to think about what inspired the artist and how that might fit with their own ideas.

The watercolours are displayed together with some of the experiments and some scribed comments from the children about what inspired their art, their thoughts about it and what they learned from it. The paintings are varied in subject matter and appearance and show the range of ways this class has explored the medium.

In this case study children have been given the opportunity to make choices about how and what they will paint and the size and shape of their painting while they all use watercolours to paint with. They have been allowed to experiment, evaluate their learning and be taught by the teacher and each other. They have been encouraged to think and talk about their work while support is available for those not ready to be completely independent. Older children with more experience of the range of media and processes can be expected to make more choices and demonstrate greater independence in their making of art if they have been taught in a way that supports this.

Using ICT tools to support learning in art and making art using digital media are also part of the art curriculum. This can engage learners in art who feel less confident in their own making skills or who have an interest in this area. Using software onscreen to create art; taking and manipulating digital photos and scanning; making videos and animations; and researching online are all areas that are common in art practice and can be used by primary-aged children. It is important to note that contemporary artists use ICT and digital media as part of their work to help them research, develop ideas, and make new and innovative work. They are often at the cutting edge of what can be done with new media visually.

As well as ensuring that we plan opportunities for children to be creative we should not underestimate the contribution of art to providing a creative and stimulating environment for children to enjoy and be inspired by. Thinking about the potential for both the inside and outdoor environment to be lively, interesting, diverse and changing places for children to work in is often a strong feature of primary schools. Displays that promote interaction and response, displays that value children's work in all areas of the curriculum and displays of artists' work all contribute to this. Increasingly primary schools are including their outdoor space as part of the learning environment with much potential for inspiring art and creativity often related to natural and manmade environments and working collaboratively and on a larger scale.

Spiritual, moral, social and cultural development

All schools must provide for the spiritual, moral, social and cultural (SMSC) development of their pupils. These aspects of the curriculum are not tied to specific subjects although there are opportunities for children to develop each of them in subject lessons as well as in other school experiences. It is important not to overlook these aspects of children's learning and to use the opportunities that the art curriculum gives you to plan for children to encounter them, talk about them and learn about them. Although they overlap and there are relationships between them it is important not to run them together and treat them as one. Eaude (2008) suggests that spiritual development relates to 'meaning'; moral development relates to 'action'; social development relates to 'interaction' and cultural development relates to 'belonging' (p. 9).

Spiritual development, the search for meaning, also encompasses areas such as faith, belief, mystery and the unknown, inspiration, ambiguity and a phrase you might have heard used in school 'awe and wonder'. It can mistakenly be equated with Religious Education (RE) and sometimes with assembly. This is a narrow interpretation and can lead to missed opportunities for exploration and learning in other subjects and areas of learning. And both making art and viewing art can provide many possibilities for exploring spiritual development. When children look at work made by artists they will try to infer and speculate to find their own meaning in it and learn about what others have taken from it.

They will learn about what has motivated artists to make their art and the inspiration and drive that have led them to devoting their lives and energies to making art. When children are making their own art you might plan starting points that allow children to investigate meaning or take them to places that inspire and have an atmosphere they can respond to.

Case study

As part of a study of places worship in RE some year 2 children are taken on visits to a local Hindu Temple and a local Christian church. They are encouraged to look for examples of art in each building and they have some time to draw from observation in order to record and respond to what they see.

After visiting each building they discuss what they have noticed, identifying colour as something significant in each place. The Hindu temple is very bright and colourful and the Christian church has several striking stained glass windows, including one designed by John Piper that is almost abstract in composition. Some children who are familiar with other places of worship contribute what they have noticed about colour in hangings, clothes and tiles. They begin to consider that a visual element they have explored in art, colour, can connect to spirituality and faith by its presence and use in places of worship.

Moral development, which helps to define the values that guide our actions, is an area that we discuss with children in relation to their own behaviour and the behaviour of others in day-to-day school life. While thinking about this we can also help children to make connections to the wider world and the bigger issues of morality beyond their day-to-day experience. We can introduce children to the work of artists who are or have been concerned with moral issues, who have drawn attention to injustice in their art or made protests about moral issues of the times. In school, moral development and behaviour is sometimes underpinned by a reward system (extrinsic motivation) although we aim ultimately for children to internalise values that guide their actions (intrinsic motivation). Children can consider why artists made their art and explore the drive, inspiration and determination that can come from within oneself compared with that imposed on us. Some children may well experience for themselves that internal drive to work on their art whether at home or at school.

Find out more

Search online for a piece of art called *La Bouche du Roi* by West African artist Romauld Hazoume to mark two hundred years since the abolition of slavery. This installation uses discarded objects found in contemporary Benin, such as petrol cans, arranged in the layout depicted by the eighteenth-century print of the slave ship, *Brookes*, used by Abolitionists in their campaign.

Images, information and videoclips of it can be found on the British Museum website, the Art Fund website and on YouTube. The print of the slave ship *Brookes* can also be found online.

Think about the possibilities for exploring larger moral issues from the past (e.g. slavery) and current in today's society (e.g. the environment) through this work of art.

Social development, the interaction with others, is an aspect of school life that underpins many of the experiences that we plan for children. Learning to relate to others; working in pairs and groups; sharing and commenting on each others' work are part of many lessons. In art lessons the atmosphere is often such that children and adults can talk more freely about themselves and what they are doing as they work practically. Some art projects will give children the opportunity to work in small or large groups to create a finished piece of art giving them a sense of being part of something bigger than any one person, as well as co-operating purposefully and supporting each other to achieve a common goal. Showing and talking about their own art to viewers, whether they are children, family or visitors to the school allows children to develop their social skills and confidence purposefully with different audiences.

Case Study

Year 4 children organise an exhibition of paintings made after a visit to the National Gallery to look at how artists have painted the sea and a visit to the seaside to draw and paint. This exhibition will be the culmination of their art experience at the school and part of their moving on to the next school activities.

They each choose a painting to show, draft and write a label modelled on those they have read in galleries, and design invitations to a preview. They invite parents, governors and friends of the school. They also look to the future and invite former pupils and staff from the schools to which they will move.

At the exhibition the children act as the curators, showing visitors around and talking with them about their work. There is a sense of achievement and excitement that comes from the completion of a project. Sharing their art work is an important aspect of this experience, but also taking charge of an event, with support from their teachers, gives them a purposeful opportunity to develop their confidence and put into practice their social skills.

In this case study children have a significant experience that is planned as part of preparing them for the move from one school to another, recognizing their achievements so far and boosting their confidence as they make the next step. Smaller-scale opportunities for developing social skills and self esteem through taking part in art activities are frequent in the primary classroom.

Cultural development, belonging to a group, can also be explored in art especially in terms of introducing children to the diversity of art made by other cultures both now and in the past. This can be an effective and interesting way in to finding out more about the cultures themselves in other subjects such as history and geography. Discovering how cultures have explored ideas and meanings visually can give children access to a range of ideas to draw upon when making their own art. It is important when choosing art from other cultures that we draw upon an interesting and diverse range of art including that made by artists working now in areas such as digital media. It can be useful to first consider the range of cultures present in the school and local community to ensure that you are drawing upon art, craft and design from these as well as introducing children to unfamiliar cultures from the past and present. Think also about cultural experiences that are meaningful and significant in your locality and in the UK so that children know about their own culture as well as that other people. This might include cultural events that happen locally every year as well as those that are one-offs such as the cultural Olympiad that supports the 2012 Olympics.

Some artists involve many people in the creation of their art: Martin Creed's *All the bells* in July 2012 and Antony Gormley's *Field for . . .* works are examples of where an artist's work depends on the involvement of communities and very large groups of people working together. This creating together to achieve and enjoy approach is a vital part of a school's ethos and mission. Participation in this kind of project can be a wonderful experience in itself as well as a chance come together as a school or community and be a small part of a larger whole.

Personal qualities

Giving children opportunities to develop personal qualities that will equip them to learn, support their well-being and be happy in future life is another important aspect of what schools aim to achieve through their ethos and curriculum. Making choices; using their initiative; taking risks and experimenting to solve problems can all be part of art lessons. Looking critically, reflecting and making judgements on their own art and that made by others are also integral to art. Following children's curiosity and allowing them to be excited and thrilled by what they see, experience and make, as well as gaining personal satisfaction and a sense of accomplishment, is all possible in the art curriculum. In addition to these personal qualities, making art and learning about how artists work helps children develop perseverance, determination and appreciate the need to work hard and be committed in order to improve and achieve.

Many art activities have the possibility of exploring and enjoying the sensory experience of making using tactile materials. Paint, pastels, clay, textiles and many other materials have visual and tactile qualities that engage children's interest quite apart from any task set for them by adults. While it is important to teach children how to use materials and develop their skills, so much can be learned by playing with and exploring the materials freely. If children are not given these opportunities to explore, practice and refine their skills they may begin to feel inhibited and less confident in their approach.

Spiritual, moral, social and cultural development and the opportunity to develop positive personal qualities have each been discussed separately in order to ensure that their relationship to the art curriculum is clear. Often there will be opportunities to explore several of these in art activities and projects in school and also in out of school learning related to the school or to art galleries.

Case Study

A group of Foundation Degree students are exploring some resources published by the Institute of International Visual Arts (2010) called 'Who are you? Where are you going?'. This resource is a set of twenty cards each showing an artwork that encourages reflection, speculation, talk about feelings and life experiences. The art is diverse, thought provoking and most of it is unfamilar to the students.

The students are asked to discuss in pairs the potential for talking about the ideas and feelings generated by the art, beginning with their own reactions and then considering the children they work with. Themes such as homes, moving, families and relationships are identified along with ideas for exploring these with children of varying ages. Some of them suggest that using pictures can provoke a wide range of responses perhaps more so than the most open of questions.

They are then asked to consider how this art could be used to talk about artists' work and inspire children's own art. They are encouraged to suggest ideas related to the themes they discussed earlier rather than ideas based on recreations or copies of the art itself. Looking at these examples of artists' work gives students an appreciation for the diverse nature of art available to share with children.

(Have a look on the website *http://www.iniva.org/learning/learning_resources/about_emotional_learning_cards* for more information about this resource.)

In this case study students explore the potential of art for inspiring talk as well as broadening the range of art they have encountered and helping them consider the way they use artists' work with children.

Connect and extend

Find the article 'Encounters with the Unexpected from Holbein to Hirst (and Back Again' by Robert Watts and published in *The International Journal of Art and Design* in 2011 (Vol 30, No 1, pp.52-61).

Consider how the discussion of issues such as ambiguity and mystery, not knowing and knowing, are an important aspect of learning in art. How can we make sure that children explore this in the classroom?

Lifelong learners

Although this book is about teaching art to primary-aged children many aspects of the art curriculum have a significance that goes beyond learning in the primary school. In school we are preparing our children to become fulfilled individuals and good citizens of the future, a future that is uncertain and changing in its demands and opportunities. Children will need resilience, flexibility and determination to meet the challenges ahead of them in adulthood.

Increasingly the world around us is full of visual imagery that children must interpret, evaluate and respond to – sometimes by engaging with and other times filtering out. The children we are teaching today in our primary schools are the citizens who will care for and value our cultural heritage in the future. They are the people who will work in the creative industries seeking to enlighten, entertain and enrich our lives.

Connect and extend

Read section 2 of Conversations and reflections: some mini case studies' in Richard Hickman's book *Why We Make Art and Why it is Taught* published in 2010.

In this section a range of people discuss their art and why they make it. Look for the impact that school and art experiences in school have had. What are the implications for your own thinking about why we teach art in schools?

What do children think about art?

Young children tend to feel positive about art. They are often willing to have a go, enjoy the process and become absorbed in it. When children of primary age are allowed a free choice of activity drawing or some kind of making activity is usually popular. Anning (2002) identified that even if children later become hesitant about drawing at school they are still engaged in it at home. Giving some consideration to what children think and feel about making art and art in school helps us understand its importance from an important perspective.

Practical task

Learning objective

● to investigate children's views on art

You will need:

● the pro forma below, a group of children

What to do:

● talk with children using the some or all of the questions listed below.

Make notes of their responses. Compare them with the discussion in the article (details below)

Question, prompt for discussion	Children's comments, views
1. What is art?	
2. Who makes art?	
3. Do you make art?	
4. Where do you find art?	
5. Why do people make art?	
6. Do you have a favourite artwork, or favourite artist?	
7. Do you like doing art at school?	
8. How often does your class do art?	
9. What are some of the art things you do at school?	
10. How good do you think you are at art?	
11. Do you look at art or talk about art at school?	
12. Do you like doing art things in your own time (when you're not at school)?	
13. Do you want to keep learning about art when you grow up?	
14. Do you think you'll keep doing art when you're a grown-up?	
15. Do you think you might be an artist when you grow up?	

Source: Primary-age children's attitudes to art, art making and art education, from The International Journal of Education Through Art, (Gibson, R. 2008), © Intellect Ltd.

Guidance notes

- Talking about some or all of these questions with children can give you an interesting insight into children's perceptions of art, artists and themselves and their school. In Gibson's small-scale study, conducted with primary-aged children in Australia, she found that children had a wide-ranging view of what art is: they could talk about the meaning and value of art with insight and depth and could talk about art in their lives now and in their future as adults.

- Taking the pupil voice into consideration is increasingly important in educational research as well as school self evaluation.

- You might consider the influence of the school approach to art on children and their perceptions when you analyse your discussions.

Connect and extend

Find and read Robyn Gibson's article published in 2008, entitled 'Primary-age children's attitudes to art, art making and art education' in *The International Journal of Education through Art*. (Vol. 4, No. 2, pp. 177–93).

Compare Gibson's findings with your own in the exercise above. Can you identify any factors that have an impact on children's attitudes to and knowledge about art? What is your role in this?

The role of adults

This chapter has called upon you to consider your own art education and current awareness of art. It has explored some of the reasons why we teach art in schools beyond the content of the curriculum in terms of making and viewing art. It is important to return to the significance of the role of adults: students, teachers and teaching assistants in the art education of children in schools in the light of these areas.

In the more distant past art education was focused on direct instruction and the idea that children should be taught the technical skills needed to use tools and materials correctly with an emphasis on copying. The role of the teacher was to demonstrate and teach skills directly with little scope for individual response and exploration. Later this was largely replaced by the idea of a more 'child-centered' approach. In this view of how children learn in art the role of the teacher would be to provide contexts and materials and allow children to create art in response to their own ideas and interests, with little if any direct teaching. Most schools would now include opportunities for exploration and expression as well as teaching children how to use tools and materials and learning and practising skills in their art curriculum. The theory that underpins teaching and learning in art can and should be explored as you pursue your course and placements in order to set your teaching in the context of the bigger picture of art education and negotiate the balance between direct teaching and allowing freedom to explore, experiment and create.

There is great potential in the art curriculum for planning learning experiences that allow individuals to respond in their own way, expressing themselves and following their own creative impulses. As teachers our role in planning activities and units of work and working with children in art lessons to facilitate, encourage and value individual responses is vital. It is important that we try to avoid ending up with some 30 outcomes at the end of a sequence of lessons or a unit of work that are largely the same or at best very similar, with no real personal expression from the children who made the art apparent: what Barnes (2002) refers to as the 'predetermined, end-product thought-trap' (p29).

There are a number of reasons why outcomes can become the same or overly similar. If we plan too tightly and restrict children's opportunities to explore, experiment and make their own choices at each stage of a unit of work any personal and individual response is squeezed out. At the early stages of learning to plan and teach art as adults we are often dependent on a scheme of work or tried and tested plans. It can be difficult to identify where to allow children choices and manage the divergent routes and outcomes that result from these. Time, space and organisation of materials and resources can be a challenge, as well as the pressure from other subjects in the curriculum. Although there may a number of challenges to the possibility of supporting and encouraging personal expression, in art it is vital to overcome these and aim to plan some opportunities for children to follow their own ideas and pathways. If we deny them this opportunity in their experience of art in school and focus solely on learning and using skills and making drawings, paintings and other outcomes, their understanding of something vital to art – the impulse and inspiration that makes people want to create art – can be stifled. Drawing on these feelings of needing to experiment and make something in order to fulfill a personal drive rather than serve a function is important in education and learning overall, and especially so in art. This drive or inspiration can lead children to be motivated learners, determined and creative in their approach and willing to persevere and work hard to achieve their goal. The sense of satisfaction from pursuing learning as well as being absorbed in a piece of work is an important aspect of being a learner.

For you as students, learning to plan learning objectives, success criteria and learning outcomes with clear ideas of what the learning will look like in other subjects, the element of uncertainty when giving children choices and allowing them to pursue a more personal impulse can be challenging. It is important to use what we know about effective teaching combined with our understanding of learning in art to plan, support and teach the subject with sensitivity. For children, often used to being set a very clear goal and indication of what learning will look like in other subjects, having more freedom in their learning can be unsettling: some children may have had little freedom or control over their own art work since their experience of art in the early years. When everyone in the class is making basically the same thing some children are more likely to compare their own art with that of others and judge themselves harshly, leading to a loss of confidence or enjoyment of the process.

Connect and extend

Read the article 'An exploration of primary teachers' understanding of art and the place of art in the primary school curriculum' written by Hallam, Gupta and Lee in 2008 and published in the *The Curriculum Journal* (Vol. 19, No. 4, pp.269–81).

Think about the three approaches to art in the curriculum identified: art as a skills-based activity, art as an expressive activity; and art as a site for cross-curricular teaching. What are the implications for the art curriculum, your teaching and the children's learning?

Conclusion

Your role as an adult preparing to or already working in school is vital to children's learning. Your beliefs and attitudes, subject knowledge and pedagogical understanding will have an impact on the children you teach imperceptibly and explicitly throughout your career. Part of your professional role will be to champion learning in all subjects for all the learners you support and teach. For some, art will be a favourite subject in which they excel and aim to ultimately pursue in further study and as a career. For many, if not most, art will be a pleasurable and engaging subject from which they can learn in a different way even if they do not go on to have anything more than an interest in the arts in later life. In the next chapter the content of the art curriculum in primary schools will be explored in more depth.

Next steps

- Develop your awareness of art in your locality and in the media.
- Look out for examples of spiritual, moral, social and cultural development in art experiences (your own and the children you work with)

References

Anning, A. (2002) 'A conversation around young children's drawing: the impact of the beliefs of significant others at home and at school'. *The International Journal of Art and Design Education*, Vol. 21, No. 3, pp. 197–208.

Barnes, R. (2002) *Teaching Art to Young Children 4–9*, 2nd edn. London: Routledge Falmer.

Eaude, T. (2008) *Children's Spiritual, Moral, Social and Cultural Development: Primary and Early Years.* 2nd edn. Exeter: Learning Matters.

Gibson, R. (2008) 'Primary-age children's attitudes to art, art making and art education'. *The International Journal of Education through Art*, Vol. 4, No. 2, pp. 177–93

Hallam, J., Das Gupta, M. and Lee, H. (2008) 'An exploration of primary school teachers' understanding of art and the place of art in the primary school curriculum.' *The Curriculum Journal*, **Vol. 19**, No. 4, pp. 269–81.

Hickman, R. (2010) *Why We Make Art and Why it is Taught*, 2nd edn. Bristol: Intellect.

NAACE (1999) *All Our Futures: Creativity, Culture and Education.* Sudbury: DFEE Publications.

Further reading

Gibson, R. (2008) 'Primary-age children's attitudes to art, art making and art education'. *The International Journal of Education through Art*, Vol. 4, No. 2, pp. 177–93.

Henley, D. (2012) *Cultural Education in England: An Independent Review by Darren Henley for the Department of Culture, Media and Sport and the Department of Education.* Available from: *http://www.dcms.gov.uk/publications/8875.aspx* (Accessed 26 March 2012).

Herne, S., Cox, S. and Watts, R. (2009) *Readings in Primary Art Education*. London: Intellect Books.

Hickman, R. (2010) *Why We Make Art and Why it is Taught*, 2nd edn. Bristol: Intellect.

NACCCE (1999) *All Our Futures: Creativity, Culture and Education*. Sudbury: DFEE Publications.

Watts, R. (2011) 'Encounters with the unexpected: from Holbein to Hirst (and back again)'. *The International Journal of Art and Design Education*, Vol. 30, No. 1, pp. 52–61.

Web resources

The Institute of International Visual Arts *http://www.iniva.org/*

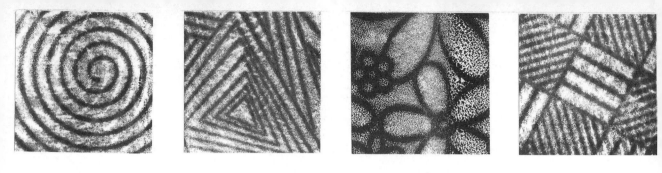

Chapter 2

The art curriculum in primary schools

Introduction

In primary schools what we teach in the art curriculum is underpinned by the requirements of the statutory curriculum. Schools interpret them in the context of the resources available locally; the expertise in the school and the interests of the children. This results in common features across schools but variations as well. If you are a student visiting a range of schools on placements these similarities and differences may be more apparent to you than if you are part of the staff working in the same school over a sustained period.

In this chapter the following aspects that underpin and affect the content of the art curriculum in a primary school will be explored:

- School policy and approach
- Subject knowledge
- Media and processes
- The work of artists, craftspeople and designers
- Linking art to other subjects
- Published schemes

Some of these are applicable to art in primary schools, such as the visual elements and the media and processes children experience. Others are the means by which schools make their art curriculum unique, such as their policy, their choices of artists and any schemes of teaching resources they use to support teachers in planning and teaching the art curriculum.

School policy and approach

Whilst statutory requirements for art in the national curriculum provide a framework for the curriculum in schools there are many decisions that schools can make to ensure that their art curriculum is distinctive and meets the needs and interests of their pupils. The school approach to the art curriculum and how it is put into practice will be guided by the school policy. The policy is likely to have been developed by the Art Co-ordinator or subject leader along with the staff of the school. The school may have a particular commitment to art or the arts more widely – this may be recognised by the award of Artsmark or involvement in the Arts Award at Discover and Explore levels. If you work in the school you may have been an active part of this process; you may have learned about it as it was communicated to staff or you may have joined the staff and found out about it in a similar way to a student on placement does. If you join a school as a student on placement you will need to assimilate and understand the school's approach quite rapidly and you will have the opportunity over a number of placements to experience and learn from a variety of different approaches, taking the most effective aspects from each to develop your own knowledge, understanding and approach.

The school policy

Schools usually have policies to guide learning and teaching. This may be an individual policy for art, a policy for 'the arts' including visual art or a policy for foundation subjects (i.e. not core subjects such as English and mathematics). Although policies are individual to the school they tend to include the following:

- a rationale and statement of aims for learning and teaching of art in the school;
- a description or guide to how the content is organised and taught in the school. This may include a curriculum map or long-term plan and a scheme of work or medium-term plan. It may also include guidance on assessment.
- a role description for the art co-ordinator or subject leader. It is likely that this will include supporting other staff and students in their roles;
- advice about inclusion and equal opportunities;
- some policies include guidance about display, exhibition and presentation of children's art work;
- a list of resources, where they are kept and guidance about how to use them. (based on Bowden, 2006).

If you are teaching art or supporting in art lessons you should ensure that you have read the policy and familiarised yourself with provisions especially in relation to the individual aims and approach of the school. It is important that children receive a consistent experience with all staff following the same approach that they have agreed together. As you read this book you will often find suggestions to consult or check with the school policy for this reason.

Practical task

Learning objective:

- to explore the school policy for art

In this practical task you will explore the school-based guidance and approach explained in the art policy. This will support your planning and teaching.

You will need:

- A copy of the art policy and the pro forma below.

What to do:

- Use the art policy to answer the following questions.

Questions	Answers
Who is the art co-ordinator or subject leader?	
What is the school vision for or approach to art?	
Is there a long-term plan or outline of what pupils will learn and when?	

Questions	Answers
Is there a list of resources for art (and how they are organised)?	
What does the policy say about how art connects to other subjects?	
What does the policy say about assessment in art?	
What does the policy say about including all pupils?	
If you are supporting pupils in art lessons is there any guidance about how to support pupils with specific needs?	
What does the policy say about display of pupils' work?	
Has looking at the policy suggested any other questions to follow up?	

Guidance notes

- When you have considered these questions, if you are left with anything that you need to clarify try to talk with the art co-ordinator.

- As a student you will need to focus on how the answers to these questions affect your placement: finding the planning and resources for the half term or unit or work that you plan to teach for example.

- As an NQT/non-specialist teacher you will have a more long-term view, thinking about the art you plan and teach with your class over the year.

- As a teaching assistant you may be especially interested in the approach to inclusion if you will be supporting individuals or groups in art lessons or have similar interests to teachers if you are covering art lessons as PPA time.

The policies for specific subjects are likely to work in conjunction with other policies that guide staff in more general areas that apply across all subjects such as learning and teaching, inclusion, assessment and health and safety. As you move around the school look around for exemplification of the art policy in classrooms and in the shared and public areas of the school. You will be able to identify some media or processes that children have explored and some artists that children are learning about. Looking at the variety of outcomes might tell you something about how much opportunity for individual response is given to children, especially in Key Stage Two. There may also be out of school learning opportunities for children to participate in art activities – schools often have after-school clubs related to art or specific crafts.

The art co-ordinator

As with other subjects or areas of learning in schools an identified teacher (or sometimes teaching assistant) will be named as subject leader or co-ordinator. Depending on the size of school and the organization of the curriculum this role may vary in name and responsibilities. In small schools staff will have several curriculum areas to co-ordinate;

in some schools subjects may be combined in different ways and in many schools the co-ordinators of core subjects may well have a much higher profile reflecting the position of that subject in the national agenda. As a former art co-ordinator I felt that the visual nature of the subject and the relationship to display meant that art was more visible and high profile than some other subjects.

One aspect of the role of co-ordinator (of any subject) is to support staff development and training. This may include leading training in school or encouraging you to seek training beyond the school. On a day-to-day basis it is more likely to include being a first port of call for your questions. If you are a student in the school, a teacher in the early stages of your career or a teaching assistant the art co-ordinator can be a great source of support to you. Bear in mind that this member of staff is likely to have class as well as subject responsibilities so choose your moment.

Art beyond the classroom

In addition to the opportunities offered in school through the statutory curriculum it is likely that there will be out of school hours learning opportunities such as after-school clubs, workshops and activities offered to children. Some of these may be centered on or have ties to art, craft and design. You can also encourage children to join in any local activities available at galleries, museums and other local places after school or in the school holidays. Many children draw, pursue crafts and make art at home and it is important that we value this interest and enthusiasm that children have for creating and making, and draw upon it to support their learning in school.

Subject knowledge

For the student, teaching assistant, HLTA, newly qualified teacher or non-specialist primary teacher the phrase 'visual and tactile elements' may be unfamiliar. These words – colour, pattern and texture, line and tone, shape, form and space – allow us to discuss specific concepts in making art and when talking about the work of artists. In this chapter each of these elements will be defined and in later chapters you will see how they connect to and underpin planning for learning and practice in the classroom.

When you teach an art lesson or an art unit of work you will have the opportunity to plan for learning in one or more of the visual and tactile elements. It may be that one or two of them are the focus of your teaching in one or more of your lessons or activities. It is important that you know which one or two you are focusing on and how they might underpin or connect to the rest of the learning planned in your unit or lesson. In many published schemes of work the visual and tactile elements for the unit are identified in the planning. They may also be identified in the long-or medium-term planning and the subject leader for art in your school will also be able to help you with this.

Some units of work may involve exploration and learning about one or two (at most three) of the elements. You will find from reading this book that there are strong connections between some elements and these complement each other. Some elements fit especially well with certain media or processes and it makes sense, for example, that we might explore pattern through printmaking or colour through painting. This does not mean that we always and only explore colour when painting. Developing your knowledge and understanding of the visual and tactile elements may give you the confidence and freedom to make connections and choices of your own when you plan units of work and art experiences.

During each year children will visit and revisit each of these visual and tactile elements consolidating and developing their knowledge and understanding of them. It is important that you take into consideration the children's prior experiences so that you can build upon these. You will find evidence of these from what you have seen displayed around the school, in the children's sketchpads, from previous planning and of course from talking with the children themselves.

Practical task

What are the visual and tactile elements?

Learning objective:

- to explore your current knowledge and understanding of visual and tactile elements.

In this practical task you will use your current knowledge and understanding to define each of the visual elements. This will help you refine and develop your subject knowledge as you support and teach art and read this book.

What to do:

- Write a short (one sentence) definition for each of the visual elements listed below.
- Focus your definition on the use of the words in the context of learning and teaching art.
- In the 'other thoughts' column note any other knowledge or understanding that you have relating to each visual element and make a note of an artist or piece of art that you think is a good example of each visual element.
- Later, come back and look again as your subject knowledge develops through experience and learning.

Visual element	Definition – general	Definition - art	Other notes
colour			
tone			
line			
pattern			
texture			
shape			
form			
space			

In this practical task you have drawn upon your prior knowledge to consider some significant ideas in art. This is an area that you can continue to develop as you observe, support and teach art; plan activities, lessons and units of work; and gain experience.

The next section of this chapter explores each of these visual and tactile elements in more depth so that you can build on your existing subject knowledge. It may be useful to return to this evaluation of your prior knowledge and add additional notes and clarifications as your understanding develops. There is further detail about the vocabulary that is used to discuss each element in Appendix 1.

Colour

When you look back at your definition of colour in the earlier exercise perhaps this is the word you felt most confident with. We use colour words in many contexts – from explaining how colour is formed scientifically to expressing personal preferences about our favourite colour and acting on these in our choices of decoration and clothes.

Knowledge and understanding about colour

When we use the word colour it can have a scientific definition and explanation but when we use it in art we are focusing more on our own perceptions of colour and its effects. Light is significant in terms of how we perceive colour, as is personal preference and our knowledge about pigments and materials.

Perhaps you remember from your own school days that colours can be identified as primary (red, blue, yellow) and secondary (violet/purple, orange, green) and that by mixing two primary colours we arrive at a secondary colour (red and blue mixed together make violet/purple). When we mix two primary colours such as red and blue to create violet/purple this colour and the remaining primary colour – yellow – are called complementary colours. When we add white to a colour the colour gets lighter and this is called a tint. When we add black to a colour it gets darker and this is called a shade. Often artists will create darker shades by mixing colours rather than using black pigment.

When you were at school you may have explored this knowledge about colour in the context of a formal exercise of mixing and painting a colour wheel. There are many other ways of exploring colour mixing that are more creative and more appropriate for primary-age children. Many of these involve mixing coloured pigment when painting and the organisation for colour mixing is discussed more fully in Chapter 7. Colour can also be explored through other media, such as collage and pastels, and through collecting, comparing and arranging activities.

Talking about colour

It is easy to assume that even the youngest children know the words associated with colour. They are often asked to identify or name objects by using or responding to a colour word: can you give me the red cube? What colour is the circle? When we are talking about colour in art we are going beyond using colour names as identifying labels. Rather we are considering how colours affect each other, how artists might choose colours to evoke certain feelings or effects, and how learners can use colour in their own work, and talking about it in an art context. This may involve detailed descriptive and technical vocabulary as well as more poetic and evocative language used in naming colours often evident on paint charts.

Tone

In general conversation we might think about the word tone as referring to the way someone speaks to us – a friendly tone or an excited tone for example. In music we might use the word tone to refer to a quality of sound. When you thought about tone in the context of art in the exercise at the beginning of this chapter perhaps you thought in terms of black, shades of grey leading to white. You may also have considered tones of the same colour from dark to light.

Knowledge and understanding about tone

When we use the word tone in art we are referring to how light affects the surfaces we are looking at. Exploring tone in art may be focused on exploring how light affects surfaces and how we represent this and use it in our own art as well as how we identify and talk about it in others artists' work.

Depending on the process or technique we are using we may be able to explore gradual tonal change through mixing paint, blending pastels, chalk and charcoal. When drawing with soft drawing pencils we can create gradual tonal changes by varying the pressure with which we press down as we draw. If we are using media such as fabric, collage or felt pens we may choose from available colours that keep distinct boundaries and our choice and placement will create contrast or transition between tones. Tone and tones of colours can be used to create a sense of space: making something appear near or further away in the distance.

Talking about tone

When we talk about tone with children it is likely that we will be using comparative vocabulary. Describing tone is often easier when we compare something with something else to say whether it is 'lighter than…' or darker than…' rather than being able to say definitively that something is dark or light in its own right unless it is very light or very dark indeed. We may also need to use words associated with talking about light such as shade and shadow. Some of the words we use when talking about tone are connected to words we used when talking about colour or can be used in combination.

Line

In day-to-day classroom life children will be hearing and responding to the word line in a variety of contexts, from lining up to move around the school safely, drawing lines under headings and using lines to mark out boundaries in games on the playground. In mathematics children will be using lines to create regular and irregular geometrical shapes. As children learn to write they are refining their skills in controlling lines to make joined marks flowing from left to right. When you thought about line in the earlier exercise you may have considered how line in art allows us to outline shapes and areas and create effects with combinations of marks and lines.

Knowledge and understanding about line

In the context of art lines do not have to be single continuous linear marks but can be as short as points or dashes. We can use lines to create outlines which can then be filled or we can place lines and marks together to create areas of tone, patterns and textures.

We can explore line using tools that leave marks, such as pencils, pens, paintbrushes and pastels. We can also use our fingers in paint or sticks in sand. We can guide and place materials that have linear qualities such as wire, thread or string. We can also use needles to sew, creating linear marks with thread on fabric.

Talking about line

When we describe and talk about line children should be able to respond to and use a range of descriptive works to express what they are doing with line and can see others doing in their art work. Using these words as they are physically making the lines can help them understand the meanings of the words in this context. Lines can often be used to outline shapes and this leads to another set of words explored more fully below.

Pattern

We are surrounded by pattern in nature and created by people. When you defined pattern in the earlier exercise perhaps this was another word you felt fairly confident with. In the natural world we can identify many different patterns. We use patterns to decorate and structure our world and in many cultures patterns have a symbolic significance. Children will often spontaneously create patterns with the materials available to them and respond to the opportunities we give them to follow and make patterns. Many sets of equipment and toys used in the classroom lend themselves to this. Children will be also exploring organised and structured patterns in mathematics using numbers and shapes.

Knowledge and understanding about pattern

In art pattern may be something created in nature, identified by our observations, and sometimes the inspiration for our own designs. It may be created by us when we place lines, marks and shapes on surfaces in a design or motif. Wenham (2003) suggests that when we are exploring pattern with children we can think about three types of pattern: linear patterns that are developed along a line; rotating patterns that are developed around a point; and surface patterns developed on flat surfaces to cover whole areas.

Children follow and devise linear pattern when they fix multilink cubes together to make repeating patterns using colour and when they build with construction toys. They may also make repeating patterns when they thread beads and found items onto a string. When doing this it is important for the child to be able to identify the beginning and end of the items that make the pattern (the motif) so that they can repeat it. This type of pattern might be used as a border. They will also experience making linear patterns when practising the flowing left to right patterns that underpin joined handwriting.

Rotating patterns begin from a middle point and may be circular like a flower, the cross section of a piece of fruit or expand outwards to fill a regular shape like patterns on tiles. These patterns often have one or more than one line of symmetry.

Repeated patterns on a surface can be made from various motifs and extended across large surfaces in any direction. We often see these types of pattern on fabric, wrapping paper and wallpaper. The surface itself and how the motifs are placed on it are important to the design and overall impression of the pattern. Sometimes a grid is used to help guide the pattern, or the motifs fit together through tessellation of shapes.

Talking about pattern

When we help children talk about the patterns they see or want to create we need words to describe the components that make the pattern. We also need to know words to describe how these are placed in relation to each other. Much of this vocabulary used is also used in mathematics. It is important to give children the opportunity to describe and explain the patterns they are making or observing with an increasingly precise vocabulary.

Texture

Everything around us has a texture that we can interact with. Young children will be exploring how the world around them feels often touching things we as adults would avoid; indeed we may need to make sure children do not touch some things for their own safety. The tactile experiences of finger painting, plunging hands in bubbles or wet sand and manipulating play dough help them learn about texture. In science children will be exploring the texture of materials as part of their explorations of the properties and characteristics of the materials around them.

Subject knowledge about texture

In art we can think about texture in two ways. Firstly, texture is how materials feel when we touch them. We begin to be able to predict how materials will feel before we touch them or touch them without looking at them and be able to name and describe them.

Secondly, texture can be represented visually by making various marks. An illusion of texture can be created even though we know we are looking at a flat surface.

Clearly tactile texture is explored through touch. When we explore tactile texture in art we may be encouraging children to take texture into consideration in their choice of materials perhaps when choosing fabrics and threads in fabric work. We may be planning experiences that allow them to explore the tactile qualities of art materials directly, such as when finger painting, manipulating clay or making an object from papier-mâché. Some children will dislike the textures involved and be reluctant to use their hands like this, preferring to use tools. When we experience works of art we occasionally may be allowed to experience some through touch although this is one sense we are often discouraged from or prohibited from using in art galleries except in special circumstances.

Visual texture, on the other hand, is explored through looking, talking about and making our own marks. We can see some textures and we can use them to create impressions by taking rubbings. We can experience making marks using textures by pressing items made of different materials into paint and printing with them or pressing items into clay or dough to leave an impression of the texture. Alternatively we can experiment with making the flat surface of paper look textured by the marks we make with pen, pencil or paint, or cutting or embossing into clay to leave a texture.

Talking about texture

When we help children to talk about texture we are building on the vocabulary that they are developing in science to describe materials and in English to bring their writing to life. When using these words and developing them in art we are perhaps being more subjective and considering how a texture might contribute to how we feel about a piece of art – the smooth, curved surface of a marble sculpture may make us want to stroke our hand along it, or the way certain fabrics look in a painting might be so realistic that we want to touch them to see if they really feel velvety or silky.

Shape

When you saw the word shape in the list of visual elements in the exercise at the start of this chapter you may have thought of shape in the mathematical sense of the word where geometric shapes have names based on their properties – triangle, square, etc. Naming, describing and exploring the properties of two-and three-dimensional shapes are important aspects of the mathematics curriculum that children investigate from their early years.

Subject knowledge about shape

When we use the word shape in the context of art it is more concerned with defining areas on a flat surface. These areas might not have a precise geometric name as they would in mathematics. Three-dimensional shapes will be discussed more fully in the section in form although of course shapes will be seen and created in two and three dimensions.

In art a shape may be made from an outline by identifying an outline with a pen, pencil, paintbrush or thread. It could be made by tearing or cutting paper or other material and placing it on a surface. Shapes can be made by printing or placing marks in a patch so that the marks together are seen as a shape. In addition to this the shapes we draw, cut or print have a background and may be placed near, next to or overlapping with other shapes. Shapes interacting together may create a pattern, a picture or the appearance of a texture.

Talking about shape

When we talk about shape in art we can use mathematical vocabulary in relation to naming two-dimensional shapes and describing types of shape and their relationships to each other. We will develop this further because we need to describe irregular shapes created by outlines.

Form

When you considered form in the exercise at the start of this chapter perhaps you found this the most elusive to define or relate to any other contexts. You may have related it to three dimensions in the same way that shape can be related it to forms in three dimensions in the same way that flat shapes can be related to representation on a flat surface. Children will often explore making small forms through making models with construction kits and on a large scale exploring forms in their environment by climbing in, on, through and under play equipment.

Subject knowledge about form

In art form can be defined as something that is three dimensional in nature. We can experience large-scale forms by moving around an object to look at it from different viewpoints including being inside and outside, above and below it. If the object is small we can pick it up and move it around to look at it from a range of viewpoints. When we experience form we may think about the form itself and the space within which it sits.

In addition to this the form that we look at and perhaps touch may be decorated with colour, line, pattern, tone, texture or shapes.

Talking about form

When we talk about form with children we may be encouraging them to use some of the mathematical vocabulary that they would use in relation to space and three-dimensional shapes. In art we might also be using many of the words that we are developing when talking about the other visual elements.

Space

When we talk about space we may again be initially drawn to the mathematics curriculum. Describing where something is in space or how objects can be moved through space is another part of the mathematics curriculum that children will have been exploring since their early years. You may also have thought about this word in relation to how children use space in PE and dance and how they move around the classroom. Considering how children use space themselves on paper in their work may also have come to mind or how they go about organising their work space at the table.

Subject knowledge about space

In art we can think about space in two ways. Firstly, we might think about space in three dimensions – how forms are made and placed in relation to each other and the environment, and how we can move around in space to see these objects from a variety of viewpoints. Secondly, we might think about how we can represent space in two dimensions to give an illusion of three-dimensional space on a two-dimensional surface. We can also consider how we use space to create patterns and use shapes.

When we think about space in three dimensions we might experience this in relation to placing our own sculptures or looking at sculptures in galleries or in the environment. In this context we need to encourage children to think not only about the form that they are making or looking at but also how it interacts in the environment in which it is placed. They will need to consider its size and scale in relation to where it is placed and the impact it has on people who see it from all angles and distances.

When we think about creating an illusion of space on a flat surface this can be an area that challenges and demoralises children when seeking to draw, paint or make any kind of pictorial representation. Learning how to give an impression of distance, using perspective and representing relative size can assume an exaggerated importance for children. Giving children experiences of their own work and the work of artists, craftspeople and designers who give them support in developing the representation of space and the understanding that it is not always the most important aspect of a piece of art can help address this challenge. It should be remembered that representing the illusion of space in two dimensions is significant in Western art but not necessarily a key idea in art in other cultures or in contemporary art so the range of art children encounter can broaden their horizons in this area.

Talking about space

Space can be described using the vocabulary of position and location that children use in their day-to-day lives and with increasing precision in their mathematical investigations. In art, some words to describe the feel of the space and how it affects us as someone experiencing it from inside or outside is also important. The impact of space on other aspects of art may also be considered – a painting or sculpture may have a more powerful and significant impact when displayed in one space than in another.

Martin Wenham's book *Understanding Art: A Guide for teachers*, published in 2003, explains each of the visual and tactile elements in much more detail and with reference to practical work and the work of artists, craftspeople and designers. This book will support your subject knowledge and can help you develop your confidence with planning and teaching art in the classroom.

Media and processes

There are many art materials available to use in primary schools, allowing for exploration of a variety of media and processes. Schools operate within the constraints of their budgets, the time and space available and the skills of their staff. It is likely that the media and processes that children experience are a planned balance between those considered to be significant enough to encounter regularly so that children can develop and deepen their skills and independence and more unusual 'one-off' experiences that will broaden their experience.

Traditionally drawing was a skill that was seen to underpin art education, being important in its own right as well as being a research tool for developing ideas in many other areas of art. Drawing is a skill that is useful across the school curriculum and beyond the educational context. At the same time many adults are quick to say that they cannot draw and therefore may lack confidence in teaching children to draw. Issues around the learning and teaching of drawing will be explored more fully in Chapter 6.

Other techniques and processes such as painting, printmaking, working in three dimensions (using clay and other materials), textiles, ICT and digital media, collage and mixed media are commonly part of the primary art curriculum. Schools can include any media that interest and inspire their pupils and reflect their culture and the cultural heritage of the local area. This can allow schools to involve a range of adults who have skills and talent in art, craft and design including students, parents and volunteers. This freedom also gives schools the opportunity to respond to the availability of new materials, techniques or processes that become available more widely, in particular perhaps digital media or the use of 'found' and recycled materials. Media and processes wilvl be explored more fully in Chapters 6 to 11.

Find out more

Techniques and processes in the school
Investigate the different art techniques and processes that children are introduced to.
These might be apparent from several sources:

● displays of children's work around the school;

● lists of resources available for art in the art policy or exploring the art cupboard;

● the long-term plan or curriculum map outlining what children will cover and when in art.

> Look for the range of techniques and processes that children encounter and any that are distinctive to the school. There might be some that are related to specific projects or people. Look for opportunities for children to revisit year by year so that can develop their skills and independence. Are there any media and processes that you would need support with if you were teach them? Is there something you could introduce and teach?

Artists, craftspeople and designers

Schools also have freedom to make their art curriculum individual and distinct through the work of artists, craftspeople and designers chosen to introduce to the children. As discussed earlier the choices schools make should be guided by the need to include experience of art, craft and design made in the past and being made now, both locally and around the world. Introducing children to original works of art as well as seeing reproductions is part of this entitlement, as is giving them an understanding of why art is made now and was made in the past. Visiting art galleries and meeting people involved in making art should also be a part of the art curriculum.

Using this freedom effectively can be a challenge for students, teachers and supporters of learning. It can feel daunting selecting from all the art, craft and design available especially for students and non-specialists in the subject. It takes time to learn about and understand the work of an artist in such a way that it can be used to inspire or support learning effectively and this can lead to a dependence on choices made in published schemes or taking the 'safe' option and sticking with known artists. Pressures of time can lead to schools rarely making changes to the artists they use as part of the art curriculum. Issues around the choices we make and their significance for learning and teaching will be explored more fully in the next chapter and in the later chapters exploring media and processes.

Find out more

Artists, craftspeople and designers in your school
Investigate the artists that children are introduced to. These might be apparent from several sources:

- displays of children's work around the school;
- lists of resources available for art and library resources;
- the long-term plan or curriculum map outlining what children will cover and when in art.

Look for the range of artists, craftspeople and designers that children encounter and any that are distinctive to the school. There might be some that are related to specific projects or people. Look for the range of opportunities. Are there any artists who are unfamiliar to you? Do you have a favourite artist whose work could inspire children's learning?

Linking art to other subjects

Although art is taught discretely in some schools, in others connections are made between two or more subjects where these would enhance learning in the linked subjects. This type of approach is sometimes called 'linked learning' or the 'creative curriculum'. When meaningful links are made these can lead to inspiring and motivating learning experiences for children and give them an opportunity to work creatively. These connections can be made through the identification of an inspiring starting point or building up to an interesting outcome that provides an engaging purpose for the learning. Activities such as visits to local places of interest, inviting visitors to the school, joining in local and national events or planning a school event are often part of this type of planning.

If learning in art, and indeed in other subjects involved, is to be effective it is important to have a clear grasp of learning objectives and opportunities in each subject. Think back to the practical activity in Chapter 1 where you evaluated activities to identify if children were learning in art or whether the learning was focused on another subject. You can use this kind of judgement and reflection to ensure that if art is connected to other subjects there is learning in art taking place and the connections are not tenuous, forced or superficial. If the art learning is merely drawing or painting a picture related to the content of one of the other key subjects there is less scope for new and creative learning in art.

Case Study

Year 3 and 4 children are working on a project that connects English and art. In English they have been reading magical stories and collecting examples of stories about birds often with magical or unusual qualities. In art they have been exploring how artists and craftspeople have represented birds in three dimensions. They have looked at objects from the British Museum Collection online and illustrations of birds in storybooks. They are going to make a magical bird of their own and write a story in which it is the main character.

In art they have been taught how to make a framework with narrow strips of card to create a bird's body and attach other features such as the neck and head, legs and wings. They will cover this with sheet materials such as tissue, plastic or fabric and have been shown how to layer these to create a feathery effect. Although all the children will make birds using these techniques there is much scope for individual choices to be made in terms of the size and shape of the form and the colours and textures of the decorative materials used.

In English the children use their bird as the main character in a magical and imaginative story. As they work on their bird sculptures they also talk about, plan and begin to write their stories. There is interaction between the making and the ideas for the story as children choose materials and colours. For some children the time spent making their bird and talking about it allows them to rehearse, refine and develop the story they will write.

The stories are made into small origami books with a photo of the bird on the cover and shared in a class assembly. Later the books are displayed in the school library with the birds hanging above.

In the case study above children worked individually to create their three-dimensional birds exploring form, colour and texture in art as well as bringing them to life as the main character in an imaginative story in English. Children were able to draw upon the choices they had made later in their stories where the tactile and visual experience of making could lead to interesting choices of vocabulary in their writing. This is one example of a meaningful connection between art and another subject; many more can be made.

Making meaningful connections between subjects in the primary curriculum while preserving purposeful learning in all subjects involved can be a challenge. When it works well it can bring learning to life in the subjects involved and lead to a more immersive and creative experience for children and teachers. In Chapters 7 to 11 connections between art and other subjects will be explored in practical tasks and case studies.

Use of published materials

Many, if not most schools will use some published materials to underpin learning and teaching in art, as in other subjects. In my experience when schools use published material they tend, over time, to change it to meet their needs so that it may become no more than a starting point or underlying structure. Some schools buy in published schemes and some local authorities have written schemes of work for their schools. There are various teachers' guides and books that can guide learning and teaching in specific aspects of art such as Meg Fabian's books on drawing (Fabian, 2005) and painting (Fabian, 2009). Another useful source of ideas and materials are the websites of art galleries and arts organisations such as the National Society for Education in Art and Design (NSEAD).

Schools make choices from these resources to support their planning and often refer to these in the long-term plan. As a student or teacher planning learning or a teaching assistant supporting learning it is your role to ensure that you adapt these plans to ensure that the objectives, experiences and outcomes meet the needs of your pupils. As you gain more experience and confidence you will increasingly use these schemes as starting points from which you develop your own ideas that relate to the interests of your pupils, the individuality of your school and the resources of your local community. One factor to bear in mind when using published schemes is that they cannot address the individual needs of your pupils, so thought must always be given to inclusion and differentiation. A significant role for students and teachers when working from scheme plans is to be selective as there tends to be too much content to realistically achieve in the time available. It is more important to choose and use some parts effectively than gallop through all the activities quickly and superficially.

As a student it can be useful to start collecting and storing ideas for teaching art both on paper and electronically so that you begin to have resources and ideas that you can draw upon to support and enhance your teaching. Taking photos and notes of ideas that you see in school and in galleries as well as saving links to useful websites will help you enormously in the future. A good starting point is the primary section of the NSEAD website.

Connect and extend

In the OFSTED publication *Making a Mark: Art, Craft and Design Education* (2012) you can explore further some of the key aspects of the art curriculum and the factors that contribute to its effectiveness. Read the sections focused on the primary art curriculum and consider them in relation to the practice you observe and your own role.

Conclusion

There is so much potential for learning in the art curriculum and art is an inspiration and opportunity to motivate and educate pupils. If you can take advantage of the opportunities offered by the curriculum you will be able to provide meaningful and effective learning experiences for your pupils. In the next chapter making connections to the work of artists, visiting galleries and working with artists will be explored more fully.

Next steps

- Check that you have a copy of the school's art policy.
- Check that you know who the art co-ordinator is and how he / she can support you.
- Check that you have a copy of the long term plan / curriculum map for the year group / key stage in which you are working / on placement.
- Pay attention to the ongoing review of the curriculum in the media and on the DfE website.

References

Bowden, J. (2006) '*The Primary Art and Design Subject Leaders' Handbook*. Corsham: NSEAD.

Fabian, M. (2005) *Drawing is a Class Act*. Dunstable: Brilliant Publications.

Fabian, M. (2009) *Painting is a Class Act*. Dunstable: Brilliant Publications.

OFSTED (2012) *Making a Mark: Art, Craft and Design Education*. Available from: *http://www.ofsted. gov.uk/resources/making-mark-art-craft-and-design-education-2008-11* (accessed: 26 April 2012).

Wenham, M. (2003) *Understanding Art: A Guide for teachers*. London: Paul Chapman Publishers.

Further reading

Fabian, M. (2005) *Drawing is a Class Act*. Dunstable: Brilliant Publications.

Three books which outline sequences of activities for Years 1 and 2, Years 3 and 4, and Years 5 and 6.

Fabian, M. (2009) *Painting is a Class Act*. Dunstable: Brilliant Publications.

Three books which outline sequences of activities for Years 1 and 2, Years 3 and 4, and Years 5 and 6.

Web resources

Arts Award: *http://www.artsaward.org.uk*

Artsmark: *http://www.artsmark.org.uk/*

National Society for Education in Art and Design (NSEAD) *http://www.nsead.org/home/index.aspx*

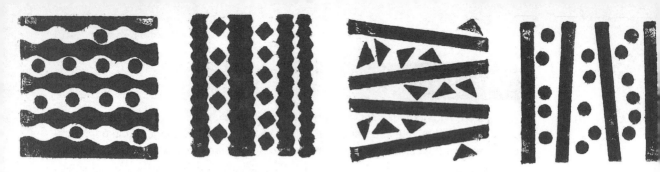

Chapter 3

Artists and art galleries

Introduction

Looking at and making connections with the work of artists, craftspeople and designers encourages us to go beyond thinking about children as makers of their own art and help them develop as discriminating and critical viewers of the art, craft and design that they see around them. Many of the children we teach will not go on to be artists, craftspeople or designers or even use art, craft and design in their working lives. All of the children we teach will go on to live in an increasingly visual environment, making their own decisions about fashion, interior décor and developing a personal style. As citizens they will encounter art in the public spaces around them and see it in galleries and museums. As Charman et al. 2006, p.54 suggest 'For those pupils who do not continue their art practice beyond school, the creative and critical skills of interpretation are equally necessary as a tool to negotiate our world of visual complexity and richness.'

It is our responsibility to give children a rich and varied experience of the work of artists, craftspeople and designers that inspires them, builds and evokes memories and feelings and broadens their horizons. These experiences can support learning and teaching by developing children's knowledge and understanding of art, craft and design from around the world and from the past so that they have a wide view of what art is as well as exploring what inspires and motivates people to make art, craft and design. Children can also learn more about the range of media and processes available to artists, especially how rapidly evolving digital media can lead to innovative art. These experiences will stimulate children to look at the world around them with curiosity so they can appreciate and be critical of the visual environment. Introducing different role models from the world of art can open children's minds to the possibilities of the range of careers available in the creative industries as well be inspired by other adults' lives and work. Children also need to develop a sense of ownership of and care for the art in public spaces and collections that they will inherit as adult citizens. Going beyond the art curriculum the work of artists, craftspeople and designers gives children a context for meaningful speaking and listening as well as enhancing and enriching other areas of the curriculum.

In this chapter the following areas will be explored:

- Making choices
- Exploring the work of artists, craftspeople and designers in the classroom
- Visiting galleries
- Working with artists

Making choices

If the opportunities available to us are to be used effectively in learning and teaching, a basic grasp of subject knowledge on the part of the teacher is necessary, while personal interest and enthusiasm are also helpful. Even if you are not a natural artist or viewer of art you can still introduce children to many exciting artistic concepts and possibilities. Schools have the freedom to make their own thought provoking and interesting choices of artists, craftspeople and designers. They have the flexibility to take the individual needs and unique features of their own community and local resources into account. Where a basic knowledge of the subject and local resources is lacking schools can resort to making obvious and safe choices or become too reliant on the choices suggested by schemes of work and published material. Being alert to national art exhibitions and local resources in galleries, museums and public spaces will allow you to make more informed and personal choices to bring your art teaching to life.

Definitions

You will have noticed the phrase 'artists, craftspeople and designers' in this book. These three words are significant and should steer us towards making a range of choices rather than choosing from a narrow group of famous fine artists.

Artists

- *A dictionary definition*: 'a person who paints or draws as a profession or hobby' or 'a person who practises or performs any of the creative arts' (Soanes and Hawker, 2008, p48)
- *A personal definition*: people who create art, especially that which is considered 'fine art' such as drawing, painting, installations, sculpture and photography.
- Artists may include:

  painters, printmakers, sculptors, photographers.

Craftspeople

- *A dictionary definition*: 'a worker skilled in a particular craft' (Soanes and Hawker, 2008, p227)
- *A personal definition*: skilled people who make decorative and/or functional objects by hand.
- Craftspeople may include:

  weavers, ceramicists, jewellery makers, felt makers, embroiderers, potters, wood carvers, stone masons, calligraphers, screen printers, batik artists, glass makers, basket makers, quilters, mosaic makers, mask makers, puppet makers, papier-mâché makers, furniture maker, knitters.

Designers

- *A dictionary definition*: 'a person who designs things' (Soanes and Hawker, 2008, p269)
- *A personal definition*: people who create or design objects and the environment, sometimes for others to make.
- Designers may include:

  fashion designers, graphic artists, illustrators, architects, milliners, glove makers, animators, product designers, cartoonists, costume designer, landscape designer, interior decorators.

Some of these examples may fit into several categories or may have a visual aspect to their role and yet not fall completely within categories of art, craft or design. These could include architects, archaeologists and cartographers. Throughout the rest of the book the word 'artists' often indicates 'artists, craftspeople and designers'.

Choosing art, craft and design to support learning in art

When you are making choices of which artists, craftspeople and designers to support your teaching it is important to consider the bigger picture of the experience the child has across one or both key stages. As Bowden 2006, p.40 states 'The programme should be broad and balanced covering a wide range of both artists and designers from a range of different genres, periods and cultures with no evident gender bias.' If all the art, craft and design that children encounter is that produced by a distinct group (men, Europeans, people who worked in the past, painters) this can skew their understanding of who produces art, craft and design entirely. It may also affect their feelings about themselves as makers of art. Having said this some works of art and significant artists are European male painters from the past and to avoid using their work entirely would deny children access to some important examples. A balance should prevail so think about the artists and artwork children will encounter over a year, key stage and whole time at primary school aiming for a wide range of experiences in the long term.

Make a list of the artists, craftspeople and designers that you are aware of. Look critically at the names of the specific artists, craftspeople and designers that you have listed. Consider them in relation to the headings in the table below.

Male artists	Female artists	Artists living and working now	Artists who worked in the past
Artists from your locality or region	Artists from the UK	Artists from places all over the world	Artists from different cultures
Art made by individuals	Art made by people working together	Art made for different purposes	Artists using different materials/processes

The choices that you make about who and what to look at, talk about and respond to should be varied and inclusive, allowing you to address issues of diversity in your curriculum. Identifying artists, who work locally and examples of art, craft and design in your local community, including public spaces, galleries and museums, is important. You can also consider encouraging children to have some choice and influence over the artists that are explored. Following children's interests may allow you to include some children who may be unmoved by traditional fine art and help you refresh your own knowledge. Animation, graphic design, comics and graphic novels, computer games, installations and the use of digital media can be motivating for older Key Stage 2 children, especially boys.

In looking more closely at the artists you refer to you may have identified some gaps. It could be that it is beyond the scope of your role to address these gaps currently. This will depend on how decisions are made about the art curriculum in the school and how much flexibility there is in making changes. Your awareness of the impact of the choices that are made and your overview of how the lesson and unit of work fits into the year, key stage and whole school experience can help you to make interesting and worthwhile connections or suggest changes in the future and make the most of the material indicated to you in existing plans.

Beyond the choices of people whose work is explored you should also consider where there are specific pieces of artwork named. It is important to remember that it is seldom that one piece of art, craft or design can represent the entirety of that person's lifetime of work. Children should not, for example, take away an impression that the only painting Van Gogh ever painted was *Sunflowers*. Where specific pieces of work are named, especially in published schemes, you should be clear about what the children are expected to learn about or from this and how it fits with their own making of artwork so that you go beyond copying the work or using it in a superficial way.

Case Study

A town centre school has audited the art, craft and design available to them as a basis for making choices about what children will look at and use in art and across the curriculum. This includes:

- a survey of the art in public spaces within easy walking distance of the school;
- consideration of the school site as an environment for art;
- a visit to and contact made with the art education officer at the local art gallery and museum, exploring the permanent collection and changing exhibtions;
- a survey of the skills and interests of parents and friends of the school;
- buying into the local authority loan scheme for orginal works of art;
- investigation of sources of funding for having artists, designers and craftspeople into the school to work and for making visits further afield to regional and national art galleries;
- investigations of local, regional national projects and awards in which schools can take part;
- investigation of internet sources and software that will support learning and teaching in art.

This audit is led by the art co-ordinator and supported by staff and governors of the school. It results in consideration of the resources, talents and expertise of the local community and how these can be used to support learning and teaching in art.

As a student, NQT or teaching assistant this case study is likely to be too big a project for you to undertake unless you have a strong personal interest in the subject or you are aspiring to be an art co-ordinator. You can, however, think about these areas in relation to the class you are teaching and plan to use what is around you effectively to support learning and teaching.

The quality and availability of resources is a significant factor in the choices you can make. If certain works of art are named in the long-term plan or scheme of work, supporting resources such as original works of art, good quality reproductions and supporting information should be available in school. The reproduction you choose should be considered in terms of scale – it may be helpful to be able to show children the actual size of a work of art by using a piece of paper to show the actual size and proportions so that they understand that all works of art are not A4 in size. If you are unfamiliar with these, finding out more about them before you begin planning, teaching and supporting is essential.

Find out more

Explore online to find the following resources and save them to your favourites:

- Google Art Project – images of art from many galleries and museums and galleries around the world.
- BBC Your paintings – a searchable database of paintings available to see in the UK and resources to use in education

LINK

- National Art and Craft Directory – an illustrated directory of artists and makers working now that can be searched by name, media and various other terms
- Engage – The national association for gallery art and education professionals, promoting access to and understanding of the visual arts through gallery education.

LINK

These are all useful websites for exploring works of art to use in the classroom and finding places to visit.

As you increasingly look around for examples of artists' work to use in your teaching it can be useful to devise a way of organising them so that you can readily access them when the time is right. Saving links to favourites, copying links to an ongoing word document and keeping a folder with images you have collected or cut out can all be useful. Another useful tool is the virtual pinboard 'Pinterest' which is a way of collecting and organising visual material online. Here you can label 'boards' by theme, pin images to them and search the boards and images of other users for images that you want to add to your collection.

LINK

Exploring the work of artists, craftspeople and designers in the classroom

There are many ways in which the work of artists can used to support and stimulate learning in art and across the curriculum. I have found that looking and talking about works of art is a way for children to explore and respond to what they see or sometimes, feel. Making connections to art they are making themselves is another way of responding to art, as long as this is planned sensitively and avoids copying. Choices can be made that support learning not only in art but in other areas of the curriculum, leading to purposeful connections being made between art and another subject.

Talking about the work of artists, craftspeople and designers

When you are planning for children to talk about the work of artists it is important to consider how you can scaffold talk about art effectively. Charman et al. (2006) suggest that whilst we can encourage children to talk about the visual elements and processes we must also equip children to interpret, explore and express ideas in relation to the art they see and experience.

When talking about art with children, especially younger children or children who are inexperienced in talking about art, having a structure to support looking and talking can help them develop and extend the vocabulary and thinking skills required. This may include a clear identification of the vocabulary and sentence structures that will be useful, some key questions and an order in which to begin questioning moving from the known to the unknown and more speculative. The level and development of the children's vocabulary should be considered as well as the needs of children learning English as an Additional Language or those who have a special educational need that has an impact on their communication and language.

Practical task

Learning objective:

● to consider the vocabulary and questions that you could use to talk about a work of art, craft or design

In this practical activity you will have the opportunity to identify the words, sentence structures, prompts and questions that you could use to talk with children about a work of art. Planning this out before you begin can help you ensure that all children are included and learn from the experience. Use what you know about speaking and listening and devising open and closed questions to help you in this task.

You will need:

● This pro forma.

What to do:

● Choose a work of art, craft or design.

● Identify vocabulary and key questions in relation to it using the headings in the boxes below as a guide.

You may wish to use Canaletto's *A Regatta on the Grand Canal* which is available on the National Gallery website. This painting can be used on an IWB and there is an opportunity to zoom in on different parts of it to focus on detail. It was painted in about 1740 and is a view of Venice during the annual carnival regatta. There is another painting by the same artist painted at around the same time called *Venice: The Basin of San Marco on Ascension Day* that you could also look at to compare.

LINK

Questions to consider:

● *What can be seen and described*: Asking children to describe what they see is a basic way in to looking at any work of art. It allows them to identify and name. This can be developed by asking them to find named items; asking what is next to, behind, furthest

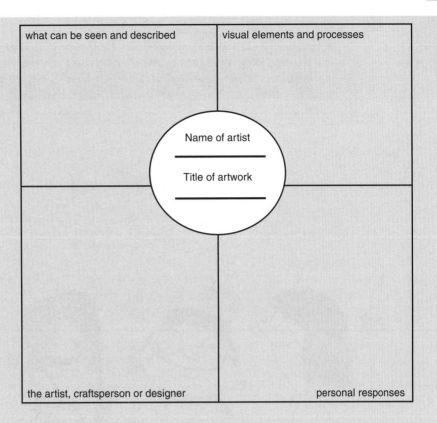

what can be seen and described

visual elements and processes

Name of artist

Title of artwork

the artist, craftsperson or designer

personal responses

away; asking children to choose a part and describe it so others can find it; or other homing in type questions. Another approach is to provide children with real items, pictures or words and ask them to find these in the work of art or use the spotlight tool on the IWB to take them on a tour of the painting before revealing it as a whole.

- *Vocabulary, visual elements and processes*: Questions and prompts in this section are likely to be underpinned by the choice of work of art that you have made. Perhaps your choice relates to a visual element, media or process that the children are or will be using and this will guide your questions. You might encourage children to look for how an artist has represented space or used colour in their work. You might aim for children to look for particular ways of using natural materials or combining threads in a weaving. With older children comparison may be drawn out between this work and other works of art the children know, or their own work. Specific vocabulary that children need in order to discuss the work should be introduced or revised.

- *About the artist, craftsperson or designer*: Questions in this section may develop as children look at the work of art. You may want to be able to share some knowledge about the artist or prompt children to devise questions so that they can do some research of their own. Children could devise their own questions that they would ask the artist if they could. Some of these questions may be more speculative and open. Some could encourage older pupils to consider the function of art, who it was made for, why it was made and how the artist prepared to make it. These questions may provide opportunities to make connections to where the art was made (link to geography), when the art was made and what else was happening at that time (link to history).

- *Encouraging personal responses and speculation*: Questions in this section could be entirely open and allow children to respond individually. This will vary depending on their age and experience and could include the feelings and memories evoked by the work and any questions children would like to ask about it. Making connections to their own work could be useful here – is there anything we can learn to help us with our own art work, for example.

    LINK

In this practical task you had a closer look at planning for talk about a piece of art. You might take elements from this approach to use at different times depending on your plan for learning. It is important to avoid being overly prescriptive – I have found that when we allow children to think about what they see without any preconceptions they can speculate and imagine more freely and creatively. As Charman et al. (2006) state 'Teaching pupils a method of looking at art does not need to place a stranglehold on what is essentially the creative act of making meaning. Rather, it offers a way of scaffolding what can otherwise seem a confusing process with no clear way in' (p. 57).

Connect and extend

Charman et al. (2006) in their book *The Art Gallery Handbook* suggest an alternative scaffold for talking about art based around:

- a personal approach,
- ways in to the object,
- ways into the subject,
- ways into the context.

You might find it useful to explore how this approach could support and develop looking at art, craft and design with children.

When introducing a work of art to children finding imaginative ways to attract children's attention is important in provoking and sustaining interest. Planning different ways in to the work of art rather than immediately looking at the entire piece helps children to look in a more focused way. Showing children small details can be an interesting way to start looking – either by covering a reproduction with a large sheet of paper and cutting windows in it to open one by one or, if the work is available online, using the highlight or zoom tool on the IWB. Taking children on a narrative tour of the work of art visiting different parts can be another way, especially if you are looking at a representative piece of art. These strategies can help children look at different parts of the work rather than become overwhelmed, not knowing quite where to look or superficially skimming over the artwork. Older children should be challenged to go on to make comparisons between works of art. Your choices of the work that children will compare should be planned to allow children to make meaningful comments that they may then go on to relate to their own work.

Case Study

At a recent local exhibition of artists' responses to visits to Venice over the Past one hundred years a group of PGCE students identified the following comparisons that could be made:

- two works of art by the same artist;
- a work of art by a contemporary artist and one by an artist who lived a hundred years ago;
- two works in the same media by different artists;
- two works of art with contrasting approaches – e.g. a detailed line drawing vs a loose, free painting;
- a work of art by a female artist and another by a male artist;
- two works of art with different viewpoints of the same place;
- two works of art with different compositions.

In this case study a relatively small exhibition was explored but it gave rise to many ideas that could be used to inspire comparisons and discussion. With a class of children a limited number of these, or perhaps only ones would be chosen to explore in depth. Along with exhibiitons many galleries and museums have educational resources available to support and guide planning and teaching.

Using the work of artists to inspire making

Some of the units of work that you teach may be inspired by or include reference to an artist's work or a specific piece of work. It is essential that this work is used thoughtfully and most especially that children are not expected to routinely copy works of art, a practice which leads to similar or even identical responses rather than individual and personal outcomes. There are many other ways of using works of art in the classroom that are more effective and inspiring to children. In the examples below exploring the human figure in motion is the underlying starting point for choices of art or artists to look at and explore.

Approach	Examples
Using the work of two artists so that children can make choices in the features and ideas they take and use.	Paula Rego – drawings for *The Dance*, 1988 Kenneth Armitage – drawing *Scurrying Figures* 1984
Using the work of an artist working in one media or process to inspire work in another.	Look at images of painted figures on Greek vases (simplified profile figures in movement, 2 colours) and make collages using these qualities
Using the work of an artist working in two dimensions as a starting point for working in three dimensions (and vice versa).	Look at images of Giacometti's depiction of figures (linear qualities) as preparation to make string prints
Using a visual element as a starting point and looking for work that exemplifies different approaches	Form – Giacometti (elongated/simplified forms), sculptures from the classical world (realism) Peter Jansen (kinetic figures)
Using the work of an artist/several artists to help solve a problem or make suggestions about how to overcome a challenge	Explore how artists have conveyed movement – catching figure mid-action (runners on Greek vases), time lapse photography (Muybridge), movement lines in cartoons
Using the work of an artist to introduce a material, tool, technique or process that the children will then apply to ideas/subject matter of their own	Peter Blake's collages using images of people – apply this to sport, dance or other physical activity.
Using the subject matter as a starting point and then asking the children themselves to find artists who have represented it in different ways before they go on to have a go themselves	Ask pairs of children to choose sport or activity that involves movement and look for two examples of this in art to share with the class.
Using abstract art to help children think about alternatives to 'making a picture of …'	Thomas Heatherwick's *B of the Bang*. Richard Long – recordings of walks in landscapes.
Using the work of an artist who works in an original or unorthodox way to get children thinking differently	'Transmission drawing' by Morgan O'Hara, responding directly to the movements of people in drawing.

LINK

Other approaches you might investigate are using several examples from the same artist to help children consider how they changed and developed over time and using two examples where one artist has responded to the work of another artist. The approaches discussed above avoid planning for children to copy the work of artists but rather inspire, teach or suggest ways forward for the art children will be making. Deciding which approach to take in any half term or unit of work would depend on the overall learning objectives you were planning to meet.

Using the work of artists, craftspeople and designers to make connections with other subjects

Your choices of the work of artists can also support meaningful links to other areas of the curriculum and enrich the overall learning experience for children. As discussed earlier it is important that when you identify and plan for these links that they are not tenuous or forced. The learning objectives relating to art and to the other subjects must be kept in mind so that you are clear about the learning which is to take place in each. This will vary from subject to subject and in relation to the chosen areas of each subject that are connected by planning.

English

There are many skills that children develop in English that require the context of another subject to make the use and application of those skills meaningful. Aspects of speaking and listening including description, speculation, narration, making presentations, participating in role play and drama can be set in the context of talking about works of art or artists' lives. Research skills such as finding information in books and on the internet, scanning and skimming, summarising and presenting can be connected to finding out more about art and artists. Many works of art and images can inspire poetry and stories.

In all of these examples the main focus of learning is English and art is providing a context for the use and application of skills. When art is the main focus of learning in the discussion and exploration of a work of art the focus is more likely to be on visual elements, how the artist solved problems and used tools and processes in their making, why the art was made and how it affects the viewer. Children will be using and developing their subject-specific vocabulary and making notes, and can also devise and write labels/catalogue entries for their work.

History

When considering connections between art and history we might identify how pictures and objects can show us what the past was like – what people wore, where and how they lived, what some people looked like and a depiction of significant events. This can enrich children's understanding of the past and what life was like for people. Older children will also explore how and why art was made in the past, as well as considering how far we can rely on what artists show us, how art might be used to persuade and inform and whether we can get a complete picture of the past by looking at the art that has survived. A further link to consider is identifying how the past and works of art and artists from the past inspire artists working now. Children can also consider how the development of materials, equipment and technology have affected what artists can make and how their work can be shared with audiences.

Geography

Similar considerations can be made in relation to geography. Art from other places can show children what those places look like, sometimes conveying aspects difficult to appreciate in any other way, such as the atmosphere, weather, colour and perhaps quality of light. These places might be real or imagined, contemporary or from the past. Comparing how artists from several times have represented a place and what that place is like now can help children consider how places and the environment change for better and for worse. Artists in the past and those working now are often inspired by places and the feelings and atmosphere of places, as well the land itself or a wish to protect the environment.

RE and spiritual development

There are opportunities to explore the way faith and belief has inspired art by looking at the art made for places of worship and made by people inspired by faith. Looking at art in churches, temples, mosques and places where people worship or contemplate can help children consider the way art can have a spiritual and symbolic meaning. In this way connections between art and religious education can be made as well as considering art in relation to spirituality outside organised worship and religions.

Science

Connections can also be made between art and science. Curiosity, careful observation and exploring materials are important in both subjects. Children can apply some of their learning in art, especially drawing, in their recording in science, learning about how a skill can be applied in different ways to meet the different requirements of a task. Scientists have used drawing and painting to record their observations (botanical illustration for example) and artists have been inspired by discoveries in science as well as what they can see with the tools scientists use in their work.

When making connections between the work of artists and learning in other subjects it is important to be clear about learning in art and in the other subject. Although physical education, design technology, ICT, mathematics, music and PSHE have not been discussed in depth here the same principles for making choices and clarity of planning apply.

Visiting galleries and museums

One aspect of using the work of artists is the unique contribution that seeing original art works can make to the learning experience. You will probably have experienced for yourself the feelings of seeing an original work of art that you know from reproductions. Reproductions tend to be misleading in terms of scale and appearance – when we encounter the original, and appreciate the size, colour, form and overall impact anew, it can be breathtaking. It is important that we help children understand to the difference and appreciate that the original work of art in its setting can inspire feelings and an understanding that it may not be possible to get from a reproduction.

Opportunities for using original works of art must be planned in at the long-term stage so that the organisation required for making visits can be undertaken in plenty of time. The school policy, guidance from the local authority and statutory requirements should be followed in ensuring that any visits are safe for adults and children.

Works of art, craft and design can be found both locally and nationally. Knowing what is available in your locality and region can allow you to make choices of art that reflect or are important in your community. Making contact with the education officer or curator responsible for school visits at your nearest gallery or museum can help you in planning for a productive visit. You should also look for works of art in public spaces such as town centres and parks as well as art at stately homes and in theatres. As well as art that is permanently displayed it is likely that there will temporary exhibitions in your locality that you can use as a focus. This requires more flexibility but liaison with gallery/museum curators or education officers can support you in planning ahead. Galleries tend to know what their exhibitions will be well in advance giving time for you to plan them in where appropriate. This can give you access to the work of contemporary artists and often there will be associated activities including the chance to meet or even work with the artist.

Preparing for the visit

Before any visit to gallery it is important that you prepare in a number of ways. Making contact with the curator or education officer to talk through any input or activities that will take place is an important first step. The curator or education officer is more likely to be able to meet the needs of your children if he or she knows about their prior experience and individual needs before the visit. Along with this visiting the gallery or exhibition yourself before you go with the children will also help you plan. Many galleries and other places of interest will allow people who are planning to bring a school to make an advance visit free of charge. If this is impossible research and find out as much as you can from the gallery's website and from talking with the staff.

Planning in terms of how it will inspire and support learning both during and after the visit will ensure that you use its full potential as a learning experience. The children will need to be prepared in terms of expected behaviour and conventions for behaviour that may be different than other places they have visited. Also, ensuring that children have the background knowledge and vocabulary to use and respond to on the visit is vital. You can do this in collaboration with the curator or education officer so that the group get the best out of the visit. This is especially important for children learning English as an Additional Language or with a special educational need related to language.

Immediately before the visit the adults who will accompany the class on the visit must be prepared in terms of health and safety, risk assessment, behaviour expectations and their own roles in supporting the class. This might involve focusing on one child or a named group of children or it might be more general. It is also important to ensure that they can support children's learning. This could involve focusing on children who will need support with their behaviour, listening to and responding to language or working practically.

Case Study

A class of Year 1 and 2 children are getting ready to visit their local art gallery as part of a unit of work based on sculpture. Before they go their teacher reviews some of the vocabulary that the curator will use. These words include:

- basic vocabulary – scuplture, sculptor, three dimensions, solid;
- words to describe position and viewpoints – behind, at the side, in front, around, above, below;
- words for the materials sculptures are made from – marble, stone, wood, clay, metal, bronze;
- words for how sculpures can be made – carved, cast, moulded, assembled.

Their teacher also reviews expected conventions of beahviour in the art gallery especially:

- walking around the gallery;
- talking quietly to each other and to adults;
- looking but not touching unless the curator gives permission.

The adults who will be accompanying the class are all present for this session so that they too are fully briefed and can support effectively. One of the adults can speak the first language of some of the children and she will support two newly arrived pupils in accessing the session.

At the gallery the curator talks with the children about two sculptures that show different ways of representing the human figure. One is Jacob Epstein's *Head of Vaughan Williams* and the other is Barbara Hepworth's *Four Figures Waiting* – both of these are cast in bronze. The children are able to use some of the vocabulary reviewed before their visit in their discussion of the sculptures.

Much of the preparation for the visit flows from the content of the visit as planned with the education officer, from the medium-term planning and from the teacher's knowledge of the children's learning in art. Whether a one-off or part of an ongoing sequence I have found that the time spent in preparation for visits is always worthwhile.

Find out more

The Art Gallery Handbook written and edited by Helen Charman, Katherine Rose and Gillian Wilson (2006) is an informative exploration of subject knowledge in relation to art galleries and how they can support learning in art and across the curriculum. It includes many practical ideas that you can use both on visits and when looking at art in the classroom – choose one to try out next time you teach art.

At the gallery

At the gallery your visit or session could be led by a curator or education officer or you might lead the visit yourself. There are a number of ways you can help children get the best from the visit. If the session is led by a curator this is a great opportunity for you to observe and learn from their practice as a specialist in their field. In the future you will be able to use some of the teaching ideas and subject knowledge in your own work where appropriate. If you lead the visit yourself it can be useful to consider some initial starter activities and a more focused activity after this.

Starter activities

When you go into the gallery it can be useful to settle the children with an introductory activity to allow them to have a look around in a purposeful way and get a sense of where they are. This could include:

Learning focus	Activity
Comparison of reproduction to original	Give pairs of children a postcard and asking them to find the work of art represented on it.
Looking carefully	Give children a picture or the name of an item that appears in some of the artworks and asking them to identify examples of it.
Inferring/looking at visual clues	Make quiz cards that ask children to look for clues in specific works of art perhaps with a main and a supplementary clue.
Reading/finding contextual information	Give children details from the label or title to the art and asking them to seek out the matching piece.
Visual elements	Ask children to look for examples of artists who have used a specific visual element – find a picture where the artist has used bright colours, find a sculpture where the artist has used curves, etc.
Time, historical context, chronology	Ask children to look at pairs of work made at different dates and find out which was made first.
Place, geographical context, location	Ask children to look at pairs of works showing different places/ landscape features / explore on a map it appropriate
Media and processes	Ask children to look for examples of a medium or process or different examples within one area such as painting or textiles.

Your choice of starter activity could be based on what the children will later go on to explore more fully and your own knowledge of the class. It could also reflect the age of the pupils and their prior experience of visiting galleries or other offsite locations. It might also relate to how busy the gallery is. At some local galleries your visit might take place before the building is open to the general public giving you more freedom to move around and use the space. At larger, national galleries this is unlikely to be the case and you will have to work around the other visitors.

Looking more closely

When you consider your main focus for learning in the gallery you should be guided by your objectives, what is available to look at and talk about, and the outcomes you have in mind for when you return to the classroom. You may have experienced for yourself how easy it is to become overwhelmed by all there is to look at in a gallery or museum and the tendency to flit from work to work looking briefly at the artworks but not responding to any in depth.

Choosing one or just a few pieces to look at more closely is an effective approach. Alternatively looking in depth at one key work all together and then giving children choice about what else to look at can allow some freedom for personal exploration. If you regularly talk about works of art with children in the classroom they are more likely to be able to talk productively and express themselves when in an art gallery looking at original work. If you have already visited the gallery and identified some prior knowledge children may need conversation will be more informed. As well as talking about works of art there is potential for using drama techniques to develop a response to a work of art: freeze framing, hot seating and dialogue improvisation can be used to place children inside a work of art and explore it from a different perspective.

Taking the opportunity to observe the curator working with children can be informative: recording children's ideas and vocabulary when they respond or noting teaching ideas that the curator can both inform future planning and teaching. In terms of support and inclusion where you have pupils with particular needs in relation to speaking and listening the support you offer in the classroom should also be available in the gallery situation and if a curator is leading the session they should be fully briefed about how to effectively include all the children. If most of the visit will be looking and talking it can be useful for adults to take notes and reminders so that when you are back at school you can prompt and help children recall what they have learned.

As well as talking about works of art children could work practically to record what they see, feel and think in the gallery. This could be in their sketchbooks or separately on paper or mini-sketchbooks made for the purpose. Worksheets, although tempting, should be avoided as filling them in can lead children to focus on the worksheet rather than the experience itself. Perhaps if absolutely necessary prompts to guide looking and help gather relevant information could be provided.

After the visit

When you return to school from visiting a gallery or works of art in another setting there a number of ways of using the experience in supporting learning in art and in other subjects. Given the time and challenge involved in planning and carrying out a trip it is very important that the experience does support learning effectively. You will have identified a connection between the gallery experience and work back in the classroom at the planning stage. Perhaps you are going to explore and respond to a similar subject or inspiration such as the figure, landscape or poetry. You may be planning for the children to work in the same media, such as watercolours, plaster and wood or textiles. You could be learning about the same visual element, such as pattern, line or space. You could also be making connections to another subject, such as exploring paintings of your locality from the past to explore both painting from observation and identify changes that have happened over time.

Using the sketches and notes or your own notes of what children said and any other materials brought back from the visit will provide a strong connection back to the experience. There may be resources that you can bring back such as guidebooks, postcards and posters and there may be resources available online. It is unlikely that you would have been able to take photos in the gallery. Keeping in touch with the gallery and sharing the children's work produced after the visit should also be considered. Curators and education staff are often interested to see what children have been inspired to do after their visit.

Connect and extend

Read Angela Eckhoff's article 'The importance of art viewing experiences in early childhood visual arts: the exploration of a master art teacher's strategies for meaningful early arts experiences' published in 2008 in the *Early Childhood Education Journal* (Vol. 35 Issue 5. pp. 463–72. Focus on the the four strategies (game play, questioning, storytelling and technical talk) explained with examples on pages 4 to 7 and consider how these might support your teaching.

Funding for trips

Taking children to art galleries and to do practical work outside the school can be costly to the school and to parents. If you are planning a trip that encourages children to enjoy and appreciate visual art especially painting and sculpture an organisation called the Eridge Trust offers grants to pay for part or all of the costs of the visit. This could support a visit to see artworks in your local gallery or sculpture park, or to go further afield. The visit need not be exclusively related to learning in art so it could be combined with another subject. Applications are normally required by the end of May for the following academic year and are quite straightforward to complete, being no longer than 600 words (see the Eridge Trust entry under Websites).

My own school benefitted from this funding on several occasions and the visits the children experienced supported their learning art and their personal development as confident and motivated learners.

Working with artists, designers and craftspeople

There are opportunities for children to meet and learn from people working as artists, designers and craftspeople. These opportunities could come about in a variety of ways including:

- through personal contact with artists who have connections with the school eg parents, governors, members of staff and their families and people living local to the school;
- through outreach activities arranged via your local art gallery. Often when exhibitions take place activities involving the artist are planned for local schools and the community;
- through having an artist to work in school as part of a one off project or ongoing initiative. Some charities and organisations fund artists to work in schools. For a list see the Further resources section at the end of this chapter.

There may be other opportunities available to you depending on where your school is – if you are close to a college or university with art students this may be a great source of people willing and enthusiastic to share their work. If your local area has an arts festivals or open studios you might find artists willing to include children as a way of reaching a wider audience for their work. If your school has a community room or large hall you might be able to hold local art exhibitions yourself, supporting the arts and artists in your community and making contact with people who might help you with the art curriculum.

When considering this aspect of the art curriculum you could use contacts with artists to develop the children's understanding of art as an opportunity for employment and personal fulfilment undertaken by people living now in the local community. Inviting artists into school to share and talk about their work allows children to learn more about what motivates people to make art and how it shapes their lives. Having an artist in residence working for a sustained period in the school with a class or year group is another way of connecting to people who make art. This is a wonderful opportunity to work with someone who has developed specialist skills in an area of art and is often a chance for children to use different materials and learn a new process or a different way of using a familiar process.

If you are going to work with someone whose job it is to make or design art it will be important that you work with them to make sure that they and the children have a positive experience. Working with children in a school setting can be very different to talking to members of the general public so you should consider how best to brief and prepare your visitor. It may be that the artist has experience of working with a range of people but you have the knowledge of your class from the inside that can be vital.

Practical task

Working with an artist, craftsperson or designer

Learning objective:

● to consider how to get the best from working with a visitor to the class.

In this exercise you will think about how to prepare for and work with an artist, craftsperson or designer in school.

You will need:

● the pro forma below

What to do:

● make notes under each of the headings below.

Unit of work	My notes
Before the unit begins	
During the sequence of lessons	
After the unit of work	

Questions to consider

● *Before the lesson/sequence of lessons*: Practicalities such as the use of time, space and resources are important to clarify well before the visit begins. Particular tools, equipment or materials may be required and could be supplied by the school, the artist or shared between them. The number of adults available to support the artist should be considered – all the usual support for individuals and groups is vital and additional adults may be needed if the activity requires. Alternatively the class might work in groups, turn by turn with the artist. Sometimes when working with a visitor a class might work for a sustained period on art rather than following their usual timetable. Making sure the routines and timings are clear is important: visiting adults may well be unfamiliar with any constraints the school day might impose. Any preparation in terms of health and safety and care of the classroom and children's clothes should also be addressed in plenty of time. Sharing information about language levels and any strategies necessary to include all children is vital to the success of the experience especially if the visitor works with children only occasionally. Checking that the visiting adult has the appropriate CRB check is also vital before the work with children begins.

- *During the lesson/sequence of lessons*: Some flexibility could be necessary, especially if the tools, equipment, materials and techniques are very new to the children. If the project is continuing over several lessons storage of partially completed work will be required.
- *After the lesson/sequence of lessons*: Continued contact with the visiting artist via email or a visit and a sharing of finished art can round off the experience and give the artist, the school staff and the children an opportunity to reflect on the experience as well as it share it with the rest of the school and parents.

Connect and extend

Read Ann Orfali's report Artists Working in Partnership with Schools: Quality Indicators and Advice for Planning, Commissioning and Delivery, published in 2004 by Arts Council England.

This report goes into more detail about the practical considerations and other aspects of working with artists in school from the perspectives of artists, schools and pupils. The later sections on indicators of quality will help you consider the contribution of this kind of activity to the life of the school, your own role and children's learning.

Conclusion

Making choices that inspire learning in art and identifying opportunities to collect ideas contribute enormously to the enthusiasm and motivation that you can create in art. The most important thing to bear in mind is that you do have the opportunity to choose from a very wide range of resources, starting points and learning outcomes. Units of work can be personal to your school and the children in your class if you want them to be. Changing what has always been done can feel like a daunting step but it is well worth the time and effort for the children and for you. In the next chapter planning for learning in art will be explored in more detail.

Encouraging children to visit galleries and museums can widen their horizons and influence their learning and lives beyond school. When I began taking classes to my local art gallery each half term I found that, over time, this led children to talk about the experiences at home, ask their parents to take them back in the holidays and ultimately to join in with holiday activities – many families had not engaged in this before.

Next steps

- Identify the different ways that learning in art will be inspired in the class/year in which you work.
- Begin to broaden your knowledge of artists, craftspeople and designers so that you have more choices available to you.

- Investigate makers of art in your locality, including people who work in school and parents.
- Investigate the original works of art available in your immediate vicinity (within walking distance perhaps)

References

Bowden, J. (2006) *The Primary Art and Design Subject Leaders' Handbook*. Corsham: NSEAD.

Charman, H., Rose, K. and Wilson, G. (2006) *The Art Gallery Handbook: A Resource for Teachers*. London: Tate Publishing.

Soanes, C. and Hawker, S. (eds) (2008) *Compact Oxford English Dictionary*, 3rd edn. Oxford: Oxford University Press.

Further reading

Charman, H., Rose, K. and Wilson, G. (2006) *The Art Gallery Handbook: A Resource for Teachers*. London: Tate Publishing.

Eckhoff, A. (2008) 'The importance of art viewing experiences in early childhood visual arts: the exploration of a master art teacher's strategies for meaningful early arts experiences'. *Early Childhood Education Journal*, Vol. 35 Issue 5 pp. 463–72.

Orfali, A. (2004) *Artists Working in Partnership with Schools: Quality Indicators and Advice for Planning, Commissioning and Delivery*. Newcastle: Arts Council England.

Schumann, B. (2009) *13 Women Artists Children Should Know*. Munich: Prestel Verlag.

Web resources

National Gallery 'Take One Picture' website: *http://www.takeonepicture.org/* Click on 'Across the curriculum' in the list on the left to take you to examples and ideas.

Arts Council England: *http://www.artscouncil.org.uk/*

Department of Culture, Media and Sport: *http://www.culture.gov.uk/*

Crafts Council: *http://www.craftscouncil.org.uk/*

Design Council: *http://www.designcouncil.org.uk/*

Creative Partnerships: *http://www.creative-partnerships.com/*

Eridge Trust email contact: *dkm.cowdy@btinternet.com* / Tel: 01223 207549

Art from India (Sir Robert Hitchams Primary school resource): *http://atschool.eduweb.co.uk/sirrobhitch.suffolk/india_art/full.htm*

Chapter 4

Planning and assessment

Introduction

As with any area of the curriculum, planning supports learning and allows us to organise content, ensure progression and consider the breadth and balance of the learning experiences. Most schools will have some or all of their planning for art in place and often plans will be reused and adapted for teaching from one year to the next. Whilst having plans in place is supportive it is important to retain some flexibility and opportunity to include new and different resources and events that can enrich learning, as well as to respond to children's and the school's interests. At the early stages of teaching it is likely that the reassurance of having plans in place will be essential for your confidence but as your teaching skills and experience develop you will increasingly value the freedom to follow your own creative ideas. In this chapter following areas will be explored:

- Long-term planning
- Medium-term planning
- Planning for learning in the lesson
- Assessing learning in art

Long-term planning outlines the content, indicating what will be covered and when. Medium-term planning sets out the expectations for a half term, unit or work or sequence of lessons. Short-term planning provides the teaching detail that can be used to support teaching or support role with the children. There are aspects of good practice in learning and teaching the class or supporting groups or individuals.

Long-term planning

The long-term plan or curriculum map outlines the general content of what will be covered and often it allocates content to specific terms or half terms in year groups or key stages. The school's art policy underpins this and gives you an understanding of the bigger picture of art in the school. It is at the long-term planning stage that links can be identified between two or three subject areas where these will enhance learning. Out-of-school visits, visitors to school and participation in local and national events can also be planned well in advance using this framework.

The long-term plan should provide a guide for the content of your teaching. When you consult a long-term plan to find out more about the next half term it is most unlikely to be in a form that you can pick up and teach directly from. It might indicate the media or process, visual elements and work of artists that may form part of the learning or it could refer you to some teaching materials. You should identify the sources of planning for each half term on the long term plan for your year group or key stage so that you are ready to consider these in relation to the class. Even if it is a familiar unit of work teaching it to a new class will require you to reflect and review before teaching it again: children's prior learning, interests and needs will be different to those of previous classes. If you are a student it is likely that your main focus on placement will be the half term you are teaching but it is important to understand the context of this half term in the bigger picture of the year and the key stage.

Practical task

Learning objective:

● to explore the long-term plan/curriculum map

In this task you will find the school's long term plan and ask yourself a series of questions to help you to reflect on how you can use it to plan and support learning.

You will need:

● a copy of the school's long term plan for the year that you are working in.

● the pro forma below.

What to do:

● Use the questions on the pro forma to explore the long term plan and make notes about what you find. Annotate the pro forma with any gaps or questions that you identify as you consider the long term plan.

Year group	What will inspire the unit of work?	Which techniques will be taught?	Which visual elements will be addressed?	Which artists, designers or craft-speople will be used?	Are there any strong and meaning-ful links to other areas of the curriculum?	Your questions to follow up
1st half term						
2nd half term						
3rd half term						
4th half term						
5th half term						
6th half term						

● *What will inspire the unit of work?*: This may be built into the unit perhaps by using a media or process; looking at the work of an artist, designer or craftsperson; by going on a visit, by working outside on or beyond the school site, making a worthwhile link to another subject area or by participating in event. If not, this is an area for you to consider and develop.

● *Which media or processes will be taught?*: You will need to know which media or processes you will be supporting or teaching throughout the year so that you can ensure you have the appropriate subject knowledge or identify gaps that you need to address. In addition to this you will need, within the broader headings of 'painting' or 'printmaking' or 'sculpture', more detail about what is expected. If the long term plan states 'painting' you need to know what sort of paint and how this experience builds on previous use of paint. You can also use this part of the long term plan to check that you have the required resources available at the time that you want to teach the unit.

● *What subject knowledge and vocabulary will underpin the learning?*: It will be important that you know which one or two visual elements (line and tone, colour, pattern, texture, shape, form and space) will underpin the learning and teaching in the unit. You will need to be sure that you make coherent connections between the specified visual elements. If no visual elements are specified you need to check which ones would best fit the media or process and artists' work stated in the long term plan and will build on children's prior experience. These will also have implications for the vocabulary and the activities that you plan to use with children.

● *Which artists' works will be viewed?*: If the work of an artist is specified it is important that you can access resources to support your teaching. You will need to check that there are good reproductions available in school or that they are available electronically. If the artists are unfamiliar to you, you may need to do some personal research so that you know some background information about them and their work and how their work relates to the techniques and visual elements you are teaching.

● *Are there any strong and meaningful links to other curriculum areas?*: When you look at the overall long term plan or curriculum map for all subjects cross-curricular links may be indentified or you may be able move content around to enable productive links to be made. It will be important that you retain the integrity of the learning in art for the children you are teaching – think back to the activity that explored this in Chapter Two.

● *Your questions to follow up:* Depending on the detail on the long-term plan that you are looking at you may have some gaps and questions that you need to follow up. Colleagues teaching the same year group, the teacher who taught the class the year before or the art co-ordinator are all people who could be of help with this.

Medium-term planning

Following on from the long term plan more detail is usually provided through the medium term plan or the plan for a unit of work that lasts half a term. The structure and content of this is likely to vary from school to school especially in terms of format and detail. The medium term plans are likely to be influenced by how learning and teaching is organised in the school. It may be that art is taught one lesson a week, every week; art may be taught in series of lessons in one week or linked to another subject and these two taught together. There are a range of sources of planning available for you to use or adapt, including units from published schemes of work that the school has collected or bought and school-devised units of work that relate to the school's interests, local resources and events. Schools may draw upon any or a combination of these sources for planning.

The structure of a unit of work

The structure of a unit of work at the medium term planning stage can be outlined following these phases: inspiring and preparing to create art; making art; and reflecting on learning. These can be followed through a sequence of weekly separate lessons over a half term or a continuous experience over a shorter period of time. They are a useful of way of helping you to think about the sorts of learning and teaching experiences that are appropriate throughout an art unit of work. The length of each phase will depend on what you plan to teach and the time available overall and is likely to vary from unit to unit.

There is more than one way of organising learning and you should be flexible so that the sequence of learning planned will support learning rather than fit into a predetermined pattern. Alternative approaches include blocking together the time available for art into a compressed period of time to allow for more intense work. This can be especially useful when using materials that are difficult to get out and put away on a weekly basis. It can also allow for children to become more absorbed in their exploration and learning because they don't have to stop and start. You might also consider pairing learning in art with another subject as long as this supports learning in both. Within lessons you should consider how time can be used effectively and the balance between your teaching and the children working practically. You should also consider how long clearing away and reorganising the classroom might take. Annotating approximate timings onto the plan can guide you and ensure that any supporting adults know how long is available for different parts of the lesson.

Connect and extend

Read Woods and O'Shannessy's article 'Reintroducing creativity: Day 10 at Hackleton School' published in 2002 in the *Curriculum Journal* (Vol. 13, No. 2, pp. 163–82).

Think about how you have seen time allocated and organised. What works effectively for art?

Inspiring and preparing

At the beginning of a unit of work you will be starting a new aspect of art with the children you are supporting or teaching. This may be a new technique or a different approach to a familiar technique. It may be introducing a different source of inspiration, starting point or work or art, design or craft. It could be a different sort of outcome involving size, scale or individual, group or whole class collaborative outcome. If you have considered the children's prior knowledge, skills and understanding you will have a clearer picture of the new learning planned for this unit.

In the early stages of a unit of work you could be planning to collect ideas in sketch-books and research from books or the internet. You might be encouraging children to explore how to use unfamiliar tools and materials freely or teaching a new technique or process. Alternatively you could be planning for children to refine and consolidate skills in using a known technique or reminding them how to use familiar tools and develop their precision and independence of use. You will probably recap on previously learned vocabulary as well as introducing new vocabulary.

This is a vital stage in a unit of work. It is very difficult to create a meaningful piece of art from nowhere. In this stage the exploration and development of ideas allows children time to become inspired, to gather the ideas and explore the tools and process that will contribute to the art they will make in the next phase of the unit. I know myself that my finished prints evolve over time from ideas in my sketchbook, responses to classes/workshops I attend, visits to exhibitions and the impetus of sharing work with others. Imagine, for example, you were given a set of watercolours and asked to make your piece of art immediately. Your response would be quite different than if you had been shown how to use the watercolours, allowed to experiment with them, looked at the work of artists that use watercolours and given some choices and ideas to inspire your painting.

Practical task

Learning objective:

- to explore the range of responses that can be inspired by the same starting point

You will need:

- the pro forma

What to do:

- take the starting point 'in the woods' and the technique of making collages. Identify as many different ideas as you can for using collage techniques to respond to this starting point. Look at the list of collage techniques in Chapter 9 to support you in this task. Aim for giving children opportunities to respond individually and creatively.

LINK

In the woods

Guidance notes

- When you are working from a starting point that you have chosen or that has been chosen for you there can be scope to inspire a wide range of personal responses even when children are using the same media to work with.

- If you are able to take children to the woods or even to a group of near by trees some children will want to respond to what they see by making quite representational collages using digital photos; collecting wood/forest type images from magazines; using papers of different sorts to recreate the scene or combinations of these. You can encourage children to go beyond the representative by getting them to sit and listen to sounds around them, lie on the ground and look up at trees and the sky as well as feeling tree trunks. This can lead some children to make more abstract collages based on their response to senses other than their vision. Also looking closely at tree trunks, bark, leaves, could lead to collages that take a tiny part and enlarge it or recreate the texture in their collage.

- If you are unable to go to the woods or trees you could make a sequence of images of woods and forests using photographic images and images from art including illustrations from children's literature. The images that you select to develop the starting point can inspire different responses than had you visited the wood. You might choose images suggestive of the mysterious and dark quality of woods in fairy tales, the stillness of winter or the bursting to life that happens in the spring. This can lead children to respond imaginatively trying to convey a sense of time or atmosphere in their collages.

- Taking this one starting point there are many possibilities for children making collages individually or together. You may have identified different ideas than those discussed above depending on your experience and interests.

In this exercise you are encouraged to approach a starting point with the idea of allowing children to express themselves in their work. With younger children this could be within the same technique, such as collage; with older children you might go beyond this allowing choice between several techniques or processes or combinations of two perhaps. As well as constructing individual and small-scale collages there is scope for planning work in a larger scale and work that is made, appreciated and then deteriorates naturally or is deliberately removed. This can also provide an opportunity for children to work together in groups making decisions about designs and allocating tasks amongst the group.

Making art, craft and design

In the middle of a unit of work you will be planning for the children to use their inspiration and experiences in exploring and developing ideas to work towards making their piece of art. By this time the children should know whether they will be working individually, in pairs, in small groups or as a whole class. They should know the scale they will be working on. Perhaps each child will make a small individual piece that will contribute to a greater whole such as making a square of fabric work which will make a collaborative wall hanging. Alternatively each child may make a larger individual piece.

At Key Stage One Children may be making a personal response within the constraints of the unit. At Key Stage Two Children may be given the opportunity to make more choices about their outcome that may take them in distinctly different directions. At both key stages there should be scope for the children's personal responses so that you do not end up with thirty identical pieces of art. Even if you end up with thirty paintings or thirty clay pots your plans should allow for some freedom for children to respond personally that will inevitably result in differences between individual pieces of work.

Evaluating and reflecting on learning

Opportunities to stop and reflect should be planned at every stage of the unit to help children make decisions and think about their art. Towards the end of a unit, as children begin to come to the end of making their artwork, plans should include opportunities for children to talk about it as they complete it and after it is finished.

At Key Stage One Children may be self assessing themselves by thinking about what they have learned and produced freely or supported by using prompts or shared success criteria. They could be describing their own work, and beginning to peer assess by talking about and asking questions about the work of other children. They could be considering what they would have done next or what they might have changed without actually making these changes. It can be useful for adults to write down children's comments for them if appropriate – perhaps annotating the comments in their sketchpad or with a photo of the art they have made.

At Key Stage Two children will be building on this supported self-and peer assessment by having the opportunity to make changes to their work in order to develop it further. This will need to be structured and supported as it is easy to do something that changes the piece of art irrevocably and leads to disappointment. Strategies leading to evaluating and developing work could include stopping just before the piece of work is finished and reviewing it whilst there is still scope for making changes, or making a copy or taking a photo of the work before changes are made.

At both key stages deciding on a title for a finished piece of work can be a purposeful final activity. This can also include a short explanatory statement about the artwork and how and why it was made. It is important that you consider when it is appropriate to evaluate and develop work within the unit and leave enough time to do this. It is easy for children to finish their piece of art towards the end of the last lesson and have no time to stop and think, and enjoy and appreciate their art and that of others. Art is often made to be shared with an audience and responded to by viewers so this should be part of the experience that you plan for children.

Case Study

In a mixed Year 1 and 2 class children look back at the collages they have worked on over several lessons. They use a short list of prompts that their teacher has prepared for them to help them consider their finished work. These prompts include:

- What are most pleased with about your collage?
- What did you find most difficult?
- What did you enjoy?
- How would you change your collage if you could?
- What have you learned about making collages?

The younger children think about their checklist with a teaching assistant to support them and scribe their responses. Some children write their own thoughts down. The teaching assistant and teacher make some suggestions for children to choose from where necessary and children also have their own ideas. Their evaluations are placed in their sketchbooks to mark the end of the unit of work. Their teacher photographs each collage and displays them on a series of Powerpoint slides that can be seen at the beginning and the end of the day by parents and visitors to the classroom.

In this case study younger children are supported to evaluate and changes are discussed but not made. With older children this evaluation stage could be planned at an earlier stage leaving time and scope to make changes. Questions and prompts would ask more of the children in terms of analysing their own work and making connections to the ideas that had led to it. In both cases the learning objectives can taken as an initial guide for the evaluative questions or prompts.

Within this stage the children's art can be shared with an audience. This is another aspect of evaluating the work – people other than the artists themselves looking at the art, making comments, asking questions and showing that they are interested in and value the children's art work. This could be through display within school or outside school, taking photos of the art and showing the photos on the IWB for parents to see either in the classroom or in an assembly. Staging a mini exhibition by displaying finished pieces and sketchbooks at home time so that parents can come in and see the work can also be a satisfying end to the unit.

Skills, knowledge and understanding

Having a clear idea of the skills, knowledge and understanding that underpin and are integral to the unit of work will support effective teaching. This needs to be indicated in your planning and may occur during any part of the unit of work. It could include introducing a new tool, media or process; exploring a visual element in a different way; looking at the work of an unfamiliar artist; or using some new vocabulary.

Building on prior learning

When planning a unit of work it is important to consider the prior knowledge, skills and understanding of the children you will be working with. Looking back over the long term plan can give you an understanding of the techniques or processes, artists' work and inspirations or contexts for previous learning in this area. Asking yourself some questions may help you make some decisions about the medium term unit you are planning or adapting. It may that with some small changes you can have a unit of work that advances learning more effectively. The chart below outlines some questions you might consider when building on the prior knowledge, skills and understanding of the children you teach. It gives some examples in the context of printmaking.

Using prior knowledge to support planning

Questions	Considerations for your planning – could you...	Examples (context of printmaking)
Which aspects of the technique/process have the children experienced before?	... introduce a new aspect of the technique/process?	The children have tried printing with objects and pressprinting in KS1 and go on to make card prints in Year 3.
How much independence did children have in using the technique/process?	... expect the children to use the technique with more independence? ... give children more choice in the response they have or the outcome they make? give children more choice in which processes they use?	The children made pressprints with help in Y1 and go on to make and print with greater independence and complexity in Y2. Children have experienced pressprint and card printing in Y1–5 and in Y6 choose between the two.
Which visual elements were the focuses of the units?	... develop a technique/process experienced with a focus on different visual elements?	The children have explored pattern and line in printmaking in KS 1 and go on to explore colour and shape in KS 2.
What inspired the art work? (observation, experience, imagination)	... aim for an outcome inspired by a different area?	Children have used natural forms as inspiration in Y4 and in Y6 use the built environment.
What scale did the children work on?	... plan for a different scale of outcome?	Children have made small prints in KS 1 and in Y3 make a large sheet of printed wrapping paper (A2)
Did children produce individual, group or whole class outcomes?	... plan an outcome that requires a shared response?	Children have made individual prints throughout KS 1 and go on to make a large collaborative textile drape in Y4.

Questions	Considerations for your planning – could you...	Examples (context of printmaking)
Which artists' work have the children looked at in relation to the technique/ process?	... inspire or relate to the work of an unfamiliar artist?	In Y3/4 children look at the work of Norman Ackroyd when monoprinting. In Y5 they explore the work of a local artist who makes collagraphs.
From which places and times and have children looked at art in relation to the technique/ process?	... use the work of an artist or art from a different place, time or culture to inspire a response?	Y1 children have looked at Indian fabrics and William Morris patterns. In Y3 they look at medieval clay tiles.
Have the children experienced the technique/ process linked to another curriculum subject?	... link the art unit to another curriculum subject?	Y3 children explore rotation, transformation and tessellation of shapes in both printmaking and maths. In Y6 children scan their small prints into the computer and develop them further on screen.
Have children linked the technique/aspect to another art technique or process?	... link two techniques or processes?	In Y2 children make wax resist backgrounds to print their pressprint animals onto.

As you plan or consider existing planning to adapt to meet the needs of the children in your class you also need to ensure that you are clear about the progress they can make in the unit of work. You might ask yourself:

● What will the children know, or know more about at the end of the unit of work?

● What will the children be able to do, or do better at the end of the unit of work?

● What will the children understand, or understand more about at the end of the unit of work?

Find out more

Investigate the resources available to support planning:

● in school – published schemes that the school has bought in;

● on the internet – websites of galleries, museums, arts organisations;

● at university – in the art room and in the library.

Planning for learning in the lesson

The format and structure of the short-term plan will undoubtedly vary from school to school and the presence or absence of some elements may well depend on the medium term plan. The medium term plan may contain sufficient detail which can be additionally annotated so that it can be taught from or it may be developed further into a series of separate short-term plans that contain the teaching detail. In this context I am referring to the plan that you will have in front of you in the lesson that you are teaching or supporting children within. The format you choose or that is used by the school should be one that supports your teaching or support and the children's learning. The plan that is being used in the lesson must be shared with or be available to all adults working in the lesson before the lesson occurs. If you are a teaching assistant who supports groups or individuals with particular needs within the lesson you will need the lesson plan in time to be able to suggest and make modifications to meet the needs of the children you work with.

Practical task

Learning objective:

● to explore a short-term plan

In this task you will take a closer look at a short term plan for art and consider it in relation to your role as a teaching assistant or teacher.

You will need:

● A short-term plan of an art lesson, the pro forma below.

What to do:

● Use the questions on the pro forma below to explore the short-term plan and make notes about what you find. Annotate the pro forma with any gaps or questions that you identify.

Look for...		Notes	Questions/ comments...
Planning	The learning objective/s		
	Success criteria, steps to success, learning outcomes		
	Resources		
	Vocabulary		
	Timings		
	Health and safety		
	Assessment opportunities		

Look for...		Notes	Questions/ comments...
Teaching and learning	Teaching and support strategies		
	Classroom management and organisation		
	Inclusion / differentiation		

Questions to consider:

- Use this completed pro forma as a basis for considering the discussion of the features of short-term planning below.

Learning objectives and success criteria

Schools usually have a policy that guides learning and teaching including the way learning objectives and success criteria are constructed and shared. This should be followed in your planning and teaching of art lessons while taking into consideration the way children learn in art, which perhaps requires a different approach that in some other subjects.

The Assessment Reform Group (2002) includes learning goals and the sharing of the criteria by which they will be assessed as one of the ten principles of Assessment for Learning: 'For effective learning to take place learners need to understand what they are trying to achieve – and want to achieve it. Understanding and commitment follows when learners have some part in deciding goals and identifying criteria for assessing progress' (p. 2). These principles can be applied when planning for learning in art although it is also important to allow space for other important aspects of the art experience to be pursued by the learner. As Bowden (2011) suggests, whilst objectives focused on children's knowledge and skills can support learning these must not override children's personal responses and individual creativity.

When you are identifying learning objectives you may be guided by suggestions in published schemes of work but it is likely you will need to modify these to make them more focused on the learning of the class you are teaching. You may also need to make some of them more small scale or break them down into a series of smaller steps related to each lesson. It is likely that you will need to express them in more accessible language for the children you teach. It is most important that you devise learning objectives that are *expressions* of what you plan for the children to learn, not what they *will* do or the context of the activity. This is a vital distinction to understand. As Clarke (2005) suggests 'the context of the learning objective is simply the activity, vehicle for fulfilling the learning objective' (p. 30). This allows children to begin to understand that what they are learning may be applied beyond the single activity or context that they are currently working on and make connections between the skills, knowledge and understanding they are learning.

Practical task

Learning objective:

- to consider effective learning objectives in art lessons.

In this task you will look critically at learning objectives in order to think about how to write clear and effective learning objectives for your lessons.

You will need:

- the pro forma below.

What to do:

- Use the learning objectives suggested below or replace them with learning objectives from your own planning. Consider each learning objective against the questions listed on the pro forma.

	Learning objective (LO)	Is the LO focused on what the children will be *learning*?	Is the LO written in language accessible to the children?
		If not, rewrite it so it is focused on learning	If not, rewrite it so it accessible to children
A	To draw what you can see through the window		
B	To explore how to create tone using drawing materials		
C	To develop the skills of observation and recording through drawing in a variety of media		
D	To draw what you can see using lines		
E	To paint the flowers		
F	To explore the colours you can make with red and blue		
G	To combine visual and tactile qualities of materials and processes and to match these qualities to the purpose of the work		
H	To make and decorate a clay pot		

Questions to consider:

- Some of these learning objectives are very firmly focused on the completion of one specific activity. LOs A, E and H merely describe the activity that the children will do rather than what they will learn by doing the activity. In rewriting these you had to identify what skills, knowledge or understanding could have been learned and write a learning objective based on this. Clearly there are many opportunities for learning within these activities so you must select and prioritise on the basis of your unit for the work and the children you are teaching. Possibilities for A could include 'to use line in your drawing' or 'to explore what a 4B pencil can do' and for H could include 'to join clay coils' or 'to carve into a clay surface'.

- Some of these learning objectives are expressed in language that is too complex to be easily accessible to most children. LOs G and C are especially challenging and are similar to those that might appear in published schemes of work. In rewriting than you need to take into consideration the age and language levels of the children you work with. Again, as well as rewriting consideration about the possible learning must be identified. LO G should be considered in relation to the visual elements and processes that the unit is based on. LO C can be more clearly connected to the visual element(s) that could underpin observation such as 'to draw what you see using lines and shape' or could focus on the exploration of drawing tools in 'to choose drawing tools that will help you draw what you see'.

- LOs B, D and F are clearly written and focused on what the children could learn. They are not specific to a particular activity in terms of context and this allows them to be revisited and developed over key stages. LO B, for example (exploring tone in drawing), will recur as children draw in different contexts such as from observation, imagination or experience. The use of the word 'explore' suggests that children have some freedom to find out and experiment. As they experience and master drawing tools, such as a range of B pencils, chalk and charcoal, pastels and pens, they will learn more about representing tone. They will also, perhaps, have other opportunities to explore tone in painting, printmaking and collage. The wording of your success criteria can modify this learning objective so children can understand some of what they might do to show learning in relation to the objective.

When devising learning objectives on planning I have found that it is useful to have already written them in child-accessible language so that as you talk about them in your teaching and share them for children to refer to you are prepared. It can be challenging to try to rephrase learning objectives from plans on the spot during your teaching.

In this activity you have evaluated learning objectives. Learning objectives are usually considered alongside success criteria. Using success criteria allows you to work with the children to clarify what the learning will look like. Your school may have a policy or guidance about how you express success criteria or steps to success as they are sometimes called. You might have in mind what you consider the success criteria for the learning objectives you have written but it is important that you include the children in expressing and discussing these. Success criteria should be expressed in child-friendly language. Have them written on your plan but be ready to modify the way you express them in relation to what the children suggest especially in terms of the language you use to express them.

One way of checking that the children understand what they will be learning is to ask them (before they start work) what they will be saying and doing to show you they are working on the learning objective. In some instances this will correspond with your expectations; if it does not this is a signal that your teaching has not had the impact you intended. In other instances, where, for example, you are encouraging children to respond openly and creatively, what children suggest will be much more diverse and open to personal interpretation.

Success criteria can be used as a focus for praise and feedback while the children work and to structure discussion in a plenary or review at the end of a lesson. You can also use success criteria as reminders and prompts as well as including differentiation where appropriate. In art it may well be the case that 'what learning looks like' encompasses a wide range of possibilities especially where children are exploring and expressing their personal and creative ideas. Devising success criteria or guidance for learning outcomes can make reference to this indicating to children that whilst they are all, for example, painting using watercolours and exploring the use of colour, there may be other areas where personal choice will have led to some significant differences in outcomes – size of work, the way the paint is applied, the use of colour and subject matter perhaps. The various ways individuals have responded can be highlighted in discussion emphasising how sometimes unplanned and unexpected things happen in art as part of the process.

Case Study

Year 1 and 2 children are drawing from observation in their sketchbooks outside in the school playground. Their teacher has shared the learning objective with them. It is 'I am learning to draw what I see'. She has demonstrated how they can look for significant and striking shapes of buildings and how they could use line to draw these and to add detail. The teacher has taken a series of photos of what can be seen from the playground and taped these together into a panaromic view that the children can look at later. On the planning, success criteria are related to using the visual elements of line and shape and being able to identify what has been drawn because some key features are clear on the drawing. With the children's help the success criteria have been expressed as:

- I have used the shapes and lines that I can see on buildings.
- My friend can take my drawing and find what I drew on a photo.

The teacher and teaching assistant use these success criteria as they work outside with the children. They use them to question, prompt and comment saying such things as:

- 'Can you show me the shapes you have used?'
- 'I can see you have drawn the triangular roof that you can see.'
- 'Can you see any details that you could add to the wall?'

When the children come back inside they swap their sketchbook with a friend and try to identify where it was drawn. The children enjoy giving clues and feedback in this part of the lesson. The teacher and teaching assistant are ready to provide a prompt by pointing to a key feature in each drawing that will home the viewer in on what was being drawn.

In this case study a clear shared-learning objective and some accessible success criteria are used to help focus children on their learning in the art lesson. This activity is a relatively short and self-contained activity. For some learning in art you might have one or more challenging learning objectives and success criteria or learning outcomes that children work on over several lessons or weeks.

Another feature of using learning objectives and success criteria is making a connection to the whole unit of work. It is important that we convey to children how their learning connects up and for what purpose they are learning. In relation to the earlier case study the children had been to see two paintings that represented well-known buildings. They would be going on to make their own paintings based on observation. The drawing activity helped them to begin to focus on the key features and shapes of buildings. Sharing this 'bigger picture' was motivating and supported children in working purposefully rather than seeing the activity as a disconnected one off.

Finally, to return to a point made earlier, whilst learning objectives and success criteria support learning and teaching, allowing children some freedom to make personal responses and express themselves is of great importance in art. Using learning objectives and success criteria with thought must be your goal so that the learning experience is not reduced to a formula and opportunities to be creative are not squeezed out.

Vocabulary

Identifying the key vocabulary that you will be using within the unit of work and in individual lessons will allow you to be clear about the meaning of the words you are using when they are used in the context of art. This has been explored in relation to vocabulary associated with visual element in an earlier chapter and will be considered witt media and processes in later chapters. When you identify key vocabulary you should think in terms of words and sentence structures. This is an area that will be of particular significance when planning to meet the needs of children learning English as an Additional Language (EAL) or children with a special educational need (SEN).

As a student or teacher you should have the overview of the whole class as well as ideas about differentiation in order to include children with EAL or SEN and how to extend the more able. Many published plans identify key vocabulary to use a starting point. As a teaching assistant you can use the identified key vocabulary on the plan as a basis for thinking about the needs of the group or individual you are supporting. You may need to take advice from the class teacher about which words are most important so you can focus your support on these. You may be able to use visual clues, labels, symbols and other aids to understanding.

 LINK

Assessing learning in art

You will certainly be familiar with assessment in subjects such as English or mathematics since these subjects are the focus of much assessment activity and training, but you may feel hesitant about or lacking in experience of making assessments of learning in art. If you have trained or been working in schools in the last few years you will also be familiar with the principles of Assessment for Learning (AfL). It is likely too that your school will have a policy that will guide your approach to assessment in relation to types, strategies and subjects.

Your approach to assessment in art should be informed by your school policy and your own understanding of assessment and AfL. Features such as giving formative feedback including using success criteria, offering useful and accessible advice about what children have done well and specific advice about how they might improve and encouraging self and peer assessment are aspects of AfL (Assessment Reform Group, 2002). Assessment in art can be perceived as different to assessment in some other subjects because of the personal and subjective nature of the subject. There are, however, aspects of art that are measurable, such as technical skills, and those that are less so, such as the individual outcomes of the children's own ideas, responses and creativity. As Bowden (2006) states 'The fact that much of the output of artistic activity in schools cannot be measured in these absolute 'right or wrong' terms does lead to view among the uninitiated that art cannot be assessed' (p. 28). It is important for you to remember that, without feedback about how to develop and improve, learning cannot take place in art as in any other subject. OFSTED (2012) recently identified that good or outstanding lessons in primary schools were characterised by: 'subtle and strategic use of assessment, focused on individual pupils' progress' (p. 16). Your role is to plan, teach and support children so that they can learn and develop in art.

When intervening to teach or give formative feedback in art lessons it is important to be sensitive to the nature of the subject. Children can easily pick up on adults having an expected or 'correct' response in mind and will be quick to judge their own work against this expectation or standard. Giving more open ended feedback can allow us to value and preserve children's own responses and avoid inadvertently pushing our own ideas at the expense of theirs.

Evidence of learning in art

There is a range of evidence of learning in art. The child's sketchbook is a valuable source of ongoing development and progress. Adding annotations on sticky notes and prompt sheets can add useful contextual detail including scribed comments from the child. Photos of the child at work, artwork in progress and finished pieces are also useful. In addition to this, observations made by the teacher and/or teaching assistant about the child at work, their attitude and their decisions enhance the quality of information available. Annotations on planning are useful reminders for following lessons or the next time the lesson or unit is taught. Displays of work also provide evidence of learning in art as do school portfolios of collected examples.

Formative feedback

Formative assessment is the assessment that we use day to day in the classroom to support children's learning and help them improve: a key part of your role. Earlier in this chapter an aspect of formative assessment, the use of success criteria, was considered. In addition to this there are a number of other strategies that you can use to give feedback to children in art. You can also consider formative feedback in relation to children's skills in making, the attitudes they demonstrate in art and their knowledge and understanding of the subject.

Strategies for using formative assessment

Some of the strategies you can use when giving feedback include acting as an 'interested observer' watching and waiting rather than being quick to comment or suggesting several alternative approaches 'you could try... or you could try...' If asked for help, demonstrating alongside the child focusing specifically on an aspect of the skill that would be helpful to their next step or solving the problem they have is a useful approach. When talking with a child using the opening 'Tell me about...' rather than 'What is it?' allows the child to articulate and describe. Asking the child to talk about what the piece of work is called or what they would tell someone about it builds on this. Acting as scribe and making a transcription of the child's responses is a useful way of recording the child's thoughts and ideas at different stages of their work. You might also provide a structure for response based on success criteria or a checklist or ask a peer to show and talk through how they are working on a similar area.

Formative assessment – making art

Supporting children to develop their technical skills in using tools, media and processes with increasing control and confidence is a key part of formative assessment – what you say and do here can make a real difference to their learning. Using pieces of work that you have created to exemplify a technical point on which children need to improve can elicit comments and give children the opportunity to look more critically. They can then apply what they have noticed to their own work.

Case Study

A class of Year 5 children are working on printmaking. They will be revisiting press printing, an aspect of the printmaking process they have used before. This time they will be expected to be much more independent and achieve a better quality of finished print. Their teacher has identified some of the things that the children need to be aware of. These include:

- moving the tile after initially putting it down, resulting in an unclear print;
- holding the tile with inky fingers so that the print is surrounded by fingerprints;
- not rolling ink across the whole tile and in particular missing out the corners;
- picking up the tile carelessly so that finger prints show on the print;
- rolling too much ink on tile so that the marks cut into the polystyrene do not print clearly.

The teacher makes prints that exemplify each of these possibilities. She asks the children to identify what went wrong and what advice they would give to someone to avoid each happening. The responses are shared with the whole class and used as a way of reminding and structuring feedback to each other. Because the feedback is applied to a set of generic examples, and no individual child's work is picked out, all feel free to say what they think and make suggestions. It gives some children confidence that, whilst things can go wrong, they can also be corrected.

As you work with children you will be able to identify where they need focused teaching in order to make progress; where they need time and opportunities to practise their skills; and what the balance between these two is. Taking care to give specific praise focused on what the child has done well and what they might do to improve or make the next step will be more effective than generic statements. You might also take into account how much support they needed from adults, from using resources and from differentiation when considering their progress in using tools, media and processes.

Formative assessment - attitudes

Noticing children's attitudes and personal qualities in the context of art lessons is another aspect of formative assessment. These have an impact on their learning and may well be different from subject to subject. Qualities such as independence, perseverance, questioning and enthusiasm play a part in learning to make art and enjoy the art made by others. You might notice how independent children are in their practical work and when they look at art; how long they are able to concentrate and sustain interest for; whether they are absorbed in their work or easily distracted; and how readily they engage with the new ideas and experiences that they are introduced to in art. You might find that some children relish the freedom that art gives them to respond in different ways and use their own ideas or that some children find this very freedom challenging and worrying. Using your formative assessment in this aspect of art will allow you to gain understanding of individuals in a different way than in more formal and less practical lessons as well as intervene to support their learning.

Formative assessment – knowledge and understanding

As well as technical skills and personal attitudes children will also be developing knowledge about art through your teaching and their own exploration. Noticing what they remember and the connections they make from lesson to lesson, and unit to unit and beyond, will give you an insight into the depth of their knowledge and understanding. Some understanding on your part of their prior experiences will help you begin to make connections, comparisons and reflections through your questioning and conversation with them and your own planning of learning.

Using assessment formatively to help children improve their art is an integral part of teaching and learning. Much of the ongoing formative assessment that is built into lessons will be oral and part of conversations with children about their work as it progresses. It is important that this feedback is clearly focused on learning and is specific rather than general. Whilst general positive comments may appear helpful and reassuring they can also be unhelpful in their lack of clarity about exactly what is being done well. Using your knowledge of the children you teach, their prior experiences as well as your planned success criteria, and thinking about the unit of work can focus your feedback, making it sensitive and effective rather than general and formulaic.

Self and peer assessment

Involving children in the assessment process is an important aspect of AfL. Helping children to assess their own work and supporting them in making peer assessment should be a part of art lessons as in any other lesson. Successful self-assessment begins with clear success criteria, steps to success or learning outcomes that are shared with the children. As discussed earlier these should be expressed in language that is accessible to the learner and used as a basis for praise and feedback throughout the lesson or unit of work. With younger children it is likely that much of this will be oral although it may be transcribed by adults so that the assessment information is not lost. It may be structured by using a short self-assessment checklist to structure the child's reflection.

Case Study

After some observational drawing Year 1 and 2 children respond to a short checklist devised by their teacher and stuck into their sketchbooks with their work. The adults who work with the children help them fill it in if necessary adding assessment comments to give a context to the children's thinking.

I can...	Bilal	
	I think...	My teacher thinks...
I can choose a 4B or 6B pencil	Yes	With TA reminder
I can look before I draw	Yes	Yes
I can draw so someone else knows where I was	Yes, my friend found where I had drawn on a photo	Used some recognsiabe shapes and details
I can suggest an improvement for my drawing	Yes, I could add more detail	Responded to chocie of improvements suggested by adult

As can be seen from this example the child's reflection together with the adult's additonal comments gives some useful assessment evidence that can be looked at along with the child's drawing. This Year 1 child is responding to adult prompts to choose appropriate drawing tools and is beginning to think about how he can improve his work by choosing from adult suggestions. Year 2 children could be making their own suggestions for improvements and children at Key Stage 2 will be expected to act on their ideas for improvement.

Self-assessment strategies such as using sentence starters may help children to articulate their own learning in a more focused manner. These could include:

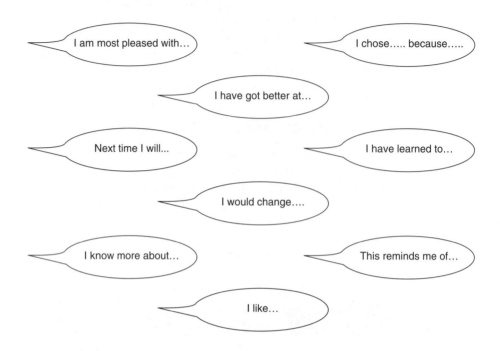

It is important to give children a focus for their self-assessment because children are prone to be harsh critics of their own work or can make general comments that do not help them articulate their learning.

When moving on to peer assessment, it is even more important to be aware of the need for tact and appropriate language with which to express oneself in relation to the work of others. Think back to comments that have been made about your own work and how poorly expressed comments might have made you feel. When planning peer assessment you might structure this by asking children to look for specific areas or features. Laying out all the pieces of work you might ask children to circulate and look for a painting where colour has been used in an interesting way, or look for a painting with detail in the foreground, or look for a painting that makes them feel happy. You might practice giving positive peer assessment comments on the work of artists, craftspeople and designers and also ask children to consider the feelings of the person receiving the feedback.

End of Key Stage assessment

There is no formal requirement for teachers to record and report children's attainment in the form of levels for art at the end of each year. At the end of each key stage teachers can judge which level description best fits the child's performance. This judgement should be arrived at by considering the child's learning over time and across a range of contexts and will not be judged in relation to a single piece of art work or outcomes of one unit of work (QCA, 2009).

The QCA (2006a, 2006b) publications *Teacher Assessment Activities Art and Design* 2006 provides materials that explore a range of assessment approaches that could be used in the classroom. These include references to levels of performance as described in the level descriptions and support teachers when making judgements at the end of the key stage. These materials may be available in your school or in the university library. They can provide you with a starting point for looking at children's work and beginning to evaluate it. This is also an activity that you should participate in with colleagues in school: looking at and talking about the range outcomes of children's learning in art and what it means for their progress and your teaching. It will help you to develop your expectations and ability to consider children's knowledge, skills and understanding as well as their creativity and attitudes. You can also look at examples of children's work in school portfolios, if these are available, as well as using any pointers in the schemes of work that you are using to guide your evaluations.

Connect and extend

Read the chapter about assessment in John Bowden's book *The Primary Art and Design Subject Leader's Handbook* published by NSEAD in 2006 and think about the ideas and points he puts forward in relation to assessing art.

Conclusion

In this chapter the stages of planning, strategies for teaching and supporting learning, and formative assessment have been explored. Your own understanding of these areas as well as your developing subject knowledge will help you teach and support effectively in art lessons. Your personal enthusiasm and interest will also support effective lessons and a positive approach from children. In the next chapter strategies for teaching and supporting learning in art will be explored in more depth.

Next steps

- Look at the long term plan to identify the techniques and processes that will be taught in the year you are working. Have you used these before? If not, have a go at them yourself so you can anticipate how to teach/support.
- Check that medium term plans and resources are available in time for you teach/support effectively.
- Look for plans available from galleries and organisations that could help to develop and enliven your planning.

References

Assessment Reform Group (2002) *Assessment for Learning: 10 principles. Research based principles to guide classroom practice.* Available from: *http://assessmentreformgroup.files.wordpress.com/2012/01/10principles_english.pdf* (accessed 23/09/12).

Bowden, J. (2006) *The Primary Art and Design Subject Leaders' Handbook.* Corsham: NSEAD.

Bowden, J. (2011) *Learning Objectives and art teaching: some thoughts and concerns.* Available from: *http://www.artinset.com/article.asp?id=313&Learning-objectives-and-art-teaching-some-thoughts-and-concerns* (accessed 20 March 2012).

Clarke, S. (2005) *Formative Assessment in Action: Weaving the Elements Together.* London: Hodder Murray.

OFSTED (2012) Making a mark: art, craft and design education. Available from: *http://www.ofsted.gov.uk/resources/making-mark-art-craft-and-design-education-2008-11* (accessed 31 March 2012).

QCA (2006a) *Teacher Assessment Activities Art and Design Key Stage 1.* London: QCA.

QCA (2006b) *Teacher Assessment Activities Art and Design Key Stage 2.* London: QCA.

QCA (2009) *Assessment in Art and Design.* Available from: *http://teachfind.com/qcda/assessment-art-and-design-assessment-subjects-assessment-key-stages-1-2-national-cur?current_search=art%20assessment* (Accessed 23/09/12).

Further reading

Woods, P. and O'Shannessy, J. (2002) 'Reintroducing creativity: Day 10 at Hackleton School' *Curriculum Journal*, Vol. 13, No. 2, pp. 163–82.

Web resources

NSEAD website – section on Health and Safety in art: *http://www.nsead.org/hsg/index.aspx*

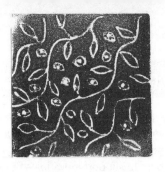

Chapter 5

Teaching and supporting learning

Introduction

In the previous chapter long, medium and short term planning were explored. The plans that you devise, adapt or use should underpin your teaching or support for learning. They give you the opportunity to think about what you will teach and how you will teach it or how best to support individuals or groups of children in a lesson. As in any subject or area of learning there is a range of teaching strategies and ways of organising learning. When you are planning an art lesson you will choose the most appropriate strategies for what you are teaching and what will best meet the needs of the children you are working with taking into account the distinctive nature of art as a subject. There may be some issues to consider that are inherent to the subject or related to your own confidence and expertise. As a student or teacher you should consider your own role and the role of any supporting adults. As a teaching assistant you should consider your own role within the team of adults in the lesson in order to support the learning of the class, group or individuals that you work with. In this chapter the following area will be covered:

- Teaching art – some approaches
- Using a sketchbook in art
- Digital media and art
- Meeting the needs of a range of learners
- Classroom management

When primary-aged children are involved in art lessons many of the teaching skills that you use all the time will of course be relevant. Art lessons, however, will be different because of the practical nature of the subject. The resources we use in art may require us, as adults, to give more thought to classroom organisation than when children are based at tables using pencils and paper or digital media. Often the working atmosphere in an art lesson is different: sometimes the room falls silent because of the intense concentration involved in drawing whilst at other times there is an excited buzz from children following their own creative ideas and sharing those of others. One feature of art lessons that will be unlike that of any other lesson or subject is the use of a sketchbook to support learning.

Teaching art – some approaches

As with using planning in any subject it is at the level of the short-term plan, the plan you have in front of you to guide what you do in the lesson, that the real detail of what to do is most valuable. Translating the planning into action – actually teaching and supporting learning requires you to choose whether to demonstrate, use resources, support independent activity or instruct directly.

Teaching detail on planning

Plans vary in their format and content. A key factor is that you can use the plan effectively to help you support children or teach children. If you are using a plan from a published scheme or a plan given to you to work from it is likely that will need to add details to help you use it effectively. If you are the class teacher or a student on placement you may have to think through the plan in relation to your classroom organisation and class. If you are a teaching assistant supporting a specified group or individual you may have to think about the plan as it applies to the needs of the child/children you work with. Annotating the plan with reminders, adding post its (were earlier called 'sticky notes') or writing on it can help you prepare so that your teaching and support is more effective. Plans from some schemes of work can be downloaded and modified electronically.

Demonstration

When you are introducing a new skill, media or process or developing a familiar one in a new direction one of the most effective ways to do this is by demonstrating it. You must therefore be clear how best to show its most important aspects or features, so that the children can respond to this in their own learning. If you are introducing something that you are less confident or less familiar with rehearse it before the lesson to make sure you can demonstrate clearly and anticipate any points to emphasise. In doing this you will also be able to identify useful tips and things to avoid that will help you demonstrate more effectively. When teaching some aspects of art it might be useful for children to have their sketchbooks and work alongside you as you demonstrate. Alternatively a visualiser with the IWB can be very useful as it allows children to see exactly what you are doing close up.

Another factor to bear in mind is that children can be eager to please adults and may want to reproduce what you demonstrate. When you plan your demonstration focus on the skill or technique rather than the content, subject or outcome that the children will be working on themselves. If, for example, you are demonstrating how to vary the pressure on the pencil when drawing to create darker and lighter tones, you could scribble or draw lines and marks rather than drawing a recognisable picture. If you are demonstrating how to use the paint brush so that the bristles touch the paper but the metal part does not, you could paint lines and marks rather than a picture that children may be tempted to try to reproduce.

As well as demonstrating to the whole class you may also use these teaching strategies with groups and individuals to support them further. The same principles can be applied and working on the children's work should be avoided. You can demonstrate using the same tools and resources that the children are using but use another piece of paper alongside the child's work rather than on the child's work. For some children teaching assistants may be deployed to support within the whole class part of the lesson to help them focus on the main teaching or to mirror the whole class teaching alongside an individual. As you observe children working you can identify those who can demonstrate to a friend, group or the class; this can be a useful experience both for the child who demonstrates and the children who learn from it.

Using examples, prompts and reminders

When teaching art you can use examples of the skills and techniques that you have made for the purpose or that you have taken from the work of artists. Depending on what you want to highlight to children it may be easier to make your own examples or it may help children make an interesting and informative link between an artist's work and their own.

When using an example to teach from it is important that you make a careful choice and that this does not steer children into copying the example. You might label the example with prompts to remind the children of the useful learning points.

Other useful visual prompts or reminders might help children who are working on their own to remember the purpose of their activity. An activity can be structured with a series of steps or instructions in words and/or photos as a reminder. Several key questions or a short checklist may remind children of what they could try out or how to overcome challenges.

Alternatively you might plan to allow children free exploration of a material in order for them to find out what can be done and what the challenges are. Only after this more exploratory phase of learning where you observe and identify key areas that children need help with will you go on to teach directly and help children share ideas and approaches. This can also be useful when children return to a tool or process that they have not encountered for some time.

Adult-led, directed and independent activity

When you plan art lessons, the way you organise teaching and learning will vary. In some lessons you may follow a similar pattern to other lessons where you begin with a whole class teaching input, followed by some guided or independent work and ending up with a plenary session to finish the lesson off. This can be adapted to art by, for example, beginning with a short drawing starter that helps children settle into the atmosphere and expectations of an art lesson. It is important to consider the proportion of time that children are actively working practically and making art as this is a crucial aspect of an art lesson. If you find that you are talking and teaching more than the children are working the balance will need adjusting. In other lessons a group rotation organisation where some children work independently and others work with the support of adults may allow for more teaching and practical work to take place. You should be guided by the organisation or management that will best fit the learning you plan to take place.

Practical task

Learning objective:

● to consider the advantages and disadvantages of different ways of organising learning

In this task you will have the opportunity to consider two main types of classroom organisation and they can support learning or be a barrier to learning.

You will need:

● the pro forma below.

What to do:

● Make some notes in each box relating to the advantages and disadvantages of each of these ways of organising learning in an art lesson. When you have finished compare them to the discussion below.

	Adult-led or directed learning	Independent activities
Advantages When would this type of activity support learning?		
Disadvantages When might this type of activity be a barrier to learning?		

Questions to consider

- *When might adult-led or directed activity support learning?*: When considering this you may have identified that demonstrating how to use a tool or follow a process step by step can give a clear model for children to follow. Tips and features that will support success can be clearly modelled. A familiar tool or process that is to be used in a new or different way can be explained. Having this clear model can boost children's confidence and reassure them before they try it for themselves. It can also be an efficient use of time.

- *When might adult-led or directed activity be a barrier to learning?*: If adult-led or directed input is to the whole class there may be some children who find the language or learning too challenging and some for whom it is not challenging enough. It may be difficult to use teaching assistants effectively in the whole class teaching part of the lesson. For some children, too much adult modelling can be discouraging as they can feel that their own efforts will not match the model they have been given. This approach can also lead to thirty similar responses based on the adult model children saw and little opportunity for individual and creative response.

- *When might independent activity support learning?*: Having the time and freedom to explore what tools will do or what effects can be created by processes and techniques allows children to develop their skills and creativity. It may be a more effective use of space and resources especially if the activity uses specialist resources or is particularly messy. They will have more autonomy and independence in their learning and the outcomes that they produce. It is also an enjoyable and positive experience.

- *When might independent activity be a barrier to learning?*: Having a go with insufficient guidance and support can be a waste of time and resources and lead to frustration. It can lead to children repeating the same outcomes and not taking steps forward in their skills, knowledge and understanding. It can be a challenge to provide enough time for children to work independently for a sustained period.

It is likely that when you plan and teach art you choose from a variety of ways of organising learning according to the time you have available, the adult support and the individual needs of the children and the learning that is planned. Ensuring that there is balance between adult-led and independent learning as well as opportunities for guided work where appropriate is something for you aim for and monitor.

Working outside

For some units of work it will be important that children work from what they can experience and see outside the classroom to collect ideas and images. This could be a relatively small-scale walk around the school grounds taking photos, sketching and making notes. It could be something more large scale like a half- or whole-day trip beyond the school entirely or partly focused on art.

When you plan for children to work outside organisation of materials and resources is crucial to supporting learning. Useful resources include:

- *sketchbooks*: Children might work in their usual, ongoing sketchbooks especially if these are portable and have a hard back that can be leaned on. Alternatively you might make small sketchbooks just for this experience. These might be more portable and user friendly for use outside especially if you concerned about weather and loss.

- *clipboards*: If the sketchbooks you are using are not hard enough to lean on each child will need a piece of stiff card or a clipboard to lean on as they draw.

- *drawing materials*: Drawing pencils, pencil sharpeners, pens and any other tools that would be useful should be available.

- *digital cameras*: Allowing children to use these will let them make their own decisions about what visual material to collect and will make the images more meaningful when back in the classroom.

- *bags*: It may be useful for children to collect things to bring back to the classroom to use. If so having a bag for each child or a large communal bag is useful.

- *other art materials*: Depending on your plans for the work outside you might take other materials – watercolours are very useful as they come in small light tins with a lid to use for a palette.

Using your school grounds and immediate local environment as a source of inspiration for learning in art can allow you to teach children the skills and establish behaviour expectations that they need in order go further afield with confidence. In the case study below, young children use their school grounds to observe and research when learning about pattern.

Case Study

A teaching assistant creates a 'looking for pattern' trail for her R Year children to explore in order to develop their observation skills and ability to recognise patterns in their environment. She uses the digital camera to take close-up photos of ten patterns that she finds around the inside and outside areas. These include the pattern on a piece of fabric, bricks on a wall, a pattern carved into a wooden bench, and some markings on a flower. She has deliberately included patterns from nature and the built environment. Each pattern is printed out, strengthened by sticking it onto a 10 cm square card and laminated. She takes the children in groups of five on a walk around the setting to look for the patterns – each child holds two cards. She has planned out a route and places to stop and look as well as some clues if they are required. As the patterns are found each is talked about and labelled with a note of where they were.

Later, children will be asked to find and photograph a pattern that they have found to add to the collection. They will use the computer to make a label saying what the pattern is and where they found it.

In this Case Study young children are given the opportunity to match and identify patterns in the world around them. This inspires description and discussion and encourages them to look more closely and with more purpose at a familiar environment. Some children continue spotting patterns at home and on their way to and from school. Without these early experiences it would be much harder for children to develop an understanding of this visual element that they can build on in key stages one and two.

Beyond the immediate school grounds children could have the opportunity to go on a trip that is solely focused on art or it may be built into a trip that is also related to learning in another or several subjects. Trips to historic sites, places of worship and places of natural beauty have potential for art as well as history, RE and geography. This is a time when meaningful links between art and another subject can be made.

Participating in events

Connecting art in school to events taking place out of school can be inspiring and add to the art curriculum as well as develop links to your local community and give you access to resources and ideas beyond the school. If you look around there may be local events such as projects, workshops and exhibitions that you can participate in. These might be through your local authority, secondary school, college or university or local arts organisations and galleries / museums.

In addition to local events and opportunities there some national events each year that you can use to focus attention on aspects of art and develop its profile in school. Each autumn term The Campaign for Drawing organises events focusing on drawing called 'The Big Draw'. You register on their website to get resources and information about events in your area or you can organise a Big Draw event of your own. Each year there is usually a theme and lots of ideas and resources available to support schools and other organisations.

 LINK

Using a sketchbook to research and collect ideas

The use of sketchbooks is common in Key Stage Two and they are now often introduced in Key Stage One. If sketchbooks are to be used effectively in the teaching of art it is important that we understand what they are, how they can be used effectively and when they might be used. Keeping a sketchbook of your own alongside that of the children can allow you to model what you are teaching. Including examples of children's work and notes can also help your practice and be a valuable source of ideas and reflection for the future. As an artist, keeping a sketchbook is a tradition that goes back centuries and examples from the past and from living artists can be used as examples to show children how they can be used to support research, thinking and making art. Each child's sketchbook is a personal record of their thinking and development as artists and can be a vital source of assessment information.

What is a sketchbook?

The term 'sketchbook' can be used to mean many things. In this discussion a sketchbook should be likened to an exercise book for art – a book in which children explore, research

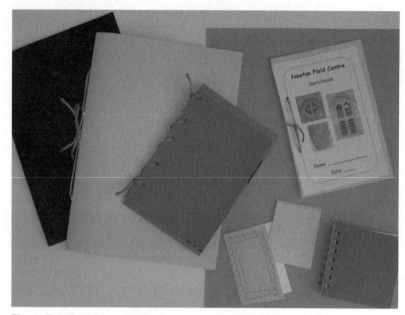

Figure 5.1 Examples of different types of sketchbooks

and record both within and outside of art lessons. It is not a scrapbook in which children's 'best' work is presented, it does not contain only drawing and it is not necessarily a neat and tidy book.

Sketchbooks are likely to vary from school to school. They should have pages of blank cartridge paper, preferably thick enough to allow children to work on both sides of each page. Some sketchbooks have pages of different colours and types of paper. If the cover is hard it can be useful as it makes the pad rigid and can be leaned on whilst working but this can be prohibitively expensive. Sketchbooks may be any size although if they are too large they can be unwieldy, hard to move around and hold, and difficult to store. If they are too small they can be constricting for children although small pads can be more portable and useful outside. The pages can be stapled, spiral bound or sewn together. Cost is usually a significant factor when sketchbooks are chosen for children. Making or allowing children to make their own small sketchbooks for a specific purpose can be an effective approach. Choice of papers (colours, types, weights) for pages and size can allow children some control over their collections of ideas.

Case Study

As part of a session exploring the use of sketchbooks a group of GTP Primary students are asked to make their own mini sketchbook. They are given the choice of ten different A5 sized papers (brown parcel paper, white cartridge paper, tracing paper, newsprint, black sugar paper, squared paper, tissue paper, card and two shades of sugar paper). They collect five sheets and staple them into a card cover. Some students choose very much at random and others employ various criteria, such as trying to match tones and colours or trying to collect a variety of surfaces.

They use their mini sketchbooks to collect research materials around the campus including drawings, rubbings, collages of collected natural materials and photos. Later they refer back to the visual information to support the making of group images based on a chosen route around the campus.

They also consider the value and potential of the sketchbook for supporting learning and giving choice to children. The issue of choosing the different pages was valued by many students. They could see the possibility of planning for children to do this as a planned opportunity to support a particular unit of work as well as way of allowing them to explore different paper surfaces and colours. Some students suggested that, instead of stapling pages into a cover, punching holes in the top and lacing them together would allow for additonal pages to be added later if necessary. Some students liked the idea of having a small sketchbook for a particular project and find it more portable to use outside than their full-size sketchbook. Others suggest the possibility of each child having a page or two to use and them making a class sketchbook for all to refer to on return to the classroom.

Figure 5.2 Using different types of paper in sketchbooks

When children first begin using their sketchbook choosing the next page or running through pages, turning a new one over each time the child perceives the marks as a 'mistake' can be a problem. To overcome this it can be useful to have a thick elastic band with each pad to keep the pages together and prevent them flapping, to identify the next page to work on and stop children from moving through pages too rapidly.

As well as a paper-based sketchbook you might consider the uses of storing work electronically in a similar manner. As schools use digital cameras and video more and more it is likely that some of the art, craft and design work that children make will be photographed and sent home rather than stored, especially work that is large, collaborative or temporary. Keeping a document file for each child including photos of children's work and other research can also be used a complementary way to the sketchbook. It is not necessary to print everything out and stick it into the physical sketchbook – perhaps a note or sticker at the relevant point in the paper sketchbook that there is additional material available electronically can serve as a reminder of this. Alternatively, and for younger pupils especially, you might maintain a shared class electronic sketchbook that you can then display on the IWB and refer to with children in subsequent lessons, using it as a reminder of prior learning.

How can a sketchbook be used?

There is huge potential for using a sketchbook in art lessons and beyond. They can be used on many different occasions in art lessons with children working directly into them and adding other material where appropriate. They might be used in other lessons and subjects or in cross-curricular projects. They can also be used outside school on visits, at out-of-school art experiences and at home or children might have specific sketchbooks for these occasions especially if you have concerns about the loss of a sketchbook that contains evidence of sustained work in art.

Practical task

Exploring sketchbooks

Learning objective:

● to find out more about how sketchbooks are used in your setting;

● to develop your understanding of how to use a sketchbook to its full potential in art lessons.

In this task you will have the opportunity to think in more depth about how sketchbooks can be used to inspire and support learning in art and consider these possibilities in relation to current practice in your setting.

You will need:

● A child's sketchbook. It may worthwhile to choose a Year 6 child's sketchbook or an example of any sketchbook that has been used for a sustained period of time.

What to do:

● Look for examples listed below.

	Example found – note details	Comment
Experimenting with/refining skills with tools/materials		
Collecting examples/pictures/reminders/photos, etc.		
Exploring a visual element such as colour/pattern		

	Example found – note details	Comment
Collecting examples of artists' work, notes about		
Photos of child at work in art lessons, annotated		
Photos of child's finished pieces of art, annotated		
Self/peer assessment relating to an outcome		
Materials collected on a visit or when working outside		
A variety of techniques and processes		
Work starting from imagination, experience and observation		
Assessment by pupil/pupil and teacher		
Work in art but related to other subjects		
Other		

Guidance note

● You might find a mixture of these different types of use of a sketchbook or a few that predominate, depending on your school's approach. A sketchbook can provide you with a fantastic record of a child's learning journey and be a reminder of prior learning and progress made. Looking at this task from another angle you might consider what the opportunities are for using a sketchbook in different parts of a unit of work: examples of this can be found in subsequent chapters.

Find out more

Search online for the Access Art website. Click on 'list all resources' and in the drop down menu select 'seeing sketch books' Here you can explore artists' sketchbooks including those belonging to a sculptor, an illustrator, an animator and a textile artist.

LINK

Some or all of the experiences related to the starting point or research would be recorded in the sketchbook so that they can be referred to in subsequent practical work. Children can look back to materials collected, notes and images made, and photos collected and draw ideas and reminders from these. This is especially supportive for younger pupils or pupils who find it harder to recall earlier lessons or experiences. Sketchbooks should therefore be with pupils in art lessons and available to consult and return to. If you keep your own sketchbook alongside those of the pupils you can model this approach.

Connect and extend

Think Inside the Sketchbook by Gillian Robinson, Alison Mountain and David Hulston (2011) is an inspiring exploration of what sketchbooks are, who uses them and how they can be used in the learning process. There are many examples of children's and artists' sketchbooks as well as practical ideas to use and develop for your own teaching.

Digital media and art

There is great potential for using digital media in art both for you as a teacher and in your teaching and support of children's learning. You can use it to support your planning; during your teaching; and as a way of recording progress and collecting assessment information. In the classroom it can be integrated into each phase of a unit of work: inspiring and preparing; making; and later evaluating and reflecting on learning. When using online sources the school e-safety policy must be followed as in any aspect of school life. Use the checklist in Appendix 2 to investigate the ICT and digital media available to you for use teaching art.

Supporting planning, teaching and assessment

At the planning stage ICT is a wonderful tool for research to enable you to find out more about artists, craftspeople and designers and examples of their work. You should consider the copyright issues related to the use of images and visual material available online. Websites such as Pinterest and Flickr can be useful resources both for finding images and collecting images together to use in teaching. You can find out more about how colleagues in other schools are planning and developing learning in art and keep up to date with resources that you can use in your teaching. Making contact with your subject association (NSEAD) and using social networking to make connections with other teachers of art can help you share ideas, access training, solve problems and get inspiration. Many art galleries have plans and activity ideas that you can use and adapt to enhance and develop planning.

As part of your teaching you might use video clips of artists at work demonstrating media and processes or talking about their work. Hardware such as the visualiser or digital microscope can be useful in art. The visualiser allows you to look at images or items with the image being projected onto the IWB and you can zoom in for a closer look. It can also allow children to see your own demonstrations close up. Tools on the IWB such as the spotlight tool can also help you focus children on certain aspects of image to look at. The digital microscope allows for an even more close view making ordinary items seem amazing. Some artists use this technology as a tool to make their art – have a look at the painting of Mark Ines Russell, who uses a microscope to look close up at small insects.

LINK

The photocopier can also be a useful tool in teaching: making copies of children's drawings so several next steps can be tried or resizing them to make them larger so additional detail can be added to help preserve an original whilst developing and experimenting.

You can also use digital photography to make supporting resources for teaching. This could include prompts and exemplifications to remind children of teaching points as well as step-by-step sequences of processes to help children recall what to do when. Labelled diagrams and layouts can help children organise materials and become more independent in choosing, setting up and clearing away. Using photos of the actual resources that children use in your classroom can make these prompts more meaningful and user friendly for some children. Filming short sequences as reminders of demonstrations can also be useful.

When assessing and recording in art, ICT and digital media provide a means of saving and sharing children's work and is especially useful when work is of large scale shared or three dimensional or if you have little storage space. Taking photos and videos of outcomes and steps along the way and storing these electronically can help overcome the challenge of storage. Displaying children's work on the IWB is an effective way of sharing outcomes with audiences as can sharing images on the school's virtual learning environment (VLE) or website so that parents can see them.

Research and collecting ideas

Digital cameras and flip cameras are versatile and useful resources and can be used by children to take still images or video clips. These can support other ways of researching and collecting images or ideas. It is important to focus children and ensure that they know what they looking for as it is all too easy take many digital photos at random. Identifying a specific focus, such as collecting examples of bright and dull colours, or collecting examples of different types of leaf, so that children look carefully and observe can focus observation and selection. It can be useful to set a certain number of photos so that children make three good choices rather than ten less useful ones – perhaps choosing which to keep and which to delete. Bear in mind that the digital camera itself and associated software will offer opportunities such as zooming in and later cropping and changing images.

In addition to taking their own images children can research images that will be useful in their art. This can give them access to a wider range of images they could not see for themselves in life. Your own preparation will be important here so that you guide them towards appropriate and useful images – creating a selection yourself from which they choose can be a way of initially limiting choice before moving towards more independence.

Case Study

A class of Year 5 and 6 children are going to be making art based on faces and portraits. Their teacher has collected a large selection of images electronically that the class can browse through at the preparation stage of a unit of work. Children are each asked to choose three images that catch their attention and save them to look at and talk about. In a conversation with peers each child identifies what it is about each image that engages them: the media used, a visual element or the subject matter itself. Later these ideas may form part of what each child goes on to make in their own art.

In the case study above older children have had the opportunity to choose images that interest them from a larger range, rather than being presented with the work of one artist chosen by the teacher. In this instance they were choosing images (faces) – on other occasions they might be looking for visual elements, such as use of line or colour, or looking for media and processes, such as different ways of decorating textiles. Using digital media can give children wider opportunities to develop their knowledge and follow their interests, selecting and explaining their choices.

Many art galleries have websites with wonderful interactive learning resources that can enrich children's learning. Increasingly there are mobile apps that can be used as part of learning in art: an example is the 'Muybridgizer' app available from the Tate Gallery where children can take a short video and see it presented as a sequence of slowed down and still images. This relates to the work of Eadweard Muybridge, an early pioneer of photography who captured people and animals in action. It allows children to create something using themselves as the subject and to use technology to present it in a similar way.

LINK

A tool for making art

ICT and digital media can be a support in creating art in other media or it can provide an exciting medium in which to create art in its own right. When working with other media and processes in art consider how some hardware and software can allow children to be more independent. Teaching children to use a photocopier or scanner to copy, expand, reduce and flip to mirror image can be very useful. When children choose images or create their own, resizing or having several copies to experiment on knowing that the original will not be lost in the process can help them make more adventurous choices of next steps. There are some inspiring examples of projects using ICT as a tool for making art to great effect on the Sir Robert Hitcham's Primary School website.

LINK

The opportunities for working on a range of scales are available as images made using digital media can be projected on IWBs, walls and large sheets. In addition to still images, designing and creating animations in two and three dimensions could be part of the art curriculum as well as making a strong link to learning in English.

As part of evaluating and recording

ICT can be a useful tool for allowing children to record progress and consider next steps. Taking photographs or scanning work at significant moments can allow older children especially the opportunity to articulate their decisions and evaluate their work. They can keep a record of each step of a shared project and identify their role in its creation. They can take photos of several views of a three-dimensional work before taking it home. When creating an image onscreen this can be saved under the same title but with a different date each time it is worked on so progress can be seen by the child and by adults supporting and later assessing.

Meeting the needs of a range of learners

All children must be included in art lessons in the same way that they would be included in any other subject or aspect of school life. Indeed art may provide a context in which many children can succeed and enjoy learning in a way that they find challenging in more formal lessons. How all children will be included in the lesson should be part of the short-term planning stage and this may include many ideas and strategies that are used across the curriculum or may require some additional planning depending on individual needs and the subject of art itself.

Some of the challenges you may need to consider are:

- fine motor control, control of tools;
- organisation of space and resources;
- sequencing of steps in processes;
- subject specific vocabulary;
- self esteem, confidence, fear of making mistakes, perception of own skills;
- behaviour/concentration.

The role of teaching assistant is vital when considering how to include and support all children. Deploying the teaching assistant effectively and ensuring he or she is fully informed about the lesson is vital. As a teaching assistant supporting a child or group in an art lesson you should consider what you know about the children, the information on the children's IEPs and any other information from the SENCo and other adults. You should then read the lesson critically with the needs of the children you are supporting in mind in order to consider any changes or additional resources that could support learning. This will help you to anticipate and pre-empt any challenges or barriers to learning in the lesson.

Given the demands of teaching assistants' time it may be that there is no support available in art lessons although the practical nature of art lessons may be a challenge. As a student or teacher you may need to consider how you will meet the needs of all children without the support of an additional adult. Strategies may include the use of visual prompts and reminders, breaking down tasks and activities into small steps, using resources such as ICT and peer support.

Practical task

Learning objective:

- to consider a range of strategies to include an individual or group

In this task you will consider how a range of barriers to inclusion might be tackled.

You will need:

- this pro forma.

What to do:

- Annotate the pro forma identifying the challenges faced by each child in an art lesson – these may be different to those faced in a literacy lesson, for example. Then suggest some ideas about how you could overcome the challenges faced by the children. You might consider one suggestion for when a TA is available and one for when there is no additional support available.

	What are the challenges for the child in an art lesson?	How could these challenges be addressed?
A child whose expressive and receptive language is below that of most of the class	On one page, facing instructions/ notes	
A child whose fine motor control is less-well-developed that most of the class		
A child who finds it hard to concentrate and has a short attention span		
A child who finds it hard sequence and follow instructions		
A child who has just arrived in the UK and begun school		
A child who has low self esteem in relation to his/her ability in art		
A child who is exceptionally talented at drawing		
A child who finds it hard to organise work space and tools		

Questions to consider:

- *A child whose receptive and expressive language is below that of most of the class*: In terms of receptive language (ability to understand language) the level of language that you are using to teach most of the class may result your teaching being inaccessible to the child. This may result in the child misunderstanding your expectations, becoming frustrated and disruptive or switching off. In terms of expressive language (ability to express oneself verbally) it may be hard for the child to ask and answer questions and describe their work. The practical nature of art lessons may make your teaching and expectations clearer to children since you are not relying on words alone but also demonstrating skills and techniques visually. You may need to consider the subject specific language that you use and ensure that you identify the key words that are essential and concentrate on these. Giving children options to respond non-verbally, such as by using facial expression, a scale of one to ten or a choice of several statements may support their response.

- *A child whose fine motor control is less-well-developed than most of the class*: The use of tools such as paint brushes, pencils, pens, needles, glue spreaders, scissors and modelling tools may be a challenge for a child with less-well-developed fine motor skills. This may result in the child being unable to create the art they want to and can see other children producing, frustration and particular challenges when working on a very small scale. Working on a large scale or allowing children some choices in their art so that children are not always expected to produce small and fiddly pieces of work can help this child. Providing appropriate tools such as modified scissors and different sizes and handle lengths of paint brushes can be helpful. Providing opportunities to develop both fine and gross motor skills is likely to be a part of the ongoing support for a child with these challenges.

- *A child who finds it hard to concentrate and has a short attention span*: The challenges facing such a child may be that he or she tunes in and out of the main teaching and then has gaps in their understanding of what to do, how to do it and your expectations. He or she may also be distracted and disruptive to the rest of the class. Considering the length of time that you expect children to concentrate without doing and joining in will be important and, again, the practical nature of art lessons may be more inclusive to the child. Breaking activities and processes down into small steps and punctuating teaching with practical activity will also be helpful. Providing reminders and prompts and using peer support can also help the child who has not been able to retain all of the steps of a process in order.

- *A child who finds it difficult to sequence and follow instructions*: There are some processes in art lessons that require children to work step by step through a sequence in order to be successful and complete their work. For children with these difficulties with processes such as printmaking may be a challenge. Scaffolding the steps with photos and short instructions will be vital as will being very clear in the demonstration of the process and the layout of each step. Pairing the child with another a child who has a good grasp of the process can also be helpful.

- *A child who has just arrived in the UK and begun school*: For a child who has just begun school in the UK getting used to the new environment, possibly a new language, routines and expectations will be a challenge in itself. It may be that art lessons are a welcome relief in that the child can make and do practically with clear visual clues from those around them. You will need to consider the child's different cultural experience and general knowledge about the UK and how this might affect the making of their own art and their response to the work of artists, craftspeople and designers. Their terms of reference might be very different to many of the other children.

- *A child who has low self-esteem in relation to his or her ability in art*: Some children have negative views of their own abilities to make art and may compare their own work harshly to the work of other children. They can be hesitant, unwilling to have a go, find it hard to move on from mistakes and be over dependent on adult support. With children like this it is important to have strategies for overcoming what they perceive as mistakes and promote a culture of having a go in order to learn. Thinking about how you praise and support is also important as well as planning art activities that are not always centered on the ability to produce representative art work.

- *A child who is exceptionally talented at drawing or another aspect of art*: It is likely that you will have one or some children who are very good at aspects of art such as drawing and whose competence is beyond that which you would expect for their age. Ensuring that these children learn and develop is also important. You may need to plan an additional or different activity for these children that allows them to make a next step or work with greater independence so that they can fulfill their potential and not feel frustrated.

- *A child who finds it difficult to organise work space and tools*: For children who find it hard to manage their work space practical lessons can be much more of a challenge as there is more scope for chaos when there are more tools and materials involved. The challenges for these children are that they can waste a lot of time searching for what they need, their tools and materials can impinge on the work spaces of others especially if a group are sharing resources and the quality of their work can be affected. Providing a well-organised working space that is clearly set up supported by straightforward rules is essential and supports all learners. For some children prompts such as shapes to return tools to, labelled trays and checklists are an additional help.

Organising the classroom

When you are teaching or supporting in art lessons it is likely that you will need to think through in more depth how you will organise the classroom because of the practical nature of the lesson. Areas such as resources, health and safety, use of space, timing and the management of any adults in the room will be important to the success of learning and teaching in art. Ensuring that you have anticipated any challenges will help you provide a supportive learning environment.

Management of resources

Art lessons tend to involve tools and materials that are not always readily available in every classroom. It is likely that you will have to collect what you need from elsewhere in the school. Planning can be used to make sure that you have enough of the appropriate resources available to you. If you are teaching the lesson, including a list of resources can act as a reminder to you or something you can ask a teaching assistant to check for you. If you are supporting in the lesson, a quick check of listed resources against what is ready for the lesson will allow you to do a final check or collect anything that is missing. In further chapters specific resources for some of the commonly taught areas of art are considered in more depth.

Management of adults

The number and roles of adults in an art lesson will vary from school to school. As the teacher you could be the sole adult teaching the class; you could have the support of a teaching assistant (TA) who will provide general support or the TA may be focused on supporting an indentified group or individual. If you are an HLTA you could be teaching the class you normally support either with or without the TA support you would normally provide. If you are a TA supporting in art you may be providing general support as directed by the class teacher or you might be supporting a group or individual with specific needs. In all of these examples communication will be important. All the adults working in the lesson need to know what will be happening and how learning for individuals and the whole class can be supported most effectively. There are some essential points to consider:

- Make sure that all the adults have access to the plan wilt enough time to read it and think about it.

- If you are supporting an individual or group with particular needs, think through how the plan will support learning for them and whether you need to suggest any modifications in order to promote inclusion. In an earlier chapter annotating teaching detail onto the plan was suggested as a way of ensuring that you are prepared for the lesson – in this example you might annotate details about how you will support and include your pupils.

- Be prepared to be flexible during the lesson as it is sometimes difficult to anticipate how long practical activities will take.

- Think about your own subject knowledge in relation to the lesson. Do you need to have a go with the resources yourself before you work with the pupils?

If you have a positive working relationship with the team of people that you work with these points will perhaps be second nature to you. If you are a student in this setting you will need to develop this working relationship quickly and ensure that the adults are fully briefed either using the systems already in place or devising ways of your own. You should be alert to taking advice from the staff who know the children best, about how they will respond in art lessons and how their learning can most effectively be supported.

Health and safety

In art lessons you will be using resources and tools that may at first be unfamiliar to children or that they do not use very often. Thinking through possible health and safety issues at the planning stage can help you to anticipate and avoid risks. When considering health and safety in relation to art you should be guided by your own school's Health and Safety Policy and any specific guidance in relation to art and health and safety in the Art Policy. You can also seek advice from the Art co-ordinator and the Health and Safety Co-ordinator in your school. Areas for consideration are:

- the materials you are using especially certain types of felt pen, dyes, glues, scrap materials, plaster of paris and clay;

- the tools you are using;

- protective clothing that is appropriate;

- the usual fire and first aid procedures;

- the use of space, how activities are set up within it, how children move around it;

- supervision that is appropriate to the number, age and levels of the children you are working with.

In addition to this maintaining a tidy and well-organised working environment contributes to a safe and productive lesson; the purposeful working atmosphere that you create in your classroom is also important.

Find out more

Clarify your understanding of the health and safety issues related to teaching art by searching for the NSEAD website online. There is some detailed guidance on health and safety in the context of art lessons available there.

LINK

Space

It is likely that you will be using more and different resources in art lessons but in the same classroom setting. In order to avoid or minimise accidents with resources it is important to think about how you will set up the room and use the space you have available effectively. You will need to consider such things as:

- the location of the sink: Is this where children will change dirty water? Is this where children will wash their hands? Is this where children will wash up equipment? Can children get to it without colliding with other children who are working? How will you organise space and timing so that the sink is not required for all these purposes at the same time?

- storage space: Where will children put their finished work? Can children take their work there or will they need adult support? Is there enough space for all children's work?

- the floor: If your room is partially or fully carpeted how will you protect this if necessary? Is there any part of the lesson that must take place on a tiled floored area? Can some children work outside?

- protective clothing: Where are aprons kept? Are they accessible to children? Are they easy to put on for children or will they need adult support? Do they protect sleeves or do sleeves need to be rolled up? Do the aprons fit? Are there enough aprons?

Giving consideration to these basic questions can help you to organise materials effectively in lessons. Organising how the space and resources within it can be used in an art lesson and most vitally making sure all adults working in the room know this can ensure that your lesson runs smoothly so that all children and adults can concentrate on teaching and learning. You may find it useful to express this as a map or a plan of the classroom or by using labels and prompts around the room.

Conclusion

In this chapter some aspects of teaching and supporting learning in art lessons have been explored. Your own experience of these as well as your developing subject knowledge will help you teach and support effectively in art lessons. Your personal enthusiasm and interest will also support effective lessons and obtain a positive approach from children. In the next chapter the teaching and learning of drawing will be explored in more depth – you may find some suggestions in this chapter apply beyond drawing and can be used in other art teaching.

Next steps

- Consider any specific needs of pupils in your class. How will you ensure that you include all children? Are there any children who particularly excel in art? How will you extend and develop them within each unit?

- Observe an art lesson in your school or next placement school. Identify the teaching strategies used by adults. How are these specific to learning in art?

References

Matthews, J. and Seow, P. (2007) Electronic paint: understanding children's representation through their interactions with digital paint. In: Herne, S., Cox, S. and Watts, R. (2009) *Readings in Primary Art Education*. London: Intellect Books. pp. 269–86.

Robinson, G., Mountain, A. and Hulston, D. (2011) *Think Inside the Sketchbook*. London: Harper Collins.

Further reading

Arts Council (2003) *Keys to Imagination: ICT in Art Education. Creating Spaces*. Available from: *http://www.artscouncil.org.uk/media/uploads/documents/publications/730.pdf* (accessed 30 June 2012).

BECTA (2009) *ICT in primary art and design: a pupil's entitlement*. Available from: *http://www.bee-it.co.uk/Guidance%20Docs/Becta%20Files/Schools/Curriculum/Art%20and%20design/02%20ICT%20in%20primary%20art%20and%20design%20A%20pupil%27s%20entitlement.pdf* (accessed 30 June 2012).

Chamberlain, A. (2010) 'Art allows all children the freedom to explore'. *START*. No. 34, pp. 12–13.

Cullen, J. And Evans, S. (2007) 'The friendship project; digital art meets PSGCE'. *START*. No. 25, pp. 26–27.

Web resources

Ideas about using photography on Artisancam: *http://www.artisancam.org.uk/pages/artforms.php?artform=photography*

A website with case studies and resources (including an image bank) to support digital media in art: *http://www.content.networcs.net/digipal/flash/digipal_intro.swf*

A website with interesting ideas and resources to support ICT/Art: *http://www.kenttrustweb.org.uk/kentict/kentict_subjects_art_home.cfm*

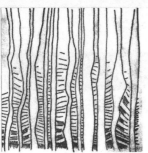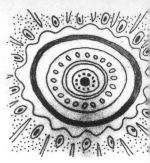

Chapter 6

Drawing

Introduction

Drawing is intrinsic to learning in the art curriculum – it is regularly used as part of the research process regardless of which media or processes will later be used and it has many applications beyond art. As such it is an aspect of art about which everyone who supports and teaches art in primary schools must have some subject knowledge of and commitment to supporting in children's learning. In this chapter the following areas will be considered:

- Subject knowledge that underlies teaching of drawing
- Teaching children to draw

Many children love to draw and become absorbed in making their own drawings in school and at home. Being able to draw to communicate, explore and record is a skill that children will be expected to use across the curriculum. Depending on their choice of career they may go on to use drawing in the world of work. Even if they do not draw as an artist in an art or design context after they leave school it is likely that being able to draw and get information from drawings will still play a part in their lives. Quite apart from this many children enjoy drawing and explore it spontaneously as a process without always thinking about the end product. If you have spent any time with children at home or in the classroom you will have noticed this. We can harness this enthusiasm and need to draw in our teaching and equip children with skills they need and the confidence to develop their drawing.

On the other hand many adults tend to lack confidence in their own ability to draw and therefore find the idea of teaching children to draw daunting. Sometimes adults retain a hesitant attitude towards their ability to draw from their own educational experiences when their own teachers perhaps gave them feedback that caused them to give up. You might have heard adults openly belittling their own skills in this area in a way that would be entirely inappropriate were they talking about other ways of communicating. Perhaps you encounter situations when it would be useful to be able to draw but you have not been given the help and opportunities that you need to learn the skills that would enable you to do this effectively. This can cause a lack of confidence and a misplaced feeling that you cannot draw. Concerns were expressed recently that 'the notion that everyone can draw is not being kept alive beyond the early years of schooling' (OFSTED, 2012, p. 52) and you play a vital role in supporting children's drawing in the next few years.

If you have experienced any of the feelings discussed above it is all the more important that you do not perpetuate these feelings with the children you are supporting or teaching. As Anning (2002) states 'An adult in a school setting may undermine the child's confidence in the efficacy of drawing strategies they have been using routinely at home, by at best ignoring or at worst responding negatively to them' (p. 198). Having a positive attitude about developing drawing skills and modelling the idea that drawing is a skill that can be developed and improved is something you can do in your role, whatever your own drawing skills are like. Fabian (2005) suggests that children need to realise that learning to draw 'will involve having a serious attitude, applying themselves and perseverance' (p. 11) and you can demonstrate this in what you say and what you do.

Connect and extend

Read the section entitled 'Focusing on key subject skills: drawing' (pp. 51–6) in the OFSTED (2012) report 'Making a mark: art, craft and design education'.

Think about how in the primary years we can build on the positive start that children experience in their early years and consider your role in giving the children you teach a positive experience of drawing that will support their enthusiasm and learning in this important area of art education.

LINK

Drawing is likely to be woven through most units of art and so it may be that each classroom has a set of basic supplies such as several boxes of drawing pencils and cartridge paper. Other types of drawing tools, especially sets of a more specialist type, are likely to be stored in a central place and used when required in planned units. Explore the list of tools and materials in Appendix 2 to find out more about the resources that support drawing in art.

In addition to the list in Appendix 2 it is important to include digital media in the range of learning opportunities that we give to children. Software that allows children to explore mark making and drawing is common on primary school PCs and laptops; children make marks with the cursor using the mouse or with their fingers on a touchpad. More recently applications that support drawing on mobile devices and tablets have become much more prominent with the inspiring examples of David Hockney's work seen in his Royal Academy exhibition of 2012 and other examples on his website. One of the advantages of these applications is that marks can be made using fingers directly onto the screen giving a direct control to the child without the need to manipulate a tool.

The subject knowledge that underlies the teaching of drawing

Developing some subject knowledge about drawing will underpin your successful planning and teaching. Some of the aspects of the learning and teaching of drawing that you may need to learn more about are:

- exploring drawing tools;
- the development of drawing skills;
- exploring visual elements through drawing;
- drawing in art lessons and beyond;
- the work of artists, craftspeople and designers.

Exploring drawing tools

When you introduce a new drawing tool or a tool that the children do not use regularly or have not used for a while, part of your planning at the earlier stage of a unit of work should include opportunities to explore the potential and qualities of the tool. If children have these investigative opportunities they are more likely to be able to use the tool with increasing confidence and control in their work. When you consider planning these opportunities your priority must be the exploration of what can be done with the tool and how to get the best from it rather than to produce a finished outcome. This is a time when children will work in their sketchbooks.

Practical task

Learning objective:

- To explore drawing tools

In this task you will have opportunity to explore the qualities of some frequently used drawing tools. You will also be encouraged to consider how you can support children in exploring these tools.

You will need:

- A pencil from within the B range (ideally 4B), black felt pen (fine, broad or marker), a biro or ballpoint pen, cartridge paper to draw on;
- the pro forma below or a copy of it.

Drawing tools	What can you do with it? Is there anything you can't do with it?	What does it feel like to use? How could it support drawing?	What challenges does it pose? How might you overcome these?
4B pencil			
Black felt pen (fine / broad / marker)			
Biro / ballpoint pen			

What to do:

- scribble with each tool to get a feel for it in your hand and how it moves. Try making marks with them at all angles;
- making lines – make some continuous lines, some parallel straight lines, some cross hatched lines (including parallel one way and then other way on top);
- making marks – make some dots, spots, short and longer dashes nearer and further apart.
- making shapes and patterns – make some circles, squares, triangles; try out some repeating patterns, colour in some of the shapes;
- making lighter and darker marks – see what happens when you press harder and then more gently as you make a continuous line; try to make some lighter and darker marks;

Figure 6.1 Mark-making exercise examples

draw some shapes and shade in one fully; try to make lighter and lighter shapes until you have an almost white/empty one.

See Figure 6.1 to examples of different marks to make. There is a fuller annotated example online.

Questions to consider:

● *What can you do with each tool? Is there anything you can't do?:* You may have found as you worked through the exercises that the tools responded in different ways.

The 4B pencil, for example, will have responded to the pressure you exerted on it so that you could make very light and very dark marks as well as many tones in between. On the other hand the felt pens do not respond to pressure as readily and a biro might fall in between. You may have found that you could create darker and lighter tones by overlapping marks and lines and placing them close together and further apart using the pens.

The biro or ballpoint pen allows you to make very fine lines and the felt pens come in different widths so that you can use three pens – fine, broad and marker, and choose within these. The pencil could vary depending on how often you sharpen it. You could start with a fine line just after the pencil has been sharpened and then as it is used it wears down, sometimes quite rapidly, to make a broader point.

Clearly the pencil can be rubbed out if you make a mark that you do not like. When working with children this can be useful or it can be a problem. The felt pens and biros cannot be rubbed out. This can mean that we accept marks we do not like and move on with the drawing regardless, as there is nothing we can do about it. This can be a good attitude to develop with children who may then apply it to their work with pencil and other media.

● *What does it feel like to use? How could it support drawing?*: As you investigated each drawing tool you may have enjoyed how the different media moved across the surface. Perhaps you haven't considered a biro as a drawing tool before although you have probably doodled with one as you talk on the phone or listen in at a presentation or meeting. How each of the drawing tools moved will have been influenced by the paper that you chose to use for this exercise.

The drawing pencil can allow you to explore and use line and tone by your own pressure on the pencil. It takes practice and experience to be able to control this and make the tone you want by exerting the appropriate amount of pressure. The felt pens and biro too support the use of line but they also allow you to explore creating tone not by pressing down harder but by placing and overlapping lines and marks. The biro can allow you to create very fine lines and sometimes the properties of biro will vary, responding to pressure and by incidental changes in the flow of ink.

● *What challenges does it pose? How might you overcome these?*: Some of the challenges posed by these tools might in other circumstances be advantages. A point made earlier about how the pens and biros cannot be rubbed out may at first appear to be a challenge but it can also be an advantage as we have to let go and just draw over marks we don't like. One of the challenges of the soft drawing pencil can be its smudginess. Again, this can be an advantage because it allows us to blend from lighter to darker and produce a large range of tones. Smudging a finished drawing can be overcome by fixing it or placing a sheet of tissue or tracing paper over it to prevent it rubbing against other pages. Soft drawing pencils can wear down quickly so you may need to be ready to sharpen them or have more pencils than you need so that you can substitute a sharpened pencil for a blunt one without the break in concentration of going off to find and use a sharpener might cause. Felt pens can make marks on children's hands and possibly their clothes. Nowadays the ink in felt pens tends to be washable – but check this on the packets before you use them. It is unlikely you would be using permanent pens in the primary school but you should check the pens to be sure. Biros can become blotchy but are very cheap and relatively expendable.

Both using a wide range of drawing tools to experiment with the marks they make and developing control and familiarity with a few basic tools used regularly are important in teaching children to draw. Teaching children to choose and use the appropriate tools in drawing, as in other aspects of art, will support children towards independence and control over their art work in the future.

The development of drawing skills

You will have noticed through your experience of working with children or by thinking back to your own childhood that children's drawing develops and changes over time. As someone who supports or teaches children as they draw it is important for you to know about stages of development and how you can support and teach children as they learn. If we do not pay attention to the development of children's drawing skills it may be that we do not give them the support they need to overcome the challenges they face as they develop their skills. If we abandon the teaching of drawing too early it can have serious consequences for children's later feelings about and confidence in their drawing skills. As an adult you may look back and feel that your drawing skills were frozen in time and you have never moved on to a stage that you would find useful in your adult life. Anning (2002) points out that 'Many children learn in the first years at school that they "can't draw"; and many adults remain arrested in the drawing capability they assumed at the age of six or seven' (p. 198). You can play an important role in avoiding this for the children you support and teach.

Early mark making

Children pick up tools and make marks with them on surfaces, at first perhaps accidentally and then later exploring what happens when they move those tools up and down, sweeping from side to side and pushing and pulling. They may be exploring how to hold the tools they make marks with and which hand to hold them in. Sometimes children will indicate what their marks relate to by naming them. This is an important stage. Barnes (2002) writes that 'Scribble is to drawing what babbling is to talk' (p.38).

At this stage we can support children by giving them a variety of tools and surfaces to investigate and by allowing them to make choices in what they will try and return to. We can talk about and describe colours, lines, shapes and marks as they make them. We can pay positive attention and encourage without always asking 'What is it?' as this can make it seem that drawings always have to be an observation 'of' something, rather than enjoying the process itself or being inspired by imagining or remembering something. We can display drawings with a label of their own choosing or just the child's name.

First representations and schema

Children begin to remember and recreate the marks, lines and shapes and use them to represent things in their drawings. Children tend to draw what they know rather than what they see. They draw about their experiences paying less or no attention to actual colours, shapes and scale. Children use their drawing to tell stories and explain the world around them. They may initiate and respond more to talking about what the drawing is about. Over time children develop ways of drawing things that appear in their drawings and this becomes the way they draw a house, a tree, a car. These schema are personal and relate to their experience. As time goes on the schemas become more developed and detailed. Space may be represented in ways that to adults appear unconventional including views from inside, outside or above, and the ground and sky may be represented by lines or colour at the top and bottom of the paper.

At this stage we can continue to ensure that children can draw with a variety of tools on different surfaces. We can help them make choices and allow them free choice of tools, surfaces and what they draw. We can begin to guide them in learning about the qualities and properties of a variety of mark making tools. When drawing from observation we can help them to look, talk about what they are going to draw and touch before they draw. We can encourage children to choose to draw from memory and imagination as well as observation.

Connect and extend

Read the article 'Young children talking and drawing' by Elizabeth Coates and Andrew Coates and published in the *International Journal of Early Years Education* in 2006 (Vol. 14 No. 3 pp. 221–41). After reading the discussion section towards the end of the article think about the implications for planning drawing opportunities for children.

Developing realism

Later, children include more and more detail in their drawing in an attempt to make their drawings appear more 'real' and representative. This can lead to frustration with the results when they compare what they were aiming to draw and what they have drawn. This might be when they begin to express a feeling of 'I can't draw'. Creating an illusion of space by using perspective can emerge as a challenge here and it should be remembered that this is an aspect of Western art and not a feature of art from other places and times.

At this stage perhaps the role of adults is most important. As children begin to realise that the way they draw something is not realistic and abandon their schemas the challenge is to find other ways of drawing. If no guidance is given at this point it is easy to give up. We can support children by helping them to look in a way that will support their drawing. We can continue to talk about what they will draw first and help them develop ways of approaching their work. We can also help children accept that when we draw we make mistakes that we can learn from and that we need to persevere in order to improve. Most importantly of all we can introduce children to artists whose drawings are non-representative and for whom drawing something that looks real is not a primary aim.

Find out more

Put 'drawing development in children' into a search engine. This will lead you to a website that compares stages in developed by Betty Edwards and Viktor Lowenfield

LINK

Put 'early drawing NSEAD' into a search engine to find Dan China's booklet: 'The Early Development of Drawing' to download.

LINK

Stages of development in drawing have been researched and written about in much greater detail than above and you should learn more about these stages, connecting them to the children's drawing that you encounter. Rough age ranges can be attached to these stages although individual children will spend longer or shorter in each of them. They may move around between stages or may miss stages out. As a student, teaching assistant or teacher you need to know enough to effectively support and teach the children you are working with. This includes knowing them as individuals and not making assumptions about where they are with their drawing. As Barnes (2002) suggests 'The stages they have been through – scribble, symbols, schema and visual realism – are each important experiences which a teacher could impede' (p. 43). In order to avoid impeding them by what we say or do or what we fail to say and do we must use our subject knowledge to underpin our planning and teaching. Barnes goes on to say 'Knowing the stages gives us the opportunity to match activities to what the children are capable of producing, and avoids forcing upon them those images for which they are not yet ready' (p. 43).

Drawing and the brain

Over recent years research about the brain has begun to have an impact on our thinking about how children learn. The brain has right and left hemispheres and scientists are continuing to investigate how these hemispheres work together. Generally the left side of the brain deals with language, maths and logic and the right side of the brain deals with spatial relationships, facial recognition, visual imagery and music. Fabian (2005) suggests that when we see a familiar item such as a house, a tree or an animal the left side of the brain supplies a name. Thereafter we stop looking at what is in front of us and rely on our internal knowledge of what the item looks like. Edwards (2012) explains that

> We tend to see what we expect to see or what we decide we have seen. This expectation or decision, however, often is not a conscious process. Instead, the brain frequently does the expecting and the deciding, without our conscious awareness, and then alters or rearranges – or even simply disregards – the raw data of vision that hits the retina (p. xxiv).

In order to develop our ability to look and then to draw we can try looking from different viewpoints so that our brain does not immediately think 'a tree' and draw our schema for tree – our internal tree picture. When I am drawing the human figure or face I make a conscious effort to look for lines, edges, tones rather than a face or features. As soon as I let an awareness of the face take over, I feel my ability to look change and become less useful for drawing. Fabian (2005) suggests looking from unusual angles and viewpoints, looking at the space around instead of the object itself or looking at reflected images.

Connect and extend

Explore the Betty Edwards' website at the link. She writes about learning to draw in an interesting way and suggests activities to help you to develop your own drawing.

LINK

Exploring the visual elements through drawing

When the learning objectives are focused on drawing it is likely that you will be exploring one or at most two of the visual elements. The chart below suggests some opportunities for exploring each of the visual elements when drawing with children.

Line	Tone
Exploring marks and continuous lines with a wide variety of drawing tools Drawing outlines, overlaps, shapes next to each other, etc. Using marks and lines to create areas of tone, pattern, texture Making lines slowly, quickly, carefully, wildly, etc.	Exploring making light and dark marks using a variety of drawing tools Exploring lighter/darker tones and contrasts Using tone to create areas, objects, textures, shapes Using tone to create an illusion of three-dimensional form
Colour	**Pattern**
Exploring applying colour using a variety of drawing tools Exploring blending tones within colours using drawing materials such as pastels Exploring making light and dark marks using colour	Making patterns using drawn marks Making patterns using lines, outlines Making patterns using tones Making patterns using combinations of… Drawing from patterns observed around us
Texture	**Shape**
Representing texture using drawn marks, lines, areas of tone	Representing 2d shapes using drawing tools to create outlines, shapes, etc Placing drawn shapes on a surface spread out, next to and overlapping
Space	**Form**
Representing 3D space in 2D using drawing tools – composition, viewpoints, creating an illusion of space Representing 3D shapes on a 2D surface Playing with space, unconventional viewpoints	Representing 3D solid objects in 2D using drawing tools Drawing onto forms to decorate them

Through each year group and key stage you will revisit visual elements through drawing in different contexts allowing children to build on their drawing skills and experience of drawing tools and surfaces. This is an area that should be thought through at the planning stage so that it is clear and can be used for planning and teaching from. You may need to think beyond the half term that you are working in now and even the year group within which you work to get a feel for the key stage so you can appreciate the child's experience as a continuum.

Some drawing materials will lend themselves to developing skills in a particular element more so than others. When we think about exploring tone white chalk and charcoal might be a popular choice as these allow us to make a dark black tone and bright white tone and we can blend them to create grey tones between black and white. Choosing a mid-tone paper will allow the white and black at each end of the tonal scale to stand out more clearly. Using chalk and charcoal with younger children can be messy and some organisation is required to protect their clothes and preserve the clarity of their work. The art software Revelation Natural Art will allow children to experiment with charcoal on screen leaving visual marks that replicate what charcoal looks like when blended.

Tone in terms of creating dark and light marks can be explored using pencils such as 4B and 6B. These soft pencils allow children to vary their pressure and make distinctly darker and lighter tones in the marks and lines that they make. The physical control of tools in order to make lighter and darker marks is a skill that requires direct teaching and opportunities to practise and consolidate. For some children it is a challenge that also has an impact on their writing where they press either very lightly so it is hard to read their written work or so hard that they indent the next few pages.

Case Study

As part of an exploration of tone in drawing Year 1 and 2 children are using 6B pencils. Their teacher has taped large sheets of paper entirely covering the tables and the children will work on these. They know that the purpose of this activity is not to create an individual finished outcome but investigate lighter and darker tones and what happens when they press harder and more gently. This gives them more freedom to experiment than if they were working towards a finished piece of work for an audience.

Their teacher asks the children to make a scribbled patch about the size of their fist on the paper and as dark as they can without going through the paper. She talks to them about how they created their very dark patches – perhaps by pressing down hard or by making close together and overlapping marks and covering the surface of the paper so it does not show through.

Next she asks them to move around to a friend's dark patch and shade a patch that is a little lighter. She emphasises the need to press a little more lightly. The children continue moving around creating and comparing tonal patches until they are making very light marks. The activity finishes with the teacher asking the children to make continuous lines but changing the pressure so that the lines get darker and lighter.

This activity falls within the early stages of a unit of work where the children will later be drawing from observation on a large scale. It allows the children to explore mark making and tone in a context where the outcome will not matter so that they can get a feel for the pencil in their hand and how to exert pressure on it to change the tones it makes. The teacher talks with the children about what they have learned and uses this to label a photo of the class working so that they can stick a copy in their sketchbooks as a reminder of the session.

This case study shows how you might create opportunities for children to explore a visual element that will underpin their later learning within a unit of work without being distracted by an individual outcome. It serves as a chance to consolidate previous experience and develop control of their mark making skills. Exploring tones from darker to lighter within a colour can also develop understanding of tone. Using a limited colour palette allows children to explore tones within one colour. Sets of pastels, coloured pencils or wax crayons often contain some tones of the same colour that can be used for this.

Drawing in art lessons and beyond

It is likely that drawing will be part of many if not all units of work in art at the exploring and developing ideas stage. From time to time it may be the main focus of a unit leading to an outcome that is a drawing or has drawing as a main part. In addition to this developing children's drawing skills should be planned as a continuous thread throughout all units, just as learning to read and write continue throughout the English curriculum. It is important that drawing is taught directly: following a scheme of work such as that written by Fabian (2005) or the teaching ideas available through the Access Art website and the Big Draw will support you in terms of your subject knowledge and teaching.

LINK

Starting points for drawing

Children should have the opportunity to draw for different purposes and reasons and their drawings should be inspired by a variety of starting points. It is important that we consider these areas when we plan drawing experiences for the children we support and teach. If you reflect upon the experiences that are given to children in their drawing throughout a year or key stage you can evaluate how they match to the areas discussed below. It may be that one area is used as a stimulus or context much more often than the others and this imbalance is something to think about in your long term planning.

Drawing from observation is often a large part of the planned drawing experience in school. This can be an increasingly challenging area for children as they may be matching and judging their own drawing to the 'real' object, person or scene that they are trying to record on paper. We need to support children to develop their skills so that they can begin to record what they see. Ensuring we choose or help them to choose appropriate tools to draw with, guiding them to look in ways useful for drawing and giving them opportunities to look at the different ways artists have drawn can be helpful.

When we ask children to draw from observation it is important that we give them interesting starting points so that they want to draw. When I draw it is sometimes because something about the landscape, the weather or the light has inspired me. On other occasions it is to gather visual information to help me make a print from or because I am inspired by what I see. When I am drawing from life it is to challenge and develop my drawing skills. Where possible we should try to give children choices within what we are asking them to draw so that there is at least a possibility of being interested in the subject matter. We should also take account of children's previous experiences so that they do not repeat the same tasks for the same purpose. If they do return to a similar or the same starting point it should be to explore it in a different media, for a new purpose or in greater depth.

Drawing from experience allows children to explore their personal experiences and memories and express their feelings on paper. When children draw spontaneously they will often draw scenes of what has happened to them in their lives. Their drawings tell stories, often including several scenes or viewpoints, and may convey feelings through the way they use tools and materials and the marks they make. They may be less concerned with making their drawings look 'real' in the way discussed in the previous paragraph and this can give them more freedom. For younger children drawing can be an easier way to communicate than writing. Drawing as a response to significant events in personal, school, national or spiritual life, such as celebrating festivals, often allows children to convey much more than they could if asked to write about the experience or memory. Talking about experiences may help children recall details to develop their work further, or a spontaneous response focused on what was significant for the child may be more appropriate.

Drawing from imagination is perhaps an area that we find more challenging to plan for in the art curriculum. Starting points for stimulating imaginative work may be responses to music, poetry or stories. Many children are interested in fantasy in literature, television, film and computer games, so they have a visual vocabulary to use in their drawing. This could be seen as a hindrance to the child's individual imagination or as a wealth of imagery to draw upon when starting out on their own imaginative drawing. It may also be more motivating for some children and boost their confidence. Drawing from imagination may also allow us to make a link to English and the children's own story illustrations and animations.

Case Study

A group of BA QTS students are exploring starting points for drawing from observation. They have begun by sharing some of the starting points for observational drawing that they can recall from their own art education. Many recall being asked to draw individual objects, and groups of objects, the landscape and the figure. In this session they are encouraged to think about some of the planning decisions and resource choices and their impact on children's engagement and learning.

One half of the group explore what children draw. They investigate a group of diverse objects to identify two key visual elements that could be explored through drawing. They consider how children can be given more choice over what they draw by collecting a varied group of objects that all lend themselves to the use of line, tone or whichever visual element is the focus of the drawing. They also discuss whether every child has to draw from the same stimulus and how far a free choice can be managed in the classroom in terms of organisation and planning for learning.

The other half of the group consider how the way viewing what will be drawn could be used to support and challenge drawing. They explore strategies such as looking closely at areas rather than the whole; using view finders; moving around to draw from a series of different viewpoints; revealing only a small part of what is being drawn and extending the area that can be seen gradually; and looking, covering, drawing from memory several times over.

Each group sets up some activities for the other to particpate in. Students participate, observe and talk about the implications for their own learning and learning in art lessons with children.

In this case study students were encouraged to think purposefully and creatively about stimulating drawing from observation by considering what they plan for children to draw from and how they go about drawing it. This helps to understand different ways that they can approach teaching drawing from observation. In later sessions they will go on

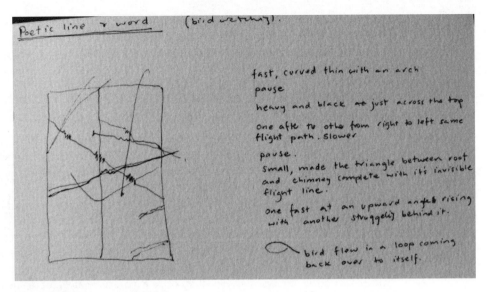

Figure 6.2 Movements of birds

to devise teaching strategies for supporting drawing and teach each other to apply their skills and get feedback on their effectiveness.

As well as drawing to explore and represent observations, experience and imagination children should also have the opportunity to use drawing to explore and record in a more abstract way. In this type of drawing their outcome will not 'look like' what they are drawing and the drawing itself when completed may not be the end product; rather the experience of making the marks in the moment is the aim. Drawing to respond to and convey a sense of movement, atmosphere or feelings is a way of approaching this. In the illustration (Fig. 6.2) you can see how an artist has responded to birds flying by drawing the movements rather than the birds themselves.

Changing the way children look at and record the familiar can also help them to move from figurative to abstract work: ask them to isolate small areas and draw them much larger; ask them to experiment with rules such as only lift the pencil and replace it five times before you have to start a new drawing; or make a rubbing and draw from it using the marks you see in your drawing. Look for examples of where artists are drawing to explore drawing and not to make a finished representation of something in order to get more ideas about this approach to drawing.

Drawing within units of work

In the early stages of a unit of work there will be many opportunities to include drawing as a means of observing, researching, gathering ideas and visual information that will be used in making a finished outcome that in itself might not include drawing. At this stage it is likely that the children will be working in their sketchbooks. They could be exploring and learning about a visual element through drawing before going on to develop it in another media or process or experimenting with drawing tools to learn about their potential. When drawing to research we might encourage children to annotate the drawing with descriptive words and phrases, written independently or scribed by us. We can encourage them to draw from several viewpoints, zoom in and look at the details. Drawing to investigate and research may be an important part of the exploring and developing stage of a unit of work and these drawings may be more of a learning process than a finished outcome.

Case Study

A class of Year 3 and 4 children are working on a unit of work that will involve observation around the built environment of the school site. The outcome of their work will be a relief clay tile of a part of the building that interests them, and they are aiming for some detail in their three-dimensional representation.

In the exploring and developing stage of the unit their first activity is to draw the front of the school building from memory on one page in their sketchbooks. The children choose to use either 4B pencils or pens. The class find this harder then they at first imagine. This is followed by going out to look at the front of the school building to compare their drawings. The children are asked to look for similarities and differences and some suggestions about how they could produce a drawing that shows a more accurate representation of the building façade. Many of them realise that working from observation will help as they will be able to look and check as they draw.

Their next task is draw from observation on the facing page to from their other drawing. Before they draw they look and the teaching asistant and teacher guide their looking focusing on the shapes and patterns that can be seen on the building. These features will support the children's claywork later in the unit. Using pens or drawing pencils will help them use lines to draw shapes and patterns without being distracted by other elements such as colour.

Another part of their research is to home in on a part of the building that interests them and draw it, paying more attention to detail – 'zooming in' on it. Some children's drawings are expanded on the photocopier and they add more detail to parts of the enlarged copy, while others use view finders and some children identify a detail and draw it freely.

The children also take some digital photos to use as reminders and take a closer look at these on the screen. Some children draw lines onto these looking for key lines and shapes – drawing onscreen or on printed out copies of the photos. They also make some rubbings of different surfaces on the school building to encourage them to think about texture when using the clay later.

In this case study the children use drawing as an integral part of their research towards a piece of claywork. Other activities in this early stage included giving children some reminders of working with clay since it had been some months since they last used it. They also tried out how they could draw into or add more clay onto their tile or add texture to create a relief effect. Although their finished outcome will not be a drawing, drawing skills were significant in the early stages of the unit.

Some units of work may be entirely focused on drawing or drawing along with another related medium with an outcome that is primarily a drawing. In these units of work you have the opportunity to pay more in-depth attention to children's drawing. Perhaps these are opportunities to tackle challenging areas such as representing space or combining drawing with watercolour, ink wash or printmaking. This might also be an opportunity to use digital media and in particular drawing software on the computer screen, more large scale on the IWB or on mobile devices.

The work of artists, craftspeople and designers

When you choose a drawing, a type or style of drawing or drawings by a particular artist it is important to choose bearing in mind your objective or learning outcome and how looking at and talking about the example(s) will support learning.

If you plan for children to explore the marks that can be made by drawing tools look for examples of a range of these. The pencil and ink line drawings of Van Gogh are a wonderful example of detailed and repetitive mark making whereas the shelter drawings by Henry Moore use light, dark and contrast of tones often using not just pencil but wax crayon and inkwash. Children's book illustrators are a great source of examples of drawing. John Burningham often uses dynamic lines and marks; Raymond Briggs uses line and colour, sometimes (as in Jim and the Beanstalk) representing one thread of the story in black line drawings, and one thread in coloured drawings, and many of Shirley Hughes's illustrations are line and colour wash or coloured pencil drawings.

Finding examples of where artists, craftspeople and designers use drawing to collect visual information, practise their skills and work thorough ideas is also useful – you may have followed a suggestion to go to the Access Art website in Chapter 3 where there are some examples of artists' sketchbooks to look at. Drawing is often a feature of hand-drawn animations and this can be a link to using ICT. The Simon's cat animations are an example of simple line drawings.

Find out more

Search for the artist Morgan O'Hara's website. Explore the performance videos to see how this artist uses drawing to respond to activities such as a dragon dance (Macau 2010), people working in a fishmarket (Japan 2003) and a dancer by a lake (Butoh, 2003). How could you encourage children to respond to what they see, hear and feel in drawing?

LINK

Teaching children to draw

When you are supporting children's drawing or teaching drawing as part of or the main focus of a unit of work there are some areas that you should consider in order to be prepared. Some of the generic teaching principles discussed in earlier chapters will apply when you are supporting or teaching drawing. In addition to these there are some other areas may need some further consideration. These include:

● rubbers and 'mistakes';
● before beginning to draw;
● viewfinders;
● teaching and supporting as children draw;
● drawing across the curriculum.

Rubbers and what to do about 'mistakes'

It is likely that you have rubbers available for general use in your classroom. Perhaps there is a school policy that guides your use of rubbers or maybe you have your own classroom rules and conventions about when and when not to use rubbers. As with other work it may be that some children often rub out until much of the evidence of their trying, thinking and investigating is absent from the page. The surface of the paper can become rough or even ripped and some or all of what you would have needed to see in order to support learning has also been erased.

In art lessons you may need to think more specifically about the place of rubbers and make this clear to children in your teaching and support. You can explain to children how important it is to make marks on paper to find out what they look like – some of these might be 'right' and some might not be what we hoped, but this does not make them 'wrong' if we can learn from them. If your classroom culture values making mistakes so that we can use them to learn from, your children may more readily understand this approach. Sedgwick (2002) suggests 'Tell the children that "wrong lines might come in useful later – please leave them there and then do the right line, or even another line that seems even more right" '(p. 14).

When you are modelling drawing you can include making a false start or a mark you initially don't want while talking through what you will do. Perhaps if is early in the drawing you might move on to another area of paper on the page, leaving the false start behind. You could continue drawing over the top and show how the earlier line becomes less noticeable as you continue to draw. For children who cannot live with a perceived 'mistake' on the page that they are working on you might have some small pieces of the same type of paper to stick over the area like a flap so that the first try is retained but covered up. It can also be useful to show children pages from artists' sketchbooks to make it clear how often they try something and move on including several first tries on the same page.

Before beginning to draw

When you are planning drawing as part of a unit of work there are a number of things that you can should consider doing with the children before they put their pencils on the paper and begin. One of the most important (and obvious) is looking. There are a number of ways you can help children to look purposefully and in a way that will support their drawing. Looking in art is different to just looking around the room to see if someone is there or glancing around to check out what is happening around us.

Looking in art is more about exploring what is going to be drawn. It will be important to bear in mind the learning objectives that you have for the task. If your aim is for children to learn more about how to use line it is important to choose things to look at that will support this objective, whereas if attention to tone or pattern is your objective you might make a very different choice of what to draw, what to draw with and what to talk about before drawing. Having made these decisions you can then consider what important features you want the children to notice and how you can talk children through what can be called 'guided looking'. Fabian (2005) states 'Children find it hard to believe that as artists their eyes are more important than their hands' (p10). She goes on to suggest that we can guide children to look 'with purpose and develop different ways of looking'.

Case Study

A class of Year 4 children are drawing from observation. They will be looking at house plants from the classroom and around the school. In this lesson the objective is for them to look closely at the shapes of leaves and draw these shapes with a focus on line. They are using fine black felt pens that they have used before in art. Before beginning their teacher asks them to walk around the classroom looking at the plants on the tables. She asks them to look for leaves with straight edges, curved edges, spiky edges and guides them to describe the shapes they see. Then she encourages them to choose to sit near a plant they are interested in rather than sit in the first available space. Once all the children are settled she asks them to move their eyes to a leaf with a shape that interests them, and then point to where it joins to a stem. She asks them to follow the outline of the leaf with their finger in the air to get a feel for the shape. It is not until the class have looked, talked and looked in more depth that they get their sketchbooks out and begin to draw. The children begin by drawing the leaf they traced in the air earlier and continue, moving to the nearby leaves, as the teacher and teaching assistant encourage them to look at the outlines they see. The emphasis is on leaf shapes rather than drawing the whole plant. After drawing for a time the children have another look around, this time for a plant with contrasting leaf shapes and the procedure is repeated.

In this case study the teacher has used the learning objective (exploring shape in outline) to guide her choice of drawing tool (pens that make clear strong fine lines) and stimulus (plants with interesting and varied leaf shapes). She has helped the children to focus their observations through talking about what they see and following the outlines with their fingers in the air to support successful drawing. This gives a clear starting point and guidance for children who could otherwise be distracted into trying to draw a generic picture of a plant.

Viewfinders and other viewing aids

A viewfinder is a piece of card with a hole cut through the middle, which can be used to isolate a part of a picture or object. It allows us to concentrate on one small part or area without being distracted or overwhelmed by the whole of what can be seen. It is a useful tool that can help children focus or organise their observation and drawing. It can support hesitant children by giving a boundary to what they are looking at and it can help children who find it hard to keep track of where and what they are looking at by bringing them back to the same area each time they look.

When you are making viewfinders for use with the children you are supporting or teaching take into consideration the size of the card. You need enough card around the hole to block out the rest of the visual information from the child's field of vision but it should not too big and unwieldy especially if each child is using a viewfinder. Think about the size and shape of the hole the child will look through. If it is too small what the child can see may be so limited it may be lacking in interest, whilst if it is too large it defeats the purpose of a viewfinder. The colour of the card that you use should also be thought about – a contrast with what is being looked at or a neutral colour so it is not distracting to the eye. It can be useful to make over time a selection of sizes and shapes of hole and colour of card so that children have a choice.

When you are using a viewfinder it is important to help the children to appreciate that the viewfinder can help them look but it is they that have to make a choice of what to look at. You can model how to place the viewfinder in different positions to look first before definitely deciding where it will go and starting to draw. It is unlikely that the first place you put it will be just the right place. For children who move around a lot you may need to help them by taping the viewfinder down once they have decided on their placement so it does not get bumped and displaced by accident.

Using a viewfinder can also be used be useful when looking at a work of art (see Chapter 3). Using the spotlight tool on the IWB will allow you to focus on some areas and hide others. This can also be a useful method of identifying areas to look at before drawing and modelling this to the whole class.

In addition to viewfinders you might sometimes consider using magnifying glasses when drawing from observation. These can support children in drawing close up and aiming for detail. Looking at items or surfaces using a Visualiser or microscope connected to the IWB or laptop can also be an effective way of taking a closer look. Clement and Page (1992) suggest using mirrors and other reflective surfaces as a way of looking at familiar items from new and unusual viewpoints.

Supporting and teaching as children draw

As you support or teach children whilst they draw there are some strategies that you can employ to help them. Some of these are approaches that you may use in many learning situations; others may be more specific to drawing. It is important to make sure that the adults supporting the class understand and agree how children will be supported so that there can be consistency. This may extend to a school-wide policy or it may be something you implement in the classroom you work in. You will also need to consider the needs of individual children within the general classroom approach and there may be aspects you approach differently to meet individual needs.

A first principle is that you show that you respect children's work and outcomes by never drawing on their work. If a teacher has ever drawn on your work you may remember feelings of unease, frustration or even anger. Clearly there will be times when a child is struggling and needs suggestions of what to do to improve. You can do this by talking and making suggestions or by drawing on a piece of paper alongside their drawing rather than on the drawing itself. If you or the child is concerned that trying out the next step might spoil the drawing you could photocopy the work and work on the copy so that the original is not lost. This can allow children to take a risk that they may otherwise be unwilling to take. If you do produce a model by drawing alongside the child try to show them just enough to help or one or two alternatives to choose from and put your modelled drawing away so that they are not tempted to copy it.

When you are giving feedback to children to help them improve their work always acknowledge the motivation, effort and perseverance that they have put into their work. We need to help children to appreciate the challenge of learning to draw. It takes hard work and regular practice to develop drawing skills just like any other area of learning. Giving children a positive attitude is crucial. If you were not given a positive attitude about drawing it is all the more important that you do not allow this feeling to seep into your own support or teaching of drawing to children. If you subtly communicate that learning to draw is an impossible task or that not being able to draw does not matter you will be denying children the opportunity to develop an important way of communicating with and responding to the world around them.

Connect and extend

Read the article 'Responding to children's drawing' by Robert Watts and published in the journal Education 3-13 in 2010 (Vol. 38 No. 2 pp. 137–53).

Think about the implications for your own learning and the way you support and teach drawing to children.

Drawing across the curriculum

There are often opportunities to draw in subjects other than art. We need to think about the purpose of these drawings, the skills that are required for these types of drawing and how they relate to learning to draw in art. As mentioned in Chapter 4 if your learning objectives are firmly related to the skills, knowledge and understanding of the art curriculum then the activity can be defined as art. If your learning objective is related to illustrating within another subject – drawing a labelled diagram of a flower or drawing a Tudor house showing the construction clearly – it is not.

Practical Task

Learning objective:

- to explore drawing across the curriculum

In this practical task you will be asked to consider when and why children are asked to draw in their school life and how the skills for different types and purposes of drawing will be different.

You will need:

- The pro forma below or a copy of it;
- a medium or weekly plan that you have worked from.

What to do:

- Look back over a weekly or medium term plan that you have observed, supported or taught from. Identify when drawing has been part of an activity. Note this onto the form in the appropriate subject row.
- Then look again at the activities that included drawing and identify the features of the drawing that were important in the activity.
- Note down any other thoughts that occur as you think, perhaps other ideas about when drawing is used in the subjects you support or teach.
- Focus on subjects other than art as drawing in the art curriculum will be discussed below.

Subject	From your planning	Features
Mathematics		
English		
PE		
PSHE		
Music		
History		
Geography		
RE		
Science		
ICT		
DT		

Guidance notes

- In this exercise you may have identified that children are often expected to draw as part of their recording and communication across the curriculum. As a student, teaching assistant or teacher who may support or teach some or all primary subjects it is useful to have thought through how drawing in these lessons may have some different features to drawing in art.

- Children may be asked to draw diagrams and charts in maths and science and in these contexts the emphasis will be on accuracy, recording details that can be labelled and some attention may be paid to scale. In DT children may be drawing designs for something they are going to make. These drawings will need to convey aspects of the design such as how parts will be joined or decorated and may show how the object looks from several view-points. Again clarity, labelling and measurement will be important. In geography, history and RE children may draw to record narratives about people and events, observations of places and artefacts and maps. Drawing maps in particular may employ specific conventions such as use of colours to indicate geographical feature, use of line to show height and use of symbols. In music children may be asked to draw what music makes them think and feel, and also draw symbols to represent music they will play. In PE children may draw out sequences of movements they plan to make in gymnastics or dance and diagrams of how games work. In English children may illustrate stories and poems to enhance their work or draw out storyboards to plan the overall structure of their story.

- When you stop to reflect on the various types of drawing for different purposes across the curriculum it will become apparent that you need to make the features of each type clear to children through your teaching. You also should make it clear when each type is required. In a science lesson, for example, you may model and teach drawing with clear lines so that the features of what is being drawn can be identified. You will show good examples of this type of drawing in your teaching so that children can see what they are aspiring to.

LINK

Some consideration should also be given to how drawing is used around us in day-to-day life and by people in their work. Adams (2006) lists many examples of trades and professions that use drawing and explains how they 'use drawing to help them understand, to help them to think, to work out problems or to enable them to communicate ideas and information to other people' (p. 1). Even if you rarely make drawings of your own you will often look at and get information from drawings in the world around you. When you use a map or look at a diagram, watch a cartoon or animation or identify a logo or symbol, you are using your ability to interpret drawings to help you or for enjoyment. As Adams points out 'In everyday life, we cannot function without drawing. It underpins our material culture. It enables us to make things. It makes things happen' (p. 4). Involving children in making and interpreting drawing in all its forms beyond its inclusion in the art curriculum is significant to their lives now and in the future.

 LINK

Conclusion

For many adults, drawing is the stumbling block that makes them think that art is not for them. When I ask adult students 'How do you feel about art?' they will, firstly, refer to drawing as if drawing is art and, secondly, using a lack of confidence and underdeveloped skills as a reason for disliking an entire subject. I have poor ball skills but as a primary teacher I had to teach throwing, aiming and catching in PE despite this – indeed it was sometimes helpful to have to work hard at these and understand the challenges children may face when developing their own skills.

The key message I would like you to take from this chapter is, firstly, that there is more to art than drawing. As you read this chapter I hope you will see that there are many ways into art and many different processes and techniques to explore. If you equate art with only drawing this is a very limited view, denying yourself and your pupils some wonderful learning opportunities. Secondly, that you can change your attitude to drawing and make sure that children develop a positive attitude to drawing through your example, teaching and support.

Next steps

- For examples of drawing have a look across the curriculum and in day-to-day life.
- Sign up for updates from the Campaign for Drawing on He Big Draw website.
- Look for a local drawing class or workshop to boost your confidence and develop your skills.

References

Adams, E. (2006) *Professional Practices*. Lancing: Power Drawing.

Anning, A. (2002) 'Conversations around young children's drawing: the impact of the beliefs of significant others at home and school'. *Journal of Art and Design Education*, Vol. **21**, No. 3, 197–208.

Barnes, R. (2002) *Teaching Art to young Children.* Abingdon: RoutledgeFalmer.

Clement, R. and Page, S. (1992) *Investigating and Making in Art.* Harlow: Oliver and Boyd.

Coates, E. and Coates, A. (2006) 'Young children talking and drawing'. *International Journal of Early Years Education*, Vol. 14 No. 13, pp. 221–41.

Edwards, B. (2012) *The New Drawing on the Right Side of the Brain.* 4th edn. London: Tarcher.

Fabian, M. (2005) *Drawing is a Class Act.* Dunstable: Brilliant Publications.

OFSTED (2012) 'Making a mark: art, craft and design education'. [online] Available from: *http://www.ofsted.gov.uk/resources/making-mark-art-craft-and-design-education-2008-11* (Accessed 31 March 2012).

Further reading

Cox, M., Cooke, G. and Friffin, D. (2009) 'Teaching children to draw in the infants school'. In Herne, S., Cox, S. and Watts, R. (eds) *Readings in Primary Art Education.* London: Intellect Books, pp. 153–68.

Fenwick, L. (2007) 'Investigating pattern'. *STart*, Vol. 24, pp. 24–27.

Fenwick, L. (2007) 'Drawing development'. *STart*, Vol. 25, pp. 22–25.

Hope, G. (2008) *Thinking and Learning through Drawing.* London: Sage.

Hughes, S. (2002) *A Life Drawing: Recollections of an Illustrator.* London: Random House.

Lee, G. (2009) 'Illustration: more than just a complement to text'. *STart*, 33. pp. 10–11.

Turk, K. (2007) 'Livening up life drawing'. *STart*, Vol. 25, pp. 12–14.

Watts, R. (2010) 'Responding to children's drawing'. *Education 3-13*, Vol. 38 No. 2, pp. 137–53.

Web resources

Examples of drawing in artists' sketchbooks: *http://www.accessart.org.uk/sketchbook/*

Henry Moore shelter drawings: *http://www.bbc.co.uk/learningzone/clips/henry-moore-s-underground-shelter-drawings-from-world-war-ii/11626.html*

Van Gogh's drawings: *http://www.vggallery.com/drawings/main_az.htm*

Shirley Hughes: *http://www.art-of-illustration.co.uk/shirleyhughes/*

Raymond Briggs: *http://www.guardian.co.uk/books/audioslideshow/2010/sep/21/raymond-briggs*

Simon's Cat – line drawn animations: *http://www.simonscat.com/*

British Museum: *http://www.britishmuseum.org/explore/highlights/highlights_search_results.aspx?searchText=drawings*

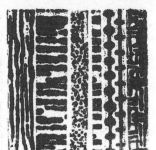

Chapter 7

Painting

Introduction

Painting can be both satisfying and challenging, providing opportunities to learn and develop skills, knowledge and understanding in art. Painting is often available to younger children, but opportunities to learn and develop their painting skills as they get older and would have more control can sometimes be less frequent. Children can explore and spontaneously discover how to paint for themselves given freedom and time, and with guidance from their teachers and teaching assistants they can develop and improve. It is limiting if they only paint irregularly and to meet prescribed outcomes. In this chapter the following areas will be considered:

- Subject knowledge that underlies teaching painting
- Teaching children to paint

There are many different types of paint and a variety of ways of applying paint for different purposes that children should experience during their primary years. These are listed in Appendix 2, where painting and painting tools are explored in depth. Throughout the primary years children should be taught and guided as well as having opportunities to explore and experiment so they can discover what they can do with paint. Planning should aim for a balance of teaching, exploring and creating with paint. Painting techniques can also be connected to other areas of learning in art. Children might apply paint directly to fabric, they might paint three-dimensional forms to decorate them or apply liquids using what they have learned about painting when making a batik or glue print.

Talking about paintings made by a range of artists working now and in the past, in the UK and around the world can inspire and support learning in art. It can open children's eyes to the many different ways to paint, what inspires others to paint and how paintings make the viewer feel. As well as learning in art, looking at and talking about paintings can support children's learning about the past in history, about other places in geography and allow them to learn about many cultures. Paint can be applied with fingers and many children can enjoy the feel of applying thick paint directly onto a surface. Changing the texture of paint can also be an interesting sensory experience. For children who dislike getting paint directly on their fingers thin plastic gloves can be used.

Children can also explore painting using software and digital media. Many art software packages allow children to 'paint' on the screen using the mouse, touchpad or using their fingers directly on the screen. They can often make decisions about the size of the paintbrush and the colours they use. The software package 'Revelation Natural Art' goes further in that children can select watercolour, colour tubs, cromar paint or acrylic paint and the marks on the screen have similar visual qualities to each type of paint. They can choose brushes of different widths and spray cans. Like a 'real' paintbrush the paint will be used up and the marks left become paler until the paint is gone and the paintbrush needs refilling. It is however, important that to recognise that painting onscreen is not an alternative to applying paint to paper, but rather an experience with intrinsic qualities of its own. As Matthews and Seow (2009) comment: 'although it is essential that children explore the messy gooeyness and splatteriness of real pigment, the smooth glide of electronic paint across a luminous glass screen is also a sensuous and enjoyable experience' (p. 285).

Find out more

Search for the website of Sir Robert Hitchams primary schools. Click on 'school websites' then click on 'ICT', then 'ICT and Art'. Explore the pages labelled 'revelation Natural Art' for ideas and case studies related to painting with ICT software.

LINK

The subject knowledge that underlies the teaching of painting

Developing some subject knowledge about painting underpins successful planning, teaching and support. Some of the aspects of painting that you may need to learn about are:

- characteristics of different types of paint;
- exploring visual elements through painting;
- developing vocabulary;
- media and processes;
- the work of artists, craftspeople and designers.

Type of paint	Definition	In school	Useful for
Powder colour	Powder pigment that when mixed with water creates an opaque painting medium	Bought in large tubs of primary colours, black and white	• Mixing own colours • Versatile – many colours can be made, adding PVA, wallpaper paste, washing powder etc can vary the consistency
Watercolour	A transparent painting medium	Bought in tins each with 12 hard tablet colours and a lid to use as a palette	• Experimenting with building up layers • Taking outside to use (very easily portable)
Ready mixed	Usually an opaque poster colour (translucent version called 'chromar' available)	Bought in 500 ml bottles	• Convenient to use in the classroom
Acrylics	Pigment in an acrylic polymer emulsion that can be diluted with water to various thicknesses	Bought in 500 ml bottles/tubes	• Can be used in different ways according to the amount of water used with it • Can be used on many different surfaces
Drawing inks/ brusho	Based on dyes rather than pigments (use with care – some does not wash out of clothing)	Bought in bottles of ink or small canisters of powder (Brusho)	• Making washes/wax resist • Can be used to dye fabric as well as on paper

Characteristics of different types of paint

Knowing about painting can allow you to find out more about different types of paint and their properties and in turn this will enable you plan and teach effective lessons. Throughout their primary years children should have the opportunity to investigate a range of paints as well as the opportunity to use the same paints over time in order to build up their confidence and skills in one area. Some of the most commonly used types of paint are listed in the chart on page 133 with an outline of their main characteristics.

Powder colour, watercolour, ready mixed and acrylic paints as well as drawing inks or pigment such as Brusho are perhaps the most commonly available in primary schools. Although storage and management of powder paint can be challenging it does provide a great opportunity for experiencing the tactile satisfaction of mixing a colour from pigment and water. The consistency and quality can be varied by the amount of water added or by using PVA glue, wallpaper paste, washing up liquid or washing powder. Watercolours, ready mixed and acrylic paint can all be mixed to create new colours as well.

Case Study

A group of PGCE students explore techniques for applying paint in order to develop their understanding of painting. They use liquid ready mixed paint of various colours and have a range of tools to apply it with, including paintbrushes, palette knives, strips of thick card and sticks. They are encouraged to experiment by applying paint with the tools, painting patches of colour roughly the size of their hand all over their paper. As these dry they paint onto the patches with controlled straight and curved lines, clusters of spots and dashes, and flicks or spatters of paint.

As the students paint many of them become absorbed in the activity of applying paint and exploring colours and marks. Some enjoy the unpredictability of flicking and spattering whilst others prefer the control of more carefully placed spots and dashes. Having time to experiment for themselves helps them think about the range of ways of applying paint and how to teach children about these in art. Many realise that whilst children could be taught how to apply paint in these ways they would also need opportunities to practise and develop them in their work.

Towards the end of the lesson they are asked to identify any challenges in terms of classroom organisation and how these might be overcome. They identify factors such as having enough space to work, protecting clothes and classroom furnishings from paint and drying the paintings. Suggestions to overcome these include children working outside; using easels; children working in groups with this as one of the activities; the role of the adult in planning beyond the painting itself to provision of aprons; where paintings will be dried and where stored.

In this case study paint and the application of paint are explored by students. In this context the students will use what they have learned to plan more effectively for learning. When teaching it is equally important for children to have opportunities to explore paint and the tools that can be used to apply it with no end point of a finished painting in mind. If they have few or no opportunities to paint freely it will be much harder for them to paint purposefully and draw upon prior learning and respond creatively.

Exploring visual elements through painting

The chart below makes suggestions in relation to each of the eight visual elements. When you are planning and teaching a unit of work that involves painting it is important to identify one or two visual elements that you will develop with the children. It is likely that this will have been done at the long term planning stage. Colour is the visual element that most readily springs to mind when we think of painting although there are opportunities for learning about many of the others.

Line	Tone
Exploring making lines and marks with a variety of painting tools such as sticks, colour shapers, sponge paddles, brushes, fingers.	Choosing, mixing and using various tones of the same colour/different colours Considering the effect that tone can have on the feel of the painting to the maker or viewer
Colour	**Pattern**
Choosing, mixing and using a range of colours – primary, secondary, complementary, clashing, etc. Exploring the feelings the use of colours can evoke – warm and cool colours, dark and bright colours, etc. Combining and using colours to create different effects	Using pattern within painting to create effects and cover areas– spots, dashes, lines, etc. Representing pattern in painting
Texture	**Shape**
Exploring thin, thick, gritty, smooth textures in paint Representing texture in painting	Exploring regular and irregular shapes in paint
Space	**Form**
Using paint to create the illusion of space through composition, perspective, etc.	Using paint decoratively on 3D forms

As you read the suggestions listed in the chart above you might have noticed that in some of these children are likely to be learning about painting itself – how to apply paint in different ways, the properties of paint and the tools that can be used. In others they are painting to produce an outcome – a painting or a 2D or 3D outcome in which painting is a part of the process, for example painting to decorate a 3D object they have made or painting a wash onto a drawing. When planning for learning it is important that you are clear about your objectives and learning outcomes and plan for some time in which to learn or refine the relevant painting skills. Colour is one of the visual elements that is often explored through painting.

When I first started teaching it was the norm that children would be given the opportunity to mix and use their own colours to use in painting. For many children the experience of mixing the powder controlling the consistency as well as the colour was a satisfying sensory experience in itself. It is an experience that is perhaps less commonly available to children in primary classrooms now but still very much worth considering because of the learning opportunities and personal satisfaction that it offers.

Exploring colour mixing

When adults mix colours for children they can ensure that they are provided with a range of colours and consistencies to experience over time. When children have the opportunity to mix their own colours they are more likely to experiment and learn about colour than if they always work from a standard set. As they look at and talk about the work of artists it will become apparent to them that artists are not using a few standard colours but are using colour in a sophisticated and creative way. Children also need the opportunity to explore this for themselves in their own work. Although allowing children to mix their own colours can seem daunting in terms of organisation of materials, space and time, the learning opportunities it provides are enormous and outweigh the organisational challenges.

When you buy ready mixed paint or powder colour it is important to buy a range of colours or pigments that will allow you and the children to mix the colours that you want; this is known as the 'double primary system'. Barnes (2002) suggests that the following pigments are needed:

- red – crimson (a dark red) and vermilion (a scarlet bright red);
- blue – Prussian blue (a turquoise) and ultramarine (a brilliant blue);
- yellow – lemon yellow and brilliant yellow;
- Black – I recommend that you have less or no black pigment and encourage children to mix their own 'black' or dark shade from a combination of other colours;
- white – you will need more white pigment.

If you plan to allow children to mix their own colours from powder pigment it is wise to develop a clear and organised approach for the work space and teach this to children. Pratchett (2007) presents an effective and well-organised system that can support children towards independence in their use of powder paint to mix their own colours. Using this as a basis for your own organisation can help you to preempt some of the problems you may be concerned about.

Practical task

Learning objective:

- To explore colour mixing with powder pigment.

In this task you will have the opportunity to explore how an organised system can support the process of colour mixing. This is based on my own experience and supplemented with ideas from Pratchett (2007). In this practical activity completing a finished painting of a subject is not important.

You will need:

- small plastic pots of red, blue, yellow and white powder colours – choose small pots and keep sets of them filled up so they can be substituted as the colour is used up. If the pots are too large it can lead to large amounts of colour being mixed and wasted;

- a spoon or broad glue spreader in each pot – each pot needs a way of moving the pigment from the pot to the mixing tray. If this is too large it will result in large amounts of colour being mixed and wasted. Younger children and children whose fine motor control is less developed may need to use spoons; older children may be able to use broad glue spreaders;

- water – choose paint pots or with younger children an ice cream container or other large flat bottomed container that is less likely to get knocked over;

- a plastic pipette/spoon – using a plastic pipette or spoon to collect water and add it to the powder on the mixing tray reduces the risk that too much water is added and washes their mixed colours away. You may find plastic pipettes as part of science equipment in school catalogues;

- a flat tray or palette to mix colours on or in – you can put out a palette with six wells to mix six colours in or use a flat tray that will allow accidental overlaps of colour, which can be interesting;

- several paintbrushes – these will be used to mix the powder with the water and frequently cleaned;

- thick cartridge paper – if the paper children are painting on is too thin it can fall apart when the paint is applied;

- table covered with waste paper or newspaper – newspaper can be considered busy and distracting so it can be more effective to cover the table with the sort of paper that is often donated to schools. It can be useful to tape the covering paper to the table to prevent it moving about.

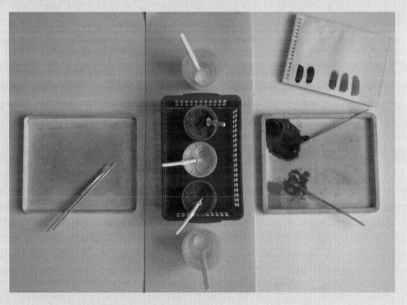

Figure 7.1 Layout of equipment for paint mixing

What to do:

- Try out the system by mixing some colours. Put out some powder onto the mixing tray, squirt some water onto the powder and mix with the brush. Keep adding water in small amounts until you achieve a creamy consistency.

- You may wish to choose one colour and mix different tones and hues of it. Try and mix the darkest colour that you can without using black pigment.

- Either as you mix or after you have mixed the colours paint them onto the paper in patches.

Questions to consider

- *How does the systematic organisation support children in independently mixing colours?*: Setting up a colour mixing table or having a system for setting up colour mixing in this way can be successful but, to be successful it also requires modelling, demonstrating and supporting by teachers and teaching assistants in the classroom. In my classroom the system was supported by a large diagram with photos and reminders on the board in front of the children. Children mixed colours in pairs and these pairs were chosen so that children could support each other. Each pair were expected to reset the table for the next pair after they had completed their activity.

- *What did you learn about colour mixing?*: Perhaps you found that rather than mixing a colour you had aimed to mix you enjoyed coming across accidental colours along the way. For many children the process itself is at least as absorbing as mixing colours to use in a painting. Colour mixing may be an activity initially planned to allow children the opportunity to explore colour rather than make a finished piece of work. Later, children may use their colours or what they have learned about colour to make a painting or just apply their mixed colours to paper to see what they look like.

- *What else did you learn?*: As well as learning about colour perhaps you also learned about texture – the consistency of the paint, whether it is thick or thin, smooth or gritty, and the possible impact of this on a painting. You may also have learned about how much water to add to the powder – too little and you get a thick paste; too much and you get a thin watery pool. By experiencing the colour mixing perhaps you began to get a feel for how much water was just right to achieve a smooth creamy consistency that would be useful and effective when painting.

- *How could you apply this in your own classroom situation?*:The system you have tried out lends itself to pairs of children taking turns. With a class of thirty children it will take time for all children to have a turn especially if your art lessons are weekly short periods. Meager (1993) describes the investigation of colour mixing using powder colour with a whole class at the same time. This approach allows all the children in the class the opportunity to experiment and as a teacher you can concentrate on teaching about colour mixing fully throughout the lesson. Clearly the preparation before the lesson and clearing up after will be extensive but it may be the most efficient way of allowing everyone to have a go; it will certainly be an exciting lesson!

Artists, craftspeople and designers and painting

When you decide to use a painting or the work of painter to inspire or inform learning in art there are so many to choose from that it can be overwhelming – this can lead to safe and obvious choices being made. We are all dependent on our own knowledge of painters and painting as well the resources available to us and we can develop this over time and in response to personal experiences and children's interests. The choices we make are significant so it is important that we seek out interesting and varied paintings and painters to look at, talk about and sometimes use to teach with.

When using paintings and painters we might be thinking about the type of paint – for example, exploring the potential of using watercolours by looking at how the work of artists who use them in very different ways can support learning. We might be thinking about how the paint is applied – when we are planning to explore mark making looking at the work of painters who apply paint in interesting and varied ways would be a good choice. We might be thinking about colour – when we are planning to use subdued and bright colours looking at artists who have used colour can be useful. We might be thinking about the subject matter – when we are planning to paint landscapes looking at the ways painters have painted from the landscape can help children think about their own responses. As you get to know more about art your confidence will develop and you will be able to go beyond the paintings and painters that you usually use and start choosing alternatives. Here are some suggestions but there are many other great choices if you want to tie your choices into your own interests and resources.

Artists who paint using watercolour include illustrators of children's books such as Jane Ray, whose paintings are delicate and vibrantly coloured illustrations of myths and legends and Michael Foreman, who uses pale washes and deep colour to illustrate his own stories and myths and legends from around the world. Elizabeth Blackadder often paints using watercolours, painting still lives of flowers, plants, objects and animals often against white or plain backgrounds. From the past it can be interesting to look at the sketchpads and watercolours of Queen Victoria; examples can be found on the royal collection website. Links can be made to animation – search on the Teachers' Media website for the animation 'The Monk and the Fish'. The animation itself is accompanied by a short programme about the making which includes the work of a watercolour artist who talks about how and why he painted as he did.

LINK

Artists who use watercolour or ink wash and line include children's book illustrators Quentin Blake and Brian Wildsmith. Botanical illustrators also often use watercolour or line and wash – you can find examples of the Victorian botanical illustrator Jane Loudon on the Victoria and Albert Museum website. Fashion designers often use this technique in their work.

There are so many artists who paint in oils and acrylics. Paintings by Impressionist artists such as Degas and Monet are often used in schools; there were two women artists who are considered to be part of this group – Berthe Morisot and Mary Cassatt. Analysing the reason for your choice could lead you away from the usual choices into some more interesting and individual areas. If you had chosen Monet because he painted from the same view on a number of occasions, look at the work of Japanese artist Hokusai, who made a series of prints of views of Mount Kilimanjaro. If you had chosen Monet because of his painting techniques, think about other painters who applied paint in similar ways, such as Seurat and Signac, or in contrasting ways, such as Bridget Riley and Mark Rothko. Remember that the painters that you choose should not all come from Europe – search the Ashmolean Museum website for Indian miniature paintings or search for the work of Chris Ofili, a painter of Nigerian heritage who began painting in the UK and now lives in Trinidad.

Teaching children to paint

If you are planning a unit of work that includes painting, being clear about the painting techniques and skills required to achieve pleasing results is important. The decisions that you make will be related to what type of paint you are planning to use, the starting points and learning outcomes that you are using, and the prior knowledge, skills and understanding that you will be building upon. Some areas for consideration are:

- use of tools;
- making paintings;
- connecting painting to other areas of art.

Use of tools

One of the most obvious skills in painting is being able to hold and manipulate the paintbrush or painting tool to make marks. When considering your choice of painting tool you should think about what will be appropriate for the children that you teach and what works with the type of paint you are using.

Gripping brushes

Long-handled paint brushes may be unwieldy for some children and they often taper making them harder to grasp securely and manipulate with control. Short-handled brushes with thick handles that are easily gripped may be a better choice. Alternatively children could be allowed to choose brushes that feel right to them from a range. Providing a choice may allow you to encourage some children to use brushes you know will suit them without picking them out a different to their peers.

Using tools other than brushes

You will have noted from earlier in this chapter there are many other tools that can be used to apply paint: paint shapers, palette knives, tooth brushes, sticks, sponge paddles. Giving children the opportunity to paint with a range of tools can help them develop their fine motor control. Using fingers and hands to apply paint can allow children to experience the tactile qualities of paint and perhaps have more or a different kind of control in its application.

Pressure applied to tool

When you model and demonstrate painting techniques it is important to allow children every opportunity to understand how to make effective marks. Younger children and children who find manipulation of tools a challenge often press down with their brush so hard that the bristles or hairs are pressed onto the paper and the metal ferrule scratches the paper. Children can be reminded in a tactile way to use the tip of the brush by asking them to practice stroking the palm of their hand with the tip of brush to get an idea of the pressure they are aiming for.

Making paintings

When we are planning for children to paint as the main part of a unit of work there are some areas to consider so that we can support their learning and success. Considering the surface on which children paint and whether and how they plan out their composition will help them prepare to paint. Ensuring that we teach what children need to know about painting techniques will also support them, as will planning to use different sorts of paint and painting.

The painting surface

It can be disappointing or frustrating for children to paint on white paper – this either leaves a white background or children struggle to fill in around what they have painted. Thinking about the surface they are going to paint on at the planning stage can help to overcome this.

Building in the opportunity for children to choose from a range of coloured papers on which to paint is one way to quickly and easily provide a background to paint on. Applying marks, rubbings, patterns or a wash is another way of approaching this. In this case it also gives you the opportunity to start children thinking about the use of space in their composition – what do you want the background to look like?

Case Study

After a visit to a farm a class of Year R / 1 children are going to paint some of the animals they saw. Before painting their teacher asks them to think and talk about where the animals were (fields) and the colours they saw (greens, browns, natural colours). Each child paints a large wash of random greens and browns as their 'field' and these are allowed to dry. As they make their washes they talk with the teaching assistant, who is helping them choose which animals they will go on paint and where they will be in their painting. This allows them to begin to think about and plan what they will paint and how they will use space in the compositions. They can give some consideration to the animals that will be in the foreground at the painting stage without leaving a white area around all their animals. Later in the week the children paint their animals onto their washes. The washes contribute to the overall effect and success of the paintings.

When we teach children how to use washes to contribute to their painting we allow them to consider the overall journey of their painting and how a painting can be built up over several stages. With older children this can be developed as they gain more awareness of using space in their two-dimensional work. This is quite a different approach to thinking of a painting as a one-off piece of work completed in one lesson or period of time. Although it has some implications for planning, classroom organisation and use of time it is a vital step towards developing independence and an evaluative approach on the part of the learner.

Another way of approaching this is to apply pattern or texture to the paper in a fairly random way and then paint on it. This could be by making a wax crayon rubbing and then washing over it with ink or Brusho or sticking ripped and cut papers onto the painting surface before painting onto it.

Children can be disappointed with their painting when it is seen as a 'coloured-in drawing' approach. Perhaps you have experienced some of the difficulties that occur when children draw out their 'painting' in pencil outline and then try to fill in these often very small and fiddly shapes with paint. Working from a combination of sketches or a plan that is visible next to their painting is one alternative. If a child needs the reassurance of some guidelines on the page painting some areas or rough outlines with a pale coloured wash that will be painted over as the painting progresses can be helpful.

Painting with watercolours

Some ways of applying paint can be used no matter what type of paint you are using and others are more suited to certain types of paint. The type of paint that you choose to use should be closely connected to the painting technique that you will be teaching. The practical exercise below is designed to help you explore the main properties and qualities of watercolour and to give a better understanding of some useful techniques and applications.

Practical task

Exploring watercolours

Learning objective:

- To explore using washes and painting on wet or dry paper.

   In this practical task you will explore the effects that can be achieved when using watercolours to paint with. Watercolours have some unique properties that can be introduced to children and will suit certain types of work.

You will need:

- Watercolour paints, the lid to mix colours in or a flat surface to mix on, thin and thick soft hair paintbrushes, a sponge paddle (optional) a pot of clean water and a large sheet of thick cartridge paper.

What to do:

1. Dampen each tablet of colour with clean water and allow it to soak in making the hard blocks a little softer and easier to use (avoid using the white tablet).
2. Using your large brush or sponge paddle, dampen a patch of the paper with some clean water. Using your smaller brush, try out some spots, dashes and continuous lines on the damp paper. Take care to use the tip of your brush when painting.
3. Repeat similar marks on an area of dry paper.
4. Mix a thin colour wash of pale green and paint it on your paper.

5. Using the palette mix some colours of your own to experiment with. Try to mix ten different greens to try out on your paper. Paint dots, dashes, lines on the area that you applied the pale green wash onto earlier.

Questions to consider

- *What differences did you notice between painting on damp and dry paper?*: When you painted on the paper that you had dampened you probably found that the paint spread out in an unpredictable manner. When you painted on the dry paper you could create crisp clear edges to the marks you made. Perhaps (when you) used the wet paper your marks were paler and more watery whereas they were more vibrant and deeper on the dry paper. As children learn about these possibilities they can begin to use them more purposefully in their work.

- *How is painting with watercolour different to painting with other paints?*: Perhaps you noticed that the colour of the paper is significant when painting with watercolours. Watercolours are transparent so the paper can show through the paint having an effect on the colour. Areas of paper can be left unpainted.

The amount of colour and water that you mix determines the depth of colour so rather than adding white to get paler tones you added more water.

When you painted a pale wash over an area of your paper then painted on it this allowed you to build up layers of colours and marks. With children you might consider helping them plan their composition so that they can apply colour washes as a background and then, either while the paper is still damp or after it has dried, paint further details.

As you paint with so much water you may have become aware of the impact that this can have on the paper. Paper that is too thin begins to disintegrate. Thicker paper is more likely to be a more durable and effective surface for watercolours.

How you used the brushes may also have had an impact on the paper. It is important to use soft brushes and use the tips of the brushes, never scratching the brush across the paper.

You may also have noticed that when your paper dried the paper was no longer flat. Finished paintings can be pressed flat under a heavy board. Alternatively for best work thick cartridge paper or watercolour paper can be stretched over a board using paper tape. This will allow the surface to be wetted and painted upon several times and it will redry stretched flat on the board. When the painting is complete it can be cut off the board by an adult using a Stanley knife.

Using watercolours to paint with is different to other types of painting. If you are going to teach children how to get the best out of these paints you must plan to teach some of the techniques and demonstrate some tips to help them towards success. Some factors to consider when planning and preparing to use watercolours are: providing the appropriate type of paper – thick, good quality cartridge paper or watercolour paper; using soft brushes of various sizes and demonstrating how to use just the tip on the paper; and making sure that clean water is readily available and changed regularly. Teaching children about washes, layers of colour, colour mixing and working on damp and dry paper, and allowing them to experiment, is an essential part of learning to paint with watercolours.

Find out more

Go to the Tate website. Search for 'Mike Chaplin', which will lead you to three short films exploring and demonstrating painting with watercolours.

LINK

When you are choosing artists who paint with watercolours to inspire the children's own use of watercolour you should consider exactly how their use of the technique will support the learning objectives you are teaching. It is important to be clear about the use of the technique and the effects that can be created rather than the subject matter if the learning objectives are focused on the process and technique.

Case Study

In this unit of work on painting the Year 2 children have been introduced to the illustrations of Jane Ray. It is likely that you have some books illustrated by Jane Ray in your classroom or library. Her work is detailed and vibrantly coloured. She usually paints using watercolours or ink and sometimes using gold or silver details. Her illustrations are often based on stories such as legends and traditional tales involving some fantasy and imagination.

The children in this class used watercolours in Year 1 and will have the opportunity to build on their prior learning of the medium as well as develop their skills. The teacher revises some of the basic elements of the technique that the children tried out in the previous year, including using the tip of the brush to paint with, mixing colours and cleaning the brush between using different colours. In the first lesson of the unit the children practise these skills.

In this unit of work the aim is to develop the children's use of colour by teaching them about buiding up pale washes and painting onto these with deep vibrant colours. The children will also be given the opportunity to develop their approach to space and composition by working on their painting on several occasions to build up a background, a foreground and additional detail. The inspiration and context for the painting is to be the stories that the children are reading and writing in their English/literacy lessons.

LINK

Watercolours also tend to be relatively portable and easy to take outside the classroom. This allows children to mix and record colours, responding directly to what they see and experience. Using them directly on the sketchpad to develop colour on pencil or pen sketches can be an effective way of collecting and recalling visual information.

Painting with ready mixed, powder or acrylic paint

Using opaque paints that cover paper and other surfaces with no transparency is another very common experience for children in school. These paints come in many different forms – hard tempera blocks, powder paint, ready-mixed paint of different types and acrylics. When you use hard tempera blocks, teach children to dampen the blocks and allow the water to soften them before beginning to paint (as mentioned above with watercolour tablets). All of these paints can be mixed so that children can make their own colours – the type of paint will have an impact on the possibilities for colour mixing. Mixing colours from dry powder perhaps gives the most scope and control to children. Acrylics and liquid ready-mixed paint can and should also be mixed by the children. Hard tempera blocks are perhaps more similar to watercolour paint in their mixing and application qualities.

Having the opportunity to explore and experiment with paint mixing and paint application is vital to children's learning. As part of the early stages of a unit of work some teaching and exploration of techniques will support what children can produce in their own work. The very wide range of ways artists have mixed and applied paint can help you in your teaching by providing examples and ideas, without copying whole paintings. One way of doing this is to identify some details (small patches or areas) from paintings and discuss them with the children, focusing on what the paint is like and how it has been applied. Using the spotlight tool on the IWB or a viewfinder on reproductions can be a practical way of doing this. Your choices of what to look at will be guided by what children will later paint – you might explore some ways that painters have applied paint by looking at the subtle use of natural colours (greens, browns) by Kyffin Williams, John Constable and Henri Rousseau; the cool, muted colours of L.S. Lowry or Vilhelm Hammershoi, the bright, vibrant colours of Elizabeth Blackadder, Chris Ofili and Brian Wildsmith or the distinct blocks of primary colours used by Piet Mondrian. In these examples the use of paint by the artist is the talking point rather than the subject matter of the paintings themselves. Children could try out several of these techniques for themselves, not aiming for a figurative or finished painting but to redevelop the range of ways they apply paint and use colour in painting.

Case Study

In the Autumn term a Year 3 class have visited their local art gallery where they have looked at and talked about two paintings, Daubigny's *St Paul's from the Surrey Side and Monet's The Thames Below Westminster* on loan from the National Gallery. The children talk about how it is possible to recognise landmarks in the paintings and infer that the artists must have worked from life and from drawings made in sketchpads. They discuss the colours in the paintings that make them think of winter – cold, dull and dark colours.

For their own paintings the class are asked to work from their own sketches drawn around the school site. They are challenged to make sure their drawings and the paintings that come from them will include recognisable landmarks and their use of colour will make us think about the time of year – winter.

In order to manage the colour mixing phase of the unit of work the class work in groups to mix a range of dull, dark and cold colours that are then stored in pots for use by the class as they make their paintings. This allows them to concentrate on colour mixing as an end in itself first and then concentrate on their paintings on a separate occasion. It allows the teacher and teaching asisstant to organise resources and support the colour mixing for a short period and then move on the paintings themselves.

The children go on to make their paintings and these are displayed alongside their preparatory sketches and scribed comments about what inspired their work and the challenges they faced.

In this case study children follow a unit of work leading to the outcome of a set of individual paintings inspired by observation of their environment and informed by other artists who have worked in a similar way. They also exercise some control over the colours of paint used and this has causes the paintings to have a distinct winter character from using colours that may not have appeared in the paintings had the paint been used straight from the bottle.

Older children, who have developed their painting skills over their primary years, should have opportunities to work on a variety of scales and have more control over how they go about making their paintings. Breaking down the painting into a series of steps and allowing time to review and reflect between each step supports children in evaluating their work and having the time and opportunity to make decisions about next steps. Alternatively, allowing children to choose between the latter approach or making a series of two or three paintings to explore their response can be another approach for children who prefer to work more quickly and instinctively. This will also allow children the freedom they need to respond creatively and is less likely to lead to a set of very similar paintings at the end of a unit of work.

Painting using digital media

Most schools have software specifically for creating images on screen. There are many available including 2Simple (2Draw, 2Animate, Photo Simple and 2Paint A Picture) and Revelation Natural Art as well as apps that involve making marks on mobile devices or tablets that appear as it drawn or painted on the screen. Using this software to create and manipulate images can allow children the opportunity to make something they could not make any other way. When planning a learning outcome it is important to consider how the qualities of the hardware or software provide a unique contribution to the learning for the individual child or class beyond that of being merely a different way to paint or draw. As Matthews and Seow (2009) identify 'electronic paint has qualities of its own... in terms of painting with light itself, in terms of colour, shape and movement' (p. 285).

Practical task

Learning objective:

- to explore some tools available for making art onscreen

In this task you will be asked to explore and analyse the tools of drawing or painting software or an app and consider the features that make it different to drawing or painting using 'real' materials.

What to do:

- Use the pro forma to try and evaluate the features of drawing or painting software or an app.

Name of the software / app		
Tools available (look for…)	Range of colours	
	Density within colours	
	Tones within colours	
	Range of tools	

Name of the software / app		
	Size of tools	
	Stamps	
	Outlining/filling shapes	
	Symmetry/transformation / rotation	
	Layers	
	Zooming in and out	
	Pasting images in from elsewhere	
How do these tools support learning in art?		
What are the challenges of using them?		

Questions to consider

- *Software or app*: These vary from those with very simple tools to having a complex range of tools. You need to become familiar with those used in the schools in which you are placed or work. You should also try to keep up with any software or apps that the children you teach are familiar with from using at home. Many children will now have access to these and be confident users of them outside school.

- *Tools*: The making of marks and lines on a background directly on the screen with fingers or stylus or via a mouse or fingers on a touchpad is a key tool to explore. The ease of this and the ways they can be used to build up patterns and images must be considered in relation to the age and physical skills of the children using the software. There are other tools listed that can then be explored and added to children's repertoire as they become ready and as they relate to other learning in art. Some software contains different layers (e.g. simple, junior, advanced, in Revelation Natural Art) so that the screen is not overly crowded with tools that younger children are not ready to use yet.

- *Benefits*: These onscreen opportunities should be considered as another way of creating art, not a substitute for painting, drawing or other practical ways of making art. They give us another way of making images that have their own inherent qualities. Being able to try out and then undo next steps will be valued by some children and being able to save versions at different stages of development can support evaluation and experimentation. Some of the tools available allow children to easily do things that might otherwise be difficult or impossible. Some children will already have a level of confidence, skill and interest that they can bring to this kind of activity in school.

- *Challenges*: Having enough time to work for a sustained period of time or a series of shorter times can be a challenge, as can having access to enough PCs, laptops or tablets. This can affect children's learning of new tools as well as creating something substantial and interesting. This will be something to consider in the long term and in relation to how ICT is organised in the school. The expense of printing images can be a challenge; showing them through the IWB and onscreen should perhaps be the way art created digitally is shared with audiences as printing them on paper rarely does the colours justice.

Painting using digital media should be considered as an additional and different way of exploring painting rather than a replacement for painting using brushes, paint and paper.

Connecting painting to other areas of art

Whilst children explore and learn about painting regularly in their primary years, what they learn about paint and how to apply it can also be applied and extended within other areas of art. When children work in three dimensions painting might form part of the decoration that they apply. This may also be the case when decorating more functional objects made in design technology. Getting paint to adhere to a range of different surfaces can often be a challenge and something the teacher must be prepared for. Sometimes it is easier to apply the paint to flat surfaces before the three-dimensional form is assembled. Connecting painting to drawing and to work in fabric and textiles can also enhance learning and allow children to use their knowledge, skills and understanding in other contexts.

Exploring line and wash

Bringing drawing skills into painting through line and wash can be an opportunity to continue to develop drawing and go further with it as well as allow children to learn about another way of using paint.

Practical task

Exploring using watercolours, drawing inks or Brusho

Learning objective:

- to explore use of line and wash.

In this practical task you will have the opportunity to explore some techniques using drawing inks or Brusho.

You will need:

- Cartridge paper, a drawing pencil and/or a black felt pen, drawing inks/diluted Brusho (or watercolours if you do not have either of these), water, a fine, soft brush.

What to do:

- Draw on the paper with the pencil or pen – perhaps try some random and irregular shapes and lines.
- Apply the colour with the fine, soft brush – partially filling the shapes, allowing some of the colour to go up to the lines you have drawn and some to go beyond them. Do not worry if the colour goes over the lines – you are not aiming to 'colour in' the lines, indeed the imprecision can add to the overall effect.

Questions to consider:

- When trying the line and wash perhaps you found that the pen lines merged into the wet colour – you might like that effect but if you do not, using permanent pens is a way around this. This technique allows the artist to draw in some detail paying attention to line and pattern, adding colour later. It can be a useful way of recording from observation directly from what is being looked at and can be used later perhaps to support another outcome such as a more 'finished' painting or an outcome using another technique.

When children work with threads, fabrics and textiles they might well use paint or painting techniques. Applying fabric paint directly to cotton allows children to use their prior experience of and learning about paint. Applying wax or paste to make batiks will also include using tools such as brushes, sticks or more specific tools (*tjanting* tool in batik). Including some painting experiences early in the unit of work can help children activate their prior knowledge, skills and understanding before going on to apply and develop it in the context of using different materials.

Case Study

A class of Year 5 children will be going on to explore batik[*] in a unit of work based around Adire cloth. This cloth is made in Africa by dyeing white cotton using an indigo blue dye. Children look at some examples of Adire that show the contrast of deep dark blue and white and look at and talk about some of the patterns used on the fabric.

Children begin by making marks freely using white wax crayons on white cartridge paper and washing over it with deep blue ink. They recall the way wax blocks out and resists the ink in the way that wax resists the dye in batik. This helps them think about how to make their own pattern for the batik they will make later.

They go on to explore making their own patterns on paper using white wax crayons to draw using lines, shapes and simplified natural forms and then washing over these with ink. After two or three versions children evaluate their ideas considering the effect of their pattern or design with a focus on the effect of the contrast of deep blue and white works.

[*](Batik – hot liquid wax is applied to cloth; when it is dry the fabric is dyed, creating a pattern)

In the case study above painting is a minor but important part of the unit of work leading to batik work on fabric. Nevertheless children enjoy this part of their art and use the wax resists as a crucial part of their research in that the wax crayons act in the same way that the liquid wax will when it resists and protects the fabric from the dye.

Connect and extend

Read the article 'What teachers can learn from the practice of artists' by Michael Jarvis published in the *International Journal of Art and Design Education* in 2011 (Vol. 30, No. 2, pp. 307–17. In this article Jarvis explores what we can learn from artists (in this context, painters) in relation to exploration and experimentation.

When you see paintings displayed in art galleries and exhibitions they usually have a label. This tends to states the name of the artist, the date it was painted, the title and the media it was painted in. Sometimes there is a statement about what inspired the artist to make the work. Providing a label is a valuable experience for children to have and helps them achieve a sense of completion. They can be encouraged to give their paintings a title and articulate their inspiration and aim in making the work as part of the evaluation process towards the end of a unit of work.

Conclusion

It is likely that children will paint at least once a year if not more frequently as part of the art curriculum. Given the complexity of the skills, knowledge and understanding involved in learning to paint, learning activities must be well planned to build on prior experiences and support new learning through both exploring and being directly taught. The adult role in planning, teaching and supporting cannot be underestimated here. Drawing upon both planned use of media and techniques as well as accidental and unexpected effects can be part of painting – this is an aspect of making art that will also be explored in the next chapter – printmaking.

Next steps

- Identify the key painters and paintings that children encounter through your art curriculum.
- Consider how these could be developed in interesting and creative ways.
- Think about trying colour mixing the next time you paint with your class.

References

Barnes, R. (2002) *Teaching Art to Young Children*, 2nd ed. Abingdon: Routledge Falmer.

Matthews, J. and Seow, P. (2009) *Electronic Paint: Understanding Children's Representation through their Interactions with Digital Paint*. In: Herne, S., Cox, S. and Watts, R. (eds) *Readings in Primary Art Education*. London: Intellect Books, pp. 269–86

Meager, N. (1993) *Teaching Art at Key Stage 1*. Corsham: NSEAD.

Pratchett, S. (2007) 'Powder and Paint'. *START*, Vol. **23**, pp. 8–11.

Further reading

Baker, S. (2010) 'Duncan Grant colour mixing'. *STart*, Vol. 35, pp. 6–7.

Fenwick, L. (2009) 'Taking the pain out of painting'. *STart*, 30, pp. 21–4.

Jarvis M. (2011) 'What teachers can learn from the practice of artists'. *International Journal of Art and Design Education*, Vol. 30. No. 2, pp. 307–17.

Schumann, B. (2009) *Thirteen Women Artists Children Should Know*. Munich: Prestel Verlag.

Water, E and Harris, A. (1993) *Royal Academy of Arts Painting. A Young Artist's Guide*. London: Dorling Kindersley.

Web resources

Brian Wildsmith: *http://www.brianwildsmith.com/*

Michael Foreman: *http://www.andersenpress.co.uk/authors/view/220*

Quentin Bake: *http://www.quentinblake.com/*

Queen Victoria's journals: *http://www.queenvictoriasjournals.org/home.do*

Jane Loudon (at the Victoria and Albert Museum): *http://www.vam.ac.uk/contentapi/search/?q=jane+l oudon&search-submit=Go*

Chris Ofili: *http://www.victoria-miro.com/artists/_6/* (teachers' pack available on Tate Britain website)

Vilhelm Hammershoi: *http://www.hammershoi.co.uk/*

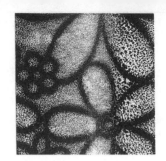

Chapter 8

Printmaking

Introduction

Printmaking is an exciting process with some intrinsic qualities that make it different from many of the other processes that you will use with children in art. Many types of printmaking allow children to produce several copies of the same image allowing them to investigate and experiment with the process and the image without obliterating their earlier work. This can allow them to feel freer to explore and be creative. Printmaking allows children to explore line, tone, colour, texture, pattern and shape. There is scope for progression towards increasingly more challenging use of the techniques and processes of printmaking. In this chapter the following areas will be considered:

- Subject knowledge that underlies teaching printmaking
- Teaching children to print

Printmaking techniques can be explored in connection with other areas of the art curriculum. Many can be applied to fabrics and textiles; others can be explored as part of developing drawing skills. Children can freely make printed paper in order to use it later when making collages or three-dimensional objects. Using ICT and digital media can help children develop prints onscreen.

Meaningful connections can be between printmaking and several curriculum subjects including mathematics. In particular, aspects of shape and space such as tessellation, symmetry and the properties of 2D shapes can be explored. Strong links can be made to design technology. Connections can also be made to other aspects of art including textiles, collage and drawing. Printmaking can be inspired by the natural and manmade worlds around us or result from experimenting with materials and techniques to use accidental and deliberate effects. Many different techniques have been used by printmakers from many cultures, times and places, and can be explored by primary-aged children.

In addition to the practical process of printmaking, ICT and digital media can be used both as part of the process and as an outcome. Using the 'stamp' feature of art software can allow children to explore printed patterns across surfaces and some software allows a large range of choices and the opportunity to scan in your own items to stamp with. Prints can be developed by adding text or images that have been collected or made onscreen and printed out.

You may be aware that many printmaking techniques that artist printmakers use require the use of a press. None of the techniques described in this chapter require the use of a press although if you do have the opportunity to allow children to work with a printmaker and use a press this will widen their understanding of the possibilities available at secondary school and beyond.

The subject knowledge that underlies the teaching of printmaking

Developing some subject knowledge about printmaking will underpin successful planning, teaching and support. Some aspects that you may need to learn about are:

- exploring printmaking skills;
- teaching the visual elements through printmaking;

- vocabulary;
- media and processes;
- the work of artists, craftspeople and designers.

Exploring printmaking skills

Printing with objects is one of the first types of printmaking that children encounter. Using objects either collected by the teacher or selected by the children themselves is an activity common in Foundation Stage or early Key Stage 1 and then abandoned later in Key Stage 1 and Key Stage 2. For younger children the excitement of pressing an object down on paper and lifting it to reveal the surprise of an unexpected shape or pattern can be absorbing and rewarding in itself. With older children it is possible to ask them to make and articulate their choices of objects, design images and patterns built from several objects and using several colours and take control of the process independently. This allows older children to achieve complex and sophisticated results across a large surface area.

Practical task

Exploring printing with objects

Learning objective:

- to explore printing from objects.

In this practical task you will explore one of the most basic printmaking techniques that many children experiment with in their early years in school. It will allow you to find out more about how to make a successful print and how to avoid some of the typical problems that can arise when children use objects to print with.

You will need:

- A flat tray, a roller, printing ink, large sheets of paper.

What to do:

1. Look around and collect ten objects that you can print with. You can consider completely varied objects or make your choices around a theme such as manmade, natural, toys, junk, household objects.
2. Put a blob of printing ink onto the flat tray and use the roller to roll it out so the surface of the tray is covered in a thin, flat and even layer of ink.
3. Press each object into the ink and then press it down onto the paper to make a print from each one.
4. You can do this several times so you can compare the difference between the first and last print – sometimes the print is clearer when there is less ink remaining on the object.

Questions to consider

- *Do you get clear and interesting prints from the objects that you chose?*: You may find that objects that have interesting shapes or textures on them make a more attractive image. You may find that some objects do not print fully because of their shape or absorbency. This is a factor to bear in mind if you are choosing objects to put on the printing table for children to use.

- *Were your objects easy to hold and manipulate?*: If you, as an adult, find the objects difficult to hold it may be all the more challenging for children. Very small objects and objects that are slippery or soft may be particularly challenging to print from. On the other hand the pattern that you get may be sufficiently interesting for you to find a way of overcoming these difficulties, such as by attaching a card/plastic 'handle' to grip.

- *Are your objects readily available in sufficient quantities for a class of children to use?*: If you plan to print from objects with a whole class or series of groups it is likely you will need to replace the objects as they get covered in printing ink. It can be frustrating for children to have to use objects already covered in ink, which may give a less clear image than when they were clean.

- *Are there any challenges using this process that you can think of for the children that you teach?*: You may have to demonstrate how to press the object down into the ink and then down onto the paper without moving or sliding the object around in order to get a clear print. This can be practised without ink and perhaps with a shape or spot on a piece of paper to 'target' the object. You may think of ways to describe the process that makes sense to the children that you teach. An example of this is to say that you must press down so hard that you can feel it all the way up your arm! Depending on the age and level of language of your pupils you may need to consider how to describe the process in a meaningful way.

- *If you were organising this activity with a group or class of children what are the implications for classroom organisation and management?*: You should consider the size of paper so that space there is for each child's paper on the table and it is not overlapping with other's or flapping over the edge of the table. Alternatively you could cover the table with paper and allow children to print anywhere. If each child is working on a sheet of paper of their own you need to consider where these will dry. Is there a drying rack available? Is it nearby so children don't have to walk around with wet pieces of paper? After they have finished where will the children wash and dry their hands? There will be other factors for you to take into consideration in relation to your classroom and the children that you teach.

It would be helpful to you as a teacher to try out any printmaking process that you intend to teach to children: this will allow you to identify teaching points and ways of organising the experience effectively.

Teaching the visual elements through printmaking

When you are planning and teaching a unit of work that involves printmaking it is important to identify one or two visual elements that you will develop with the children. It is likely that this will have been done at the long term planning stage.

Line	Tone
Drawing and mark making onto polystyrene tiles, into plasticine Drawing onto a surface in monoprinting Lines created with string on a tile Lines created with glue on a tile	Choice of tones within one colour of ink and/or paper when printing Understanding the need for some light and dark contrast to make the image visible
Colour	**Pattern**
Choice of colour of ink and paper when printing – matching, contrasting, complementary, etc.	Exploring and creating different types of pattern – repeating, rotating, transforming, symmetrical, tessellating Using single or combinations of objects to create patterns Using tiles to print with physically and on screen
Texture	**Shape**
Exploring natural and manmade textures to make prints/rubbings from Choosing textures to make planned effects Printing from collage tiles	Using regular and irregular shapes to create prints Exploring mathematical aspects of shape – repeating, rotating, transforming, symmetrical Use of stencils/cut outs Exploring what happens to shapes when they are printed – text (mirror image)
Space	**Form**
Using the space of the printing tile/paper – composition Printing around edges, in borders, across the whole surface, using a grid, in rows and columns Placing – next to, overlapping, leaving spaces between	Printing to decorate 3D forms Using printed paper/card/fabric to construct 3D forms

There are some visual elements that lend themselves to exploration through printmaking. The opportunities for repeating and reprinting allow children to explore pattern and pattern making in many different ways. Being able to take rubbings or print from textured objects or create images and patterns from reassembling textured papers gives much scope for exploring the texture of surfaces beyond merely making rubbings. Printmaking can also be a vehicle for exploring tone, line and colour as well as underpinning the exploration of form by allowing children to quickly create a lot of decorated paper, card or fabric with which to create three dimensional forms.

Case Study

In a unit of work on printmaking with a Year 1 class two visual elements are identified in long term planning as the main focus of the learning and teaching: pattern and line.

Pattern is at the heart of the unit of work and the children are given the opportunity to explore and identify manmade patterns in the immediate environment, on Indian fabric and on reproductions of a range of tiles. They find, photograph, draw and talk about patterns in the exploring and developing ideas stage of the unit of work. The children's understanding of how patterns are designed is a focus for learning.

The other visual element that the unit focuses upon is line. Whilst exploring patterns the children are asked to draw using line, find examples of the use of line in the patterns they are looking at, try out a selection of tools that make lines and explore straight, curved, continuous, broken and other types of lines.

The children each draw upon their exploration of pattern and line to design and make a press print tile of a pattern created by lines drawn into the polystyrene. When they evaluate their work they are encouraged to look at how line has been used in the design of their patterns. They all print in black printing ink on white paper to allow their designs to be easily compared and focus on the use of marks and lines.

Whilst working on this unit other visual elements such as shape, colour and space play a part but are not the main focus of learning and teaching at the early stages. Later, children freely print their polystyrene tiles using any colour of paper and printing ink to explore the variations and allow them to exercise more choice after the focused learning apparent earlier in the unit.

The learning experience in the case study above begins with a tight focus on two visual elements in particular and then allows more personal freedom to use the technique towards the end of the unit. The printmaking technique used – biro line and mark making onto polystyrene – supports this.

Practical task

Learning objective:

- to explore line through a simple printmaking technique.

In this practical task you will have the opportunity to see what you can do with lines on a surface. This will allow you to consider how choice of technique and visual element should support each other.

You will need:

- A piece of card 15cm X 15 cm, some double-sided sticky tape, some string, scissors to make the printing tile.
- A flat tray, roller, one colour printing ink, paper to print on.

What to do:

1. Make the tile – first experiment with the string by cutting it and placing it to create patterns and shapes or by curing it around continuously without cutting. When you are happy with your pattern cover one side of the card square with the double-sided tape and recreate your pattern sticking the string firmly on the sticky surface.
2. Print from the tile – put a blob of printing ink onto the flat tray and roll it out so the surface is flat and even; roll the roller over the ink and then over the surface of the tile aiming to transfer the ink to the string. Pick up the inked tile and place it carefully on the paper. Roll over the back of the tile with a clean roller pressing as hard as you can.

In this practical task the nature of the material used to make the printing tile is linear and supports exploration and learning about linear marks and continuous lines.

Key vocabulary

When you are planning for a printmaking experience or unit of work it is important that you identify the key vocabulary that the children will need to understand, respond to and use when working. This is especially significant for children learning English as an Additional Language (EAL) and some children with special educational needs (SEN) who may be challenged by encountering new vocabulary or familiar words with slightly or completely different meanings when used in the context of an art lesson. Key vocabulary can be considered in relation to the printmaking process itself and the visual elements you are exploring – this model is often demonstrated on published plans and schemes of work. In this unit which is called 'Investigating Pattern' the vocabulary is listed as:

- printing skills, e.g. stencil print, stippling, block print, roller, printing ink, calico, hessian;

- visual and tactile elements, eg geometric shapes, space, symmetry, identical, reflective, rotate, translation, pattern, repeat, motif

(QCA, 2000, p. 1). Clearly as an adult who knows the children in your class you will be able to identify a more precise and useful list of vocabulary, some of which may be focused on the needs of individuals. You will also be able to make useful connections to vocabulary being learned and used in other contexts – in this example there is some mathematical vocabulary. This may be one of the factors that cause you to choose to teach this unit of work alongside or shortly after mathematical work on shape and pattern.

Case Study

In the unit of work on printmaking with Year 1 discussed above many of the children are learning English as an Additional Language (EAL). It is therefore crucial that the teacher identifes the key vocabulary that the children will be responding to and using in their art lessons. It is important for the teacher to be aware of words that are new to the children and words that they have heard and used in other contexts and may have a slightly or completely different meaning in art lessons.

In this unit of work the teacher identifies the following:

visual elements

- pattern – repeating, regular, decorative, words for shapes within patterns – square, triangle, circle, etc.;
- line – straight, curved, curling, continuous, broken, thick, thin, (extended to wide, narrow, fine, broad, spiral, loop where appropriate).

tools and materials

- felt pens (fine and broad), rollers, pencils, biros, rollers, trays, printing ink, pressprint.
  the process
- Press down, roll over, roll on top of, place, lift up.

In addition to this the teacher thinks about when children will be talking about their work and identifies some sentence starters:

- 'I like this pattern because ...'
- 'I chose this pattern because ...'
- 'My pattern is ...'
- 'I can see .... in my pattern.'
- 'I could change my pattern by ...'

A clear focus on the identified vocabulary will support the children's learning in art and in language development generally. This analytical approach to the vocabulary your pupils will learn and use is likley to be something you apply across the curriculum to support the pupils learning EAL in your class.

Printmaking processes

There are many different printmaking techniques that are suitable to explore in the clasvsroom with primary-aged children. The chart below summarises those commonly used in schools along with basic information about each.

A summary of basic printmaking techniques

Technique	Definition	Examples
Printing from body parts	Applying paint to a body part and then pressing down it on a surface.	Children use their own hand prints to create a plain coloured hand on which they will draw or paint *mehndi* patterns as part of Diwali celebrations.
Printing with objects	Placing natural or manmade objects into paint then pressing it down on a surface.	Children choose up to three objects and three colours to create a repeating pattern across the whole surface of a larger piece of paper.
Printing from constructed tiles	Making a textured surface using card or textured collage materials, applying printing ink to with a roller then pressing it down on a surface	Children each choose and stick textured wall paper on a card tile the shape of a stone after observing and feeling the textures of weathered stone on an old building. They make prints from these to recreate a large collaborative wall.
Printing from drawing into a block	Drawing into a polystyrene surface, rolling printing ink on it then pressing it down on a surface.	Children create a linear picture by drawing into press print. They print these in a range of coloured printing inks on coloured paper experimenting with the contrast between ink and paper.
Printing from string	Making an image or pattern from string stuck on a card.	Children create a swirling pattern inspired by watching water in a stream. They practise making their pattern, then draw it on a piece of card. The card is covered with double-sided sticky tape and then they place the string on the lines they drew earlier.
Monoprinting	Rolling printing ink on a flat surface, drawing directly on it and placing paper on it to take the print or drawing through paper on to the inked surface.	Children create a monoprint of an imaginary creature by making a monoprint – some children draw freehand having experimented in their sketchpads and others draw through a photocopy of their chosen drawing from their sketchpad.
Blocking out/ stencils	Rolling printing ink on a flat surface, placing paper shapes on the ink to block out, placing paper on the ink and rolling to take the print.	Children cut or tear long thin strips of thin paper. They place these at random or by design on the inked surface. A piece of paper is placed on top and rolled over. The process is repeated with another colour of ink and more strips of paper. Rubbing over with wax crayons or graphite sticks can produce a similar effect.

Before you begin to teach children about a particular type of printmaking it is important that you try it out for yourself so that you understand how it works and can identify ways of teaching and supporting children effectively. Anticipating any challenges that may occur and helping children overcome them through advice and organsiation can help make the experience more satisfying and successful. Alternatively you may plan for children to experiment freely and then pick up what emerges: an example of this is when children print using letters or numbers and realise that they must be reversed in order to print the right way round. Discovering this for themselves is often a powerful and memorable learning experience but should be discovered before a lot of time and effort has gone into designing and making a print block. The practical task below takes you through one technique, monoprinting, and also gives you a structure that you could apply when trying out others.

Case Study

A group of BA QTS students who are exploring drawing and printmaking experiment with monoprinting as a process that connects the two. They watch a demonstration of how to monoprint noting the set up of tools and materials. These include a flat smooth surface, such as a smooth table top, a piece of perspex or MDF, flat trays, hard rollers, printing ink, pencils and biros, masking tape and paper to print on.

They watch as their tutor puts a blob of printing ink on the flat tray and rolls it out so the surface is flat and even. She then rolls ink onto the smooth surface aiming for an even covering. She places a piece of paper over the inked surface gently and tapes it across the top. She makes marks and draws on the back of the paper, pointing out to the students that she does not rest her hand on the paper whilst drawing. She points out how the tape allows her to lift the paper to see the results and put it back down to continue drawing.

Students go on to explore this process for themselves to find out more about the practicalities of organising it and the potential for learning and creativity. Some students like the way that a drawn monoprint has a slightly 'fuzzy' residue of ink that adds to the attractiveness of the image. They also realise that it can be a great way of freely exploring markmaking and drawing and that children could choose a drawing from their sketchbook, have it photocopied and then draw through it if blank paper worries them. Later in the session students experiment with layers of several colours on the same print.

Some students find that pressing their hand on the back of the paper can result in too much ink getting onto the surface and almost masks out the drawing. They identify that when working with children they may need to demonstrate how to draw on the back while leaning their hand on the paper and allow them to practice perhaps on newspaper. Their tutor also shows them some frames made from thick corrugated card that can be placed around the edge of the drawing surface for the hand to rest on without affecting the surface.

During the session students produce a lot of prints quite rapidly and realise that the supply of smooth surfaces could be an issue, or the cleaning of the table tops as you go along and when finished, especially if the table is used for 'clean' activities most of the time. Organising drying such a large amount of work must be thought through too.

LINK

In this case study students find that making monoprints is a completely different sort of printmaking in that each print is unique and a great many can be produced relatively quickly. This allows freedom to experiment and explore the process, immediately learning from experience. This type of monoprint can be produced in several colours by drawing through the paper and one colour of ink, moving onto the next colour and then the next. The colour of paper can enhance the print and, when dry, collage can be added to develop the image further.

Artists, craftspeople and designers and printmaking

Connections can be made between the work of printmakers and the printmaking techniques used in schools. When you are researching the work of artists to use you will come across additional types of printmaking defined below. Although it is not necessary for primary-aged children to know about all of these in detail both you and they will encounter these words when you explore prints made by artists. Some of these techniques or processes have connections to the printmaking you will teach or support at primary school.

Term	Definition	Link to school printmaking
Collagraph	A print made from a collaged surface	Using textured papers, card, fabric, string and glue to print from
Drypoint	A print made from scratching into the surface with a sharp point	Drawing into polystyrene tiles
Engraving	The incising of marks, an incised block or the print itself	Drawing into polystyrene tiles
Etching	Prints created on metal where the surface texture is created using acid	
Intaglio	An imprint produced by rubbing ink into grooves (usually on a metal surface) and then printed through a press	
Linocut	A print produced by cutting into a lino block with tools	Drawing into polystyrene tiles
Relief	Impression produced by applying ink to the surface of the printing block or plate – the uncut surface prints and the cut areas allow the paper to show through	Drawing into polystyrene tiles
Screen print	Printing using a frame covered in fine mesh through which is ink is forced onto the paper below – areas are often masked-off using stencils	Blocking out ink on a surface using paper
Stencil	A shape used to mask out to create an image	As above
Woodcut	A print produced from a block of side-grain wood or manufactured board	Cutting into polystyrene tile
Wood engraving	A print produced from a block of end-grain wood using engraving tools	As above

Definitions adapted from Desmet and Anderson, 2000.

When you make connections to the work of a printmaker it is important to be able to choose one that relates to the learning experience. You could be looking for someone who uses the same or a similar technique: monoprinting, relief printing or collage printing, for example. Alternatively you could be looking for someone who has made / makes prints inspired by the stimuli you will be using: landscape, nature or their imagination, for example. As well as looking to the past and to other places for examples of prints and printmakers there are many artists making prints now. Prints are often more affordable as original works of art than paintings or sculpture so it may be easier for you to have access to them and their makers.

A familiar starting point for finding prints is to look at the illustrations in children's books. Artists' prints have often been used to illustrate stories and poems. Edward Bawden made a series of linocuts illustrating Aesop's Fables; Chris Wormell makes woodcuts to illustrate his books, often based on animals; Patrice Aggs makes hand-coloured etchings, such as the ones for Philip Pullman's *Count Karlstein*, and Flora McLachlan makes prints inspired by myths, legends and fairy tales.

Exploring how printmaking has been used for decoration will allow you to explore the technique in different times and cultures. Indian woodblocks and fabrics created using this method can be used to allow children to print with the blocks, look at the designs and then make their own prints on paper or fabric. William Morris designed handmade wallpapers inspired by nature. There are many examples of printed patterns used decoratively on the clothes children wear and the fabrics around them. Although these are now mass produced they were initially designed by someone.

Many artists working now work wholly or partially in print in varied and interesting ways. Lucy Skaer's prints from a deconstructed chair as part of her Turner Prize exhibit in 2009 can inspire children to think about viewpoints and the potential of everyday objects for print-making. Some printmakers use printmaking techniques to make three-dimensional objects. Many of Banksy's works contain an element of printmaking, primarily using stencils. Print-making has also been influenced by digital media with prints being created and/or printed using new technology. There are some interesting examples on the websites listed below.

Find out more

About the printmaking techniques artists use

Find the Victoria and Albert Museum website. At the 'what's in the V & A?' tab at the top of the screen, click on 'prints'.

1. Scroll down to the 'Study Room resource: printmaking techniques' and open this. Here you can explore different types of printmaking and explore examples.

 LINK

2. Scroll down to the 'Printing 1450–1520' and open this. Here you can see a short film demonstrating how to make a woodblock print based on medieval playing cards.

 LINK

3. Scroll down to 'The V & A's Computer Art Collections' to find examples of prints partially or entirely created using digital technology.

 LINK

Teaching children to make prints

Printmaking is a wonderful technique to explore with children because there are so many possibilities – it can give you and the children a real chance to experiment, learn from accidental effects and make choices. When planning for a successful learning experience there are some significant factors to consider:

- organisation of space and resources;
- physical skills.

In addition there are a number of possibilities that can be explored. In chapter printmaking in relation to connecting to children's prior learning was explored. In this section the following ways of approaching printmaking will be presented:

- connecting printmaking to other areas of art;
- developing an extended printmaking experience;
- working individually and in groups;
- making connection to other curriculum subjects.

Organisation of space and resources

For successful printmaking it is important to work in an organised space. As a teacher you are likely to plan this in your classroom and if possible you could include a 'messy' table for children to apply ink at and a 'clean' table where children print on their paper. You may have a tiled or practical area available to use for 'messy' art and this may be equipped with a sink and a drying rack. The layout should be explained and modelled to the children you are working with so that they understand your expectations and how its organisation will help them produce successful art work.

You should consider the tools and materials that are required at each table and the most efficient way of laying these out. An example of this is when you are printing from tiles with string on. You will need a roller in each tray of ink to ink up the tiles. You will also need to keep some rollers clean to roll across the back of the tile exerting pressure

Figure 8.1 Printing table 1: putting ink onto the tile (dirty table)

Figure 8.2 Printing table 2: printing onto the paper (clean table)

to make your print. The easiest way to do this is to place the ink trays and the ink rollers on the 'messy' table and the clean rollers on the 'clean' table. It is again important that you explain and model this so that children understand why they cannot grab any roller and use it for any purpose. Drawing a map or diagram for you and your support staff or to share with the children may help. You can also distinguish 'clean' and 'inky' rollers by attaching a coloured ribbon or sticker to the handle of the rollers that will stay clean. Another consideration will be where to keep paper to print on so that it is accessible but stays clean. You should also decide who will monitor and replenish ink. Older key stage 2 children could take on this responsibility but for younger pupils who may put out too much ink adult support will be required.

Physical skills

From experiences of printmaking that you may have had or from undertaking the practical tasks earlier in the chapter you will have begun to come to an understanding of some of the skills that underpin printmaking. It is important for your planning and teaching that you identify the specific skills required within your unit of work or lesson and that you take into consideration children's existing skills and prior experiences in this area. The need to place the object or tile down on the paper, keep it still, apply pressure to it and then lift it up is the basic difference between printmaking and other art techniques, which, by contrast, require tools to be moved around to make marks.

Within the various printmaking processes children will be challenged to use their fine motor skills effectively in a different context than they are used to in the classroom. They may be using a pen or pencil but to make marks into a surface that resists their tool – plasticene or polystyrene, for example. They may be using tools they have never used before, such as hard or sponge rollers that require some pressure to be exerted upon them to get the effect that they want. They may need to place objects or tiles precisely on a place on the paper without moving it around and then pick it up and replace it on exactly the same spot in order to get the effect they have planned. The knowledge that you have of your children will allow you to plan strategies to support some or all pupils in developing the skills they need.

It could be that you have to build in additional practice of some skills, deploy support staff effectively or partner children with supportive peers. ICT can support learning in this area and allow children to develop their understanding without the physical demands of printmaking. It is possible to scan one printed image and manipulate it in a 'printmaking like' manner on screen for children who find the physical process of printmaking impossible. Children can also manipulate stamps on the screen to create patterns. There are several websites that allow children to create a pattern or design a pattern tile and print it out. Links to these are available in the list of websites at the end of this chapter. These activities can also be a useful part of a printmaking unit of work for all children and will support you in making a connection between ICT and art.

Even in the simplest of printmaking processes there a number of steps that must be carried out in sequence in order to achieve a successful result. For children who find sequencing and remembering a series of steps in the right order printmaking can be a challenging process. But it can be an excellent opportunity to develop sequencing and following instructions in a practical and purposeful context. Making sets of step-by-step instructions of some printmaking processes that can serve as prompts or a model to use to make your own class-specific prompt cards matched to the needs of the children you are working with can be useful. Printmaking can also be a context in which to apply the learning that takes place in literacy or English lessons on the non-fiction text type of instructions.

 LINK

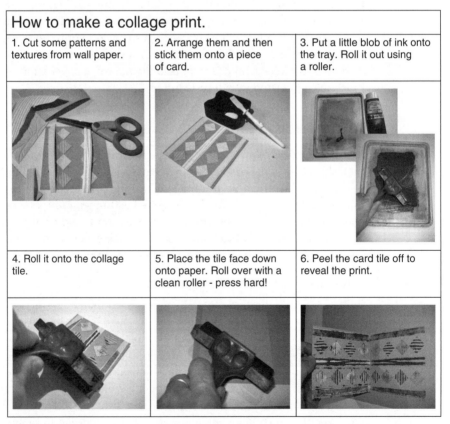

How to make a collage print.		
1. Cut some patterns and textures from wall paper.	2. Arrange them and then stick them onto a piece of card.	3. Put a little blob of ink onto the tray. Roll it out using a roller.
4. Roll it onto the collage tile.	5. Place the tile face down onto paper. Roll over with a clean roller - press hard!	6. Peel the card tile off to reveal the print.

Figure 8.3 Example of step by step prompts

Connecting printmaking to other areas of art

Some printmaking techniques are useful for creating backgrounds and interesting surfaces that can be used to work on using paint, print or drawing or to provide materials for use in collage. Using the whole surface of a large piece of paper and working individually or as a group can provide children with the chance to experiment freely, learn from each other and enjoy the sensory and creative experience.

Printing with objects across the surface is one way to create backgrounds and some of the other printmaking techniques that lend themselves to this are listed below.

Type of printing	How to	Example
Rolling over printing	Cut or rip shapes from paper. Place these below a large sheet of paper on a flat surface. Roll over with a hard roller and a little printing ink. Move the shapes and roll again, perhaps with a different colour.	Cut leaf shapes, some with patterned blade scissors and roll over in shades of green to create a background for painting, printing or collaging flowers on.
String roller printing	Tie and knot string around a hard roller. Roll this through printing ink and onto paper.	Print in browns on brown papers to create tree bark paper to use for collage.
Sponger roller printing	Use sponge rollers with patterns cut into them (stripes, spots, etc.) or put masking tape or string around a sponge DIY roller.	Use randomly on white paper using pastel shades of paints, to paint on later with bolder brighter colours.
Marbling	Fill a large shallow tray with about 2 cm of water. Drop marbling ink onto the surface. Place paper on the surface to take a 'print' from the water surface.	Use as a watery background for printing, painting or collaging fish and sea creatures on.
Bubble printing	Make a mixture of water, washing-up liquid and paint, ink or brusho in a container with no lid. Use a straw to blow in to this to create bubbles that rise above the surface of the container. Take a print from the bubbles.	Use silver and neon colour bubbles on dark paper to create materials for using in fantasy and imaginative work.
Sponge printing	Use sponges cut into shapes at random or more purposefully to print with all over a surface.	Print brick shapes in purposeful patterns as a built environment background.

This may mean that you include some printmaking at the beginning of a work on painting or collage in order to allow children to create interesting surfaces to work on or that you include these more independent activities within a printmaking unit and keep the outcomes to use in later units; the long term plan can help you organise these connections.

Printmaking processes can also be applied to fabrics and textiles by using the same or a similar process but using fabric paint/ink on cotton or other textiles. These could include printing with objects, block printing and string printing. It could also include types of printmaking that relate more closely to use with fabrics and textiles such as stencilling and screen printing. Trying out these processes on paper can be a useful way of allowing children to prepare and design before moving on to working on fabric.

Creative connections can also be made between printmaking and collage techniques. Prints can be taken from collage materials that have interesting textures. Prints can be enhanced by adding collage such as images and text as well as natural and manufactured found materials to the print surface either during or after printing.

Case Study

A class of Year 3 children explored the stonework on some local buildings whilst on a trip to a field centre. Outside the building each child focused on one stone and firstly looked at the size and shape to begin to see that no two stones were the same. They were then guided to look more closely at what they could see on their chosen stone: marks, lines, patterns and colours. They felt the textures on the stones: there were smooth patches and rough patches as well as some pieces of fossil. They made rubbings from these stones using graphite sticks on thin paper.

Inside the field centre each child drew their stone shape on a piece of card and cut it out, some with adult help. Using a collection of textured wallpapers each child ripped and cut textures to make up their stone and moved them around until they were happy with the arrangement. When satisfied they glued the papers down to create a textures block from which to print.

Each child printed their stone several times on a choice of natural stone coloured papers using a limited colour range to experiment with the interplay of ink and paper colour. They also printed their stone on a whole class collaborative wall to display in the classroom. On return children explored making prints from textured papers, learning about the parts of the surface that hold the ink and print and the gaps that reveal the paper.

In this case study children explored the creative possibilities of both collage and print-making using collected, found and recycled papers to make printing blocks. In this case they had abstract and surface textures to choose from but if you look in DIY stores you will see that there are many textured wall papers that have textures based on repeating patterns and natural motifs such as leaves, flowers and grasses. All of these are a great source for making print blocks with and lead to an interesting range of prints.

Developing an extended printmaking experience

When you plan a unit of work entirely around printmaking children will have an opportunity to create a print and experiment with it, building on their skills and developing their understanding of the technique more fully. As children move into Key Stage Two it is important that children build on their prior experiences of printmaking and are challenged to achieve more complex and interesting results throughout an extended experience.

Case Study

Children in later Key Stage 2 research African animals by looking at photos and exploring some Oxfam wrapping paper that features simplified animal shapes decorated with patterns. As part of their unit of work in art each child will design a two plate card print to print individually and as part of a larger collaborative picture.

Each child designs a simple animal in outline shape and creates two identical cards to use to make their print. One card is left plain and the other is decorated using card, string and collage materials. Some children base their patterns on their observations of animal coats and others choose a more decorative approach. Each child marks the back of their patterned and plain piece of card so that when they are printing they know which way round to place the cards they are printing from.

Initially each child prints one print using a light colour for the plain shape and darker colour for the pattern. All the children evaluate their prints and consider any changes or improvements they wish to make. A few children decide to add more to their decorated card; several remake their patterned card so it is less 'full' allowing the patterns to be seen more clearly. At this stage children also refine their placement so that they can print one card exactly on top of the other and use the marks on the back of the card plates to ensure that they put ink on the correct face of the card.

Next children print freely, experimenting with colour combinations and creating sheets containing three or four animals. They also make a wax resist background to print their animal on as an individual outcome. Finally each child prints their animal on a piece of fabric to make a large collaborative hanging for the school entrance hall.

LINK

In this case study older children use printmaking to follow through a number of steps. They draw upon prior learning and experience of techniques and can make a number of decisions printing freely, evaluating and learning, leading to the creation of both individual and collaborative outcomes over half a term. At the planning stage, breaking this unit of work down into a series of steps was crucial to classroom organisation, use of classroom space and use of time within lessons and across the weeks.

Connect and extend

Read Anne Desmet's book *Primary Prints: Creative Printmaking in the Classroom*, published in 2010 by A&C Black.

Look at her project based around buildings as an example of a sustained printmaking experience. Try out some of her ideas to extend the range of printmaking activities you plan for children.

Making connections to other curriculum subjects

Connections between printmaking and other curriculum subjects can be made to strengthen learning in both subjects. In the example below a connection is made to mathematics in order to put some mathematical learning into practice and explore it creatively.

Case Study

A class of Year 2 children have been learning about two-dimensional shapes: naming them and exploring their properties including the number of sides and the number of corners. They have been using mathematical vocabulary including side, edge, corner, curved, straight, overlapping, tessellating and, also, regular and irregular as well as shape names.

The class are asked to draw and cut out two different shapes each from newsprint. The only constriction is that the shapes must all have straight sides and be of a size no smaller than their hand. This leads to children creating a variety of irregular straight-edged shapes. As the children cut their shapes out they sort them into groups by number of sides (e.g. three sides, four sides) onto larger labelled sheets so that roughly the same number of shapes with three, four or five sides or more are made. They are aiming for a lot of shapes to use and discard in the print making activity.

For the printmaking activity a large piece of perspex (or a table top) is used. Yellow paint is rolled over the surface using a sponge roller. Ten children are asked to each choose a shape and place it on the paint surface so it is not touching any other shape. A large piece of white paper is placed on the surface, taped to the table at one end and pressed down to take a print. Before the paper is lifted the children make a prediction – what colour will the shapes be? The paper is lifted to reveal white shapes where the paper shapes blocked out the yellow paint.

The paper shapes are peeled off the surface, which is now rolled with orange paint. Another ten children each choose a shape to place down. Paper is placed down and pressed again. Once again, the children try to predict what might happen – when the paper is lifted there are some white shapes, some yellow shapes and an orange background. Some new shapes have been created by overlaps.

Finally the paper shapes are peeled off, the table is rolled with red paint and the last ten children place shapes on the surface. The paper is pressed down and then peeled off to reveal white shapes, yellow shapes, orange shapes and a red background. The paper is placed where the whole class can gather around to see it and talk about what they have noticed. In relation to shapes children can see that new shapes have been created by overlaps, shapes within shapes can be seen and some interesting irregular shapes have been covered by others and are now lost to the viewer.

In the case study above this could be considered as an early approach to screenprinting where an image is created by blocking out and letting the surface show through. Children learn that when shapes are placed randomly some interesting parts of the print can be obliterated later – they can be challenged to find out how to protect and retain these. Later in art children can make individual or group prints based on different versions of the same shape or combinations of shapes, planning and predicting rather than working randomly as they were previously. It is an opportunity to teach children some of the basic possibilities of this type of printmaking before going on to explore it in more depth, perhaps on fabrics.

In terms of mathematical learning children are more able to recognise irregular shapes and are more aware of how shapes can be created from overlapping or placing next to other shapes. In Case Study 8.6 the outcome is a large piece of printed paper to which all the children in the class have contributed. There are no individual outcomes to this activity. It is a relatively quick activity and creates excitement each time the paper is peeled off the surface to reveal a new image.

There are many opportunities to link printmaking and make prints in connection with other curriculum subjects; for example many experiences that children have – poems, stories and use of lettering and texts in English; close observational drawing in science;

visits to heritage sites in history; visits to other places in geography and places of spiritual significance in RE – may inspire the making of prints as a response.

Conclusion

Printmaking is a huge area of art encompassing many techniques that can be used separately or in combination. It can give children opportunities to work individually and with others to create larger-scale works where their own contribution can be identified. Accidental and unexpected effects are valued and enjoyed in printmaking; children can be surprised and excited by what happens as they work. We are surrounded by examples of prints and printmaking, including original artists prints, making this an area where we can give children the opportunity to see original work and perhaps talk to the artists who make it.

Next steps

- Look for some examples of printmaking in your school and immediate environment.
- Find some useful websites and save them to your favourites for use to develop your subject knowledge or to use with children.

Reference

Desmet, A. and Anderson, J. (2000) *Handmade Prints: An Introduction to Creative Printmaking Without a Press.* London: A & C Black.

Further reading

Desmet, A. (2010) *Primary Prints Creative Printmaking in the Classroom.* London: A & C Black.

Desmet, A. (2010) 'DIY school prints'. *Printmaking Today*, Vol. 19, No. 4, pp. 28–9.

Dyson, M. (2008) 'Stamp design'. *STart*, Vol. 28, pp. 19–21.

Hilton, L. (2009) 'Urban places and open spaces townscapes and cityscapes from 2D to 3D'. *STart*, Vol. 32, pp. 14–18.

Web resources

Find examples of the prints of Patrice Aggs, Flora McLachlan and Chris Wormell on this website: *http://www.art-of-illustration.co.uk/*

Find examples of the work of Edward Bawden on the Cecil Higgins Art Gallery and Museum website and a short film about him, his prints and how to make a linocut here: *http://www.artisancam.org.uk* click on 'activities' and then on explore 'linoprinting'.

Find Lucy Skaer's chair installation here: *http://www.lissongallery.com/#/exhibitions/2009-10-14_lisson-presents-6*

Design and print out a tile here: *http://www.vam.ac.uk/vastatic/microsites/1312_artsandcrafts/design_a_tile/tool/*

Chapter 9

Collage

Introduction

Collage gives children a wonderful opportunity to explore a wide range of materials and create interesting and varied pieces of art by choosing, placing and arranging. This can be particularly engaging for children who are critical of their drawing skills and lack confidence in art as a result. Planning learning experiences based around collage can focus on the use of collected and recycled materials, making projects and units of work economical and responsive to the resources available locally. In this chapter the following areas will be considered:

- Subject knowledge that underlies teaching
- Teaching children to use collage techniques

Collage often provides the opportunity for combining a range of materials and techniques in a mixed media approach. Collage techniques can be used as a way of creating decorated surface on which to paint, draw or print; it can be used to add detail and texture to a painting or print; or it can be a way of creating interesting papers to use in sculpture. In addition there is great potential for using ICT as part of a unit of work involving collage or as the main outcome.

Although collage can be regarded as an activity more suited to younger children it would be a mistake to dismiss collage as 'cutting and sticking' and restrict this area of art to the early years and Key Stage 1. Cox and Watts (2007) note that collage 'can be perfectly simple or endlessly complex' (p. 73). As children's abilities to use tools and make choices of materials and their placement develop increasingly sophisticated and creative results can be achieved.

In addition to the practical materials and tools that you can use in collage there is much potential in using ICT and digital media both as part of the process and to create the finished piece. Finding or making text to print out and use as part of a collage can be useful. Searching for images online, copying or scanning images or using digital photos taken by adults or children can be used in a collage and can also be manipulated and changes made on screen before printing out.

The subject knowledge that underlies the teaching of collage

Developing some subject knowledge about collage will underpin successful planning, teaching and support. Some aspects that you may need to learn about are:

- collage tools and materials;
- visual elements that can be taught and developed effectively through collage;
- vocabulary to use;
- media and techniques;
- artists, craftspeople and designers who work with collage.

Collage tools and materials

There are many materials that can be collected and used to make a collage. Children can be given complete freedom or opportunities to explore different types of collage and use groups of materials depending on the unit of work they are involved with. The collection and arrangement of collage materials provides a valuable built-in opportunity to evaluate and make changes before the final piece is made.

Case Study

In a mixed class of Reception and Year 1 children the teacher and teaching assistant have planned and resourced the opportunity for the children to freely create collages for half a term. At the medium term planning stage they identified the skills the children will develop, the tools they will use and the materials that will be available, some of which will be available throughout the half term whilst others will be replaced weekly to maintain interest and variety. A trolley is set up that contains:

● a variety of surfaces to stick materials onto including different shapes, sizes, thicknesses, textures and colours;

● a variety of materials and items to use for sticking;

● plain and patterned scissors;

● glue sticks and PVA in small pots along with glue spreaders.

Nearby there is a display board to which children can attach their collages. This gives them the opportunity to share their work with each other and pick up ideas to try as well as reclaim their work and continue to develop it. Each week the teacher or TA spends some time observing, teaching and supporting the child-initiated learning in this area of the classroom and they also draw the children's attention to the collages that are being made to highlight what works well and the variety of approaches that can be tried when using these materials. The adults are able to introduce ideas where necessary as well as promote the ideas brought by the children – at one point a child makes a miniature collage using very small pieces of pasta, pot pourri and paper and, when this is shown to other children, working small takes off and dominates the sticking table for about a week. The adults support this interest by seeking small items to add to the trolley during the week. Towards the end of the half term children take digital photos of two of their outcomes and tell the adults about them as a record of their work before some of it is displayed around the school and the rest goes home.

In the case study above younger children are given some freedom to create and experiment with no finished outcome in the adults' minds or on their planning. The focus is on developing and improving skills and using the children's own ideas within the overall area of collage. This can result in a more varied set of outcomes from the class than had the children been guided towards making a collage based on a theme or using a limited range of materials. There is no reason why older children cannot be given these choices.

Find out more

About the resources available to you locally
Search online for your local scrapstore. Identify:

● where it is;

● the costs involved for joining/visiting;

● the materials available.

Teaching the visual elements through collage

The chart below makes suggestions in relation to each of the eight visual elements. When you are planning and teaching a unit of work that involves collage it is important to identify one or two visual elements that you will develop with the children. It is likely that this will have been done at the long term planning stage.

Line	Tone
Using linear materials such as string, thread, wire, wool, twine that can be manipulated into curved and straight lines Using linear materials that are straight such as twigs, dowelling, strips of card	Using tones of the same colour Exploring the effect of contrasting tones – placing pale next to deep or bright next to dull
Colour	**Pattern**
Exploring the same, contrasting, matching colours Creating new colours from overlapping Choosing using different tones of the same colour Choosing and placing colours next to each other for effect–contrast/clash/matching	Creating patterns from collage materials based on their colour, shape, tone, texture, etc. Creating different types of pattern – repeating, geometric, etc. Using collage materials that have patterns on them
Texture	**Shape**
Exploring textures of collage materials freely Making choices related to textural qualities such as smooth, soft, hard, bumpy Graduating textures from smooth to rough, from soft to hard Contrasting textures for effect	Using random and planned shapes Using regular and irregular shapes Creating shapes by choosing, cutting or tearing Exploring the shapes created by cutting away and leaving a hole (negative shapes) Exploring the new shapes created by overlapping
Space	**Form**
Exploring composition by placing and rearranging collage materials Experimenting with scale by reducing and expanding on the photocopier or on the computer screen	Using collage to make or decorate 3D forms Creating relief images

The visual elements that you focus on when making a collage depend partly upon the materials you plan to use. If you have materials of many different colours colour will clearly be the focus of learning: children might choose and place materials of different colours to make varied effects or collect and arrange different tones of the same colour in their work. Texture will be important and can also lead to rubbing and printmaking activities. There is also scope for exploring patterns through placing collected items as well as choosing from materials that are patterned, such as papers and fabrics.

Another aspect of collage is that images such as photos, pictures and other graphic material (adverts, maps, cards, lettering, text, etc.) can be chosen, changed and used in combination to construct a new image or piece of art. These could be found by children using resources brought from home, available in school, found online or digital images they have photographed themselves. This may allow them to explore aspects of shape, space and form that they would find challenging to draw or paint for themselves.

Practical task

Learning objective:

● to explore shape and space in the context of collage.

In this practical task you will have the opportunity to consider how using the reducing and expanding feature of the photocopier can be used to explore shape, scale and space in a unit of work focused on collage. This is something that could be undertaken with the support of an adult when working with younger children or more independently when working with older children.

You will need:

● black pens; paper; scissors, glue, access to a photocopier, a piece of white A3 paper.

What to do:

1. Either draw or find (clip art or from a book) some black line drawings of several of the following: a person, a flower, a household item, a door/doorway, a window, a wrapped present.
2. Cut them out leaving the black outline visible.
3. Photocopy your chosen drawings so that you have two sets.
4. Add more linear detail and decoration to one set drawings.
5. Take one set of the drawings to the photocopier and create two new sets: one by reducing and one by expanding.
6. Cut out your new sets and arrange all the drawings on a piece of coloured paper. Experiment with contrasting the original sizes and the larger and smaller versions to create imaginary scenes using the new scale of items as part of the effect. Arrive at a scene that you find interesting and will inspire a story or description.
7. Stick your drawings on the A3 paper.
8. Copy your collage so that you have a 'finished' version to develop further.

Questions to consider

- *Creating or collecting the drawings to use*: You might have used existing line drawings from clip art or found in a book or perhaps you drew some items yourself. If you were including this in a unit of a work, making the drawings could be an early part of the unit. These could be from observation, from looking at line drawings or from tracing over photos in catalogues to create linear representations. In order to create a collection of drawings to use the class could work collaboratively creating three drawings each and then all choosing and using from the photocopied collection.

- *Reducing and expanding*: Would this be feasible for the children you are teaching to do for themselves? As mentioned above the role that the children take in using the photo-copier will vary. If you plan for children to take a major role younger children could be supported by a TA whereas older children might be expected to learn the process and work independently. The photocopier's position may also be a factor especially if it is a long way from the classroom. If children's involvement in this aspect of the unit of work is less important, you or a TA could reduce and expand ready for the next lesson.

- *Cutting out*: Perhaps you cut your items out carefully or perhaps just roughly around the outline. If you are sticking them onto the same colour paper, as you are in this activity, it is less important to cut exactly around. This is an area you could consider if trying this with children. Adults could cut out the copies roughly and the children could trim them more carefully where needed. This will relate to any overlapping or placements at the next stage.

- *Arranging*: How long did you spend experimenting and exploring the effects you could create? At this stage it is important to have some time to try out different placements rather than rush to stick them down. When doing this with children it would be important to make sure there was no glue available so that they could instead concentrate on this stage and really try out different versions of their compositions. You might use this stage to explore the effects of contrasting scales especially where you have items that are much bigger or smaller than expected or than they usually are in relation to each other.

- *Sticking down*: How did you do this? Perhaps you used a glue stick and had some scope to peel off and replace or perhaps you used PVA because you were sure where the pictures were going to go. If you are going to copy the final picture to create the finished outcome, just sticking down quite roughly could be enough. If you have used PVA, ensure that the picture is fully dry before copying so that you do not get PVA onto the photocopier bed.

There is much scope for working both individually and collaboratively in art at different stages of this activity, as well as linking to English and other subjects. The collection of drawings that the class use can be planned together to relate to an imaginary or known story and each scene could be constructed to further the story, which can then be told or written in English lessons. Colour and decoration can be added at any stage. Backgrounds can be constructed to reflect the story setting, using other collage techniques perhaps.

Key vocabulary

When you plan a unit of work based partly or wholly on collage techniques it is important to identify any words that will be used: these might be entirely new, familiar but used in a different context, or an opportunity to consolidate and re-enforce. Vocabulary could be considered in relation to, firstly, the materials being used and their characteristics and, secondly, the technique itself and the tools and skills involved.

There are many opportunities for naming and describing materials when using collage. This could be in terms of collections and which materials fall within these – papers, including tissue paper, gummed paper, newspaper, shiny paper, wax paper. Alternatively it could relate to characteristics such as textured, reflective, smooth or translucent. Choosing and using these materials to make a collage can allow children to explore the materials and their characteristics firsthand so that when they are required, perhaps in science or DT to explore and use materials in relation to their properties, they have some experience of them. Whilst choosing and discarding descriptive and comparative vocabulary will be vital, ensuring that adults plan to and support children in articulating this should be a part of any plan.

Making collages will also involve vocabulary related to the type; this is explored more fully below. In addition the tools children use and possibilities of the technique itself will also require some specific vocabulary. If children are making a decoupage emphasis will be on words such as flat, smooth, next to and overlapping. In many different types of collage placing materials will be a large part of the process and positional vocabulary such as next to, on top of, overlapping, to the right of will be vital when talking about the children's work. With younger children this may be used and modelled by adults; indeed it would provide a good practical opportunity to consolidate these words.

Collage techniques

There are many different collage techniques that are suitable to explore in the classroom with primary-aged children. The word collage is taken from the French word *'coller'* which means 'to glue'. The chart below summarises those commonly used in schools along with basic information about each.

A summary of basic collage techniques

Technique	Definition	Examples
Collage	An image made from gluing a selection of materials onto a flat surface.	Children tear and glue coloured tissue paper onto a plastic surface using a lot of PVA glue. When the glue is dry the collage is peeled off the surface to create a translucent image. Each side is decorated with glitter / sequins to complete.
Decoupage	Cut-out images/photos are pasted onto a surface so that it appears they are painted directly on it when varnished over.	Children collect images from magazines and newspapers around a theme identified by an adult or chosen themselves. They glue down their chosen images after arranging and rearranging to find the composition they find most attractive.
Assemblage	Constructed from collected and found elements, including three-dimensional items.	Children collect ten items (both natural and man-made) on a walk around a local wood. They use these as a basis for an assemblage representing their experience. They link to English by writing short impressions and including these as part of their assemblage.
Photo montage	Collages made from photos or parts of photos, made by hand on paper or digitally onscreen.	Children create an imaginary scene using a mixture found and created images. They use the photocopier to resize some of these to change usual scale. They use the scanner to scan the finished scene and show each on the IWB. Some children use the IWB pens to draw into the scene and add handwritten and typed text.
Digital collage	Collage constructed entirely using digital technology and displayed onscreen.	Children choose a place of personal significance or interest and take some photos of it digitally. They manipulate these onscreen, cutting them, rearranging them, resizing them, to create a semi-abstract representation of the place that conveys its essence rather than representing it figuratively.

As well these types of collage there are other activities that are very close to being collage – techniques tend to overlap. One example of this is placing material or objects to make a temporary flat or three-dimensional image such as making a Rangoli pattern using coloured petals, seeds and small stones or collecting items based around a theme and arranging them before photographing.

You may have noticed that two techniques have not been mentioned so far. One is the screwing up of small pieces of coloured tissue paper to fill in pre-drawn shapes. Perhaps you spent time screwing up tissue when you were at school – think about what the learning in art could have been when you were doing this. Whilst this activity could be part of creating scenery for a play or large-scale display for the school the opportunities for individual learning tend to be limited. The other technique is making mosaics from small pieces of pre-cut paper, card or tile. There is some possibility for individual creativity in this depending on how it is planned but at worst it is simply filling in large areas with specified pieces to someone else's plan. Making a mosaic can be a worthwhile whole school project but should not take time away from art lessons unless the contribution to each child's learning in art can be identified.

Artists, craftspeople and designers who make collage

There are many examples of artists, designers and craftspeople using collage or collage techniques in their work. The technique of gluing papers onto surfaces was first named as collage in the early twentieth century when artists such as Picasso, Braque and Schwitters began to incorporate fabrics, paper, text, picture, wood and other materials into their paintings. Look for the work of Margaret Mellis (*Sobranie Collage*, 1942 and *Number Thirty Five*, 1983) in the Tate online catalogue. Matisse also used cutting and placing later in his life. *The Snail* is a frequently used example of this aspect of his work but look also for other examples of his use of the same technique to widen your and the children's experience.

LINK

In more recent times photographs and digital photography have been increasingly used by artists in collage or to make photomontages. The cover of the Beatles' *Sgt Pepper's* LP (by Peter Blake) is a very familiar example of using photos of people: collecting and arranging people who could not possibly be present together in the same room. David Hockney's use of polaroids of a landscape placed slightly separately in a grid pattern and photographs overlapping to make a large composite view are examples of the use of photos in collage. It is important to bear in mind that this is a difficult technique to allow children to explore on paper individually unless you are prepared to take and print many photos. It is something that could be explored digitally, perhaps.

There are some very accessible examples of the use of collage techniques in the illustrations for children's books. Polly Borland's illustrations for Lauren Child's retelling of *The Princess and the Pea* (Child and Borland, 2005) has three-dimensional dolls house room sets and two-dimensional collaged and drawn figures photographed to illustrate the story. Jeannie Baker's illustrations for several children's books including *Window* (1991) and *Where the Forest Meets the Sea* (1987) include the use of many natural materials to create detailed landscapes often with a theme of protecting the environment. Eric Carle uses collage constructed of papers that he has collected and used to make bold and brightly coloured illustrations for many stories familiar to younger children. There is an interesting video clip where he demonstrates how he works on his website.

LINK

Tony Cragg's work *Britain Seen from the North* demonstrates an interesting use of a collection of abandoned items arranged on a large scale within two outlines. Perhaps this could be described as a collage or perhaps a sculpture. Each item is attached to the wall within the outlines paying attention to the colour, size and texture overall. Whilst most schools will not have space for each child to work to this scale there could be scope for thinking about working collaboratively in a similar manner to create a large, temporary outdoor arrangement which can be photographed or a smaller-scale piece based on individually devised themes. Look up Susan Stockwell's collages, based on themes such as maps and money – these can seen on her website. Her work also moves into three dimensions using selected collaged paper to make dresses and other items.

> ### Find out more
>
> Find the Victoria and Albert Museum website. Enter the word 'collage' in the search.
> Browse the range of images of collage available, looking out for those that interest you in
> terms of technique or subject matter. Think about how these would relate to your teaching.
>
> **LINK**

Teaching collage

Collage techniques allow children to explore and make choices leading to personal creative outcomes. When planning for a successful learning experience there are some significant factors to consider:

- organisation of space and resources;
- the elements of the process.

In addition there are opportunities to:

- explore collage techniques in art;
- combine and mix media;
- make links to other curriculum areas.

These will be explored more fully later in this chapter.

Organisation of space and resources

As in any art lesson the organisation of space in the classroom and the resources required for each lesson or the unit of work is important to the overall manageability and success of the experience.

At the early stages of a collage unit of work when children are choosing from materials it will be necessary to consider where they will do this and how they will store their collections. It can be useful to have a named bag for each child into which they can put their choices – the size will depend on the materials available to choose from. This will allow each child to feel that their materials are safe and ready for the next stage and allow you to put most of the remainder away, perhaps keeping a smaller selection for further choices later.

The nature of the materials being used will also influence your organisation of resources. If natural materials are being used, for example, they might deteriorate quite quickly so pressing them or drying them could be appropriate. Alternatively you might compress the unit of work so that the materials are chosen and used quickly before they are spoiled.

At the sticking stage the glue to be used should be considered. Glues used in schools are washable but it is sensible to plan to avoid getting glue onto children, their clothes and the classroom. Teaching children how to use glue efficiently by, firstly, providing them with the right type of glue and tools to apply it and, secondly, covering them with aprons and the tables with paper will go a long way towards achieving this. In addition ensuring that collages can dry without sticking to each other and be available for further work where necessary is also important to work out in advance.

Case Study

A class of Year 5 and 6 children are planning individual collages to express their feelings and thoughts about a line of poetry that they have chosen for themselves. This will allow them to identify some words that evoke feelings, mental images or thoughts. The starting point is deliberately open to allow the children to choose from poems they know from school and those they have found themselves. As they research and begin to choose some children wish to include song lyrics and this idea is offered to all.

When they have identified their line of text they then begin to consider a personal and creative response using collage techniques. Their teacher reminds them of some different approaches, which they have encountered during earlier experiences of art, and tells them of some new ones. She encourages them to consider finding and using both 'real' and 'virtual' images and items initially before deciding whether to produce an onscreen collage, a paper-based collage or a mixture of the two.

For the purposes of organising their collection of images and material each child has a named bag in which to place real material and a named folder on the computer to save found images and images they have photographed or scanned for themselves. As part of their collection their teacher organises them to talk in pairs, giving each other a 'tour' of the material collected and discussing how it relates to the line of text and their personal response. This helps them articulate their choices and discard some materials as well as preventing them collecting at random or becoming too distracted.

In this case study older children are given a lot of freedom with the task that has been set. In order to keep the artwork on track the teacher provides some structure so that children do not lose sight of their ultimate aim. Children are also given the choice of collage techniques and materials, allowing for personal creativity so that their finished art is likely to be different from child to child. There is also a connection to English in that children are reading and choosing meaningful pieces of text and considering how words can evoke feelings and both abstract and representational images in the mind of the reader.

Stages of the process

When you are planning a unit of work involving collage it is important to consider the various parts of the technique so that you can identify how best to plan for and support children's learning. These include: collecting, selecting and discarding; cutting/tearing; placing and arranging; joining or attaching and developing. Depending on your plans these stages might be spread out in a series of lessons over half a term or combined within a shorter period of time. Each one will be explored more fully below:

Collecting, selecting, discarding

It will be important to plan for children to make some choices about what they will include in their collage and what they will choose not to include. This will be related to the overall unit of work. You could plan a limited choice – natural materials collected from a walk in the local area; pictures focused on a theme from magazines; materials with interesting textures, reflective and shiny properties or within one colour – or you could plan for a freer choice. The plans you make for this stage will relate to the resources available to you and the ideas you have for the outcome of the unit of work. Bear in mind that allowing choice at this stage could result in a more varied outcome and more opportunities for children to follow their own ideas rather than conform to a predetermined outcome. Providing children with a named bag or envelope in which to keep their chosen material is a useful way of organising at this stage.

Cutting or tearing

When using some materials children will have to reshape them to use them effectively in their collage work. Tearing papers of different types can result in varied and accidental edges that are more interesting than cut edges. When cutting you need to plan for adults to support in this area in order to help children avoid frustration. If the developing of cutting skills is not the main learning objective there is no reason why adults could not cut along lines drawn by children. Another factor to consider is the size – children will often draw shapes too small and intricate to realistically be cut out. This can be addressed by encouraging them to cut freehand without drawing, to think about the size of the shape being cut out and tearing.

Placing and arranging

This is a crucial stage in designing and making a collage and should not be hurried. The presence of glue will tend to short circuit the careful consideration and trying out needed for success at this stage. You can model the arranging and rearranging to try out different compositions so that children begin to understand that they can achieve different effects by placing next to, further away, overlapping or discarding altogether. At this stage it may also be necessary to select more or different things to use in the composition. The interplay between the background and what is being stuck to it should also be considered.

Joining or attaching

How you plan for children to join their collage together will depend on the materials used and the planned outcome. In some instances the outcome could be temporary and recorded by a photograph before being dismantled. When glue is used the type of glue and application technique should be right for the collage. When gluing flat onto large areas PVA or PVA diluted with water can be painted on the surface with a large brush or sponge paddle and items placed on it and pressed down. When gluing smaller items, or aiming for some parts to stick up or remain unattached, use a glue spreader, a small brush or a glue stick. Sellotape, masking tape, double-sided sticky tape and other types of attachment could also be considered.

Developing

It may be that the collage will be worked on in several lessons, developing and refining it. This is especially true when using collage techniques with older children who make more complex designs and are able to sustain attention on the same piece of work over a longer period of time. Collage is a particularly good opportunity to allow children to review and evaluate their work and suggest and make changes to improve and develop along the way.

It is advisable to make the teaching decisions about each of these stages at the medium-term planning stage so that you can build in choice, independence and time to make an individual response.

Exploring collage techniques in art

A variety of collage techniques can be explored by children working individually or working together in small or large groups. There are also opportunities for working on a range of scales and creating work that is permanent and more temporary collages perhaps similar to installations. When planning units of work based on exploring collage techniques there is much scope for giving children choices so that they can respond to starting points and express their own ideas.

Case Study

A class of Year 4 children are preparing to join in a whole school celebration of the Hindu festival of Diwali. They have been given the task of creating large rangoli patterns beside each entrance into the school. They have identified six entrances and the class has been divided into six groups of five. In the week approaching the festival the children research rangoli patterns online. They collect examples and look for the main features of the designs, finding that images from nature, including flowers, leaves, fish, birds and butterflies, are used, they are symmetrical patterns, they can be square, rectangular or circular, they are brighly coloured and made from all sorts of local and available materials.

Using this research as a basis each group evaluates their space and plans the appropriate size and shape to fit and then goes on to design the rangoli pattern itself. Intially they experiment with small-scale designs of the same proportion. The teacher and TA help with working out the proportion. When they have settled on a design they identify the materials that they will use to construct the collage. They can choose from items that are readily available in the classroom, natural materials from the school grounds and some scrap materals brought in by staff.

On the day of the Diwali celebrations each group takes their design and materials to their location and begin construction. They draw the design on the ground in outline and fill the spaces with the materials: some groups have chosen recycled paper and plastic materials of bright colours; others have chosen autumn leaves and seeds; and others have chosen fabrics. The finished rangoli patterns are varied and a step beyond chalk colourings often prevalent in schools at Diwali. As soon as the rangoli patterns are finished they are photographed so that each child can have a record of their group work in their sketchpad, annotated with their role and thoughts. Visitors to the school enjoy the varied rangoli patterns that greet them as they enter the school.

In this case study children design, select and place materials without sticking them down and the finished piece of art is temporary. The process of planning, design and construction is collaborative and allows children to connect their art to a celebration from a world religion. Since they are Key Stage 2 they are given more independence to lead the design and choice of materials whilst also paying attention to the main features traditionally expected in a rangoli pattern.

In contrast to this temporary and collaborative approach collage also offers scope for children to work individually following their own imaginative ideas. Because children can find and select existing images from a wide range of sources they can use them to create new and unexpected combinations and layouts. This can lend itself to images inspired by imagination and fantasy as well as leading to surreal and abstract work. Looking for images of items that do not usually fit together is a way of exploring this, as well as considering the scale of the chosen items in relation to each other or their location in unexpected contexts. Children can also cut images up and insert other images within them and around them to change and develop them.

There are a wide range of sources of visual material for this kind of collage. Pictures can be collected from magazines and newspapers; children can take their own photographs to use; online material can be used where appropriate. ICT tools can be supportive in this kind of activity, allowing children to work onscreen to manipulate images by resizing, stretching or changing colours and copy images so that they can repeat and change them in different ways. Pictures can be created on paper and onscreen, where they can then be projected large scale giving children another perspective on their effect.

Connect and extend

Find the Kurt Schwitters i-map animation on the Tate Gallery website (link below). Play the animation to find out more about Schwitters – his life and a particular collage *Opened by Customs* 1937–8.

Think about the ideas connect to your learning about teaching collage in the classroom – qualities of papers, the meaning that might be attached to come items, how items are positioned and overlapped and the part dull and bright colours play in the composition.

LINK

Combining and mixing media

There are opportunities to use collage techniques in combination with other aspects of the art curriculum to create mixed media pieces. This might be by using another technique such as drawing, painting or printmaking to create papers or backgrounds to use in making collages. It might be by adding collage detail to a drawing, painting, print or sculpture or using collaged material to work in relief or in three dimensions. Using digital media could also be used as part of these approaches.

Creating the papers which children will then go on to use to make collages can be a wonderful opportunity for children to freely experiment with techniques such as colour mixing in painting; printing using rollers with string tied around them; marbling; and many more. Experimenting with mark making and then photocopying the sheets, reducing and expanding them can result in some interesting papers to use in collage. When children work in this way they are collectively making the raw materials that the class will go on to use for their collages. There are several ways of organising this:

- materials could be saved from a unit of work on printmaking, drawing or painting;
- materials could be deliberately made during such a unit then kept to use in a later collage unit of work;
- creating the materials could be planned for the initial stage of the collage unit of work.

Having more varied materials to use to make collages can enhance the quality of the experience and help children make connections between different parts of the art curriculum and understand that techniques and processes can be combined to great effect. When combining two or more art techniques or processes in this way children can work over several stages, thinking about how they are going to develop their work rather than making a one-off. This connects us back to the need to support children in reviewing, evaluating and then developing their artwork unit of work.

Case Study

In a previous unit of work Year 1 children were experimenting with mark making. Early in the unit of work their teacher planned for them to make marks on a large scale to help them work more freely and feel less constricted. They worked in pairs using large wax crayons on A2 paper. Each pair made two sheets trying out a range of marks: one focused on clusters of small marks, flowing lines, patches made using the crayons sideways; the other took rubbings from flat surfaces around the immediate classroom.

When they had completed their large sheets they flooded them with washes made from Brusho (see Chapter 6) using large soft brushes and sponge paddles. The colour washes brought the mark making to life and made them stand out. Later in this unit of work the children went on to work individually developing their mark making into some drawings and the mark making experiment sheets were storied ready to use in the next unit of work based on collage.

In the collage unit of work children chose sections of their earlier sheets as backgrounds for their collages. Some children also cut shapes from the leftover parts of sheets to stick on to develop their background more fully. Later they went on to make imaginary creatures to add to the foreground of their collages in a contrasting style (using small 3D items and fabrics) so that the two techniques working together created an effect of distance and was more satisfying as a finished piece of work.

In the case study above planning ahead allowed a connection between one unit of work and another and enhanced the overall experience of the children. When working with older children they could have had more input into the process so that they could take more of a role in deciding on the processes or colours that they would use at a later date. An alternative is to make sure that spare pieces of paper used to experiment with are kept to use as and when appropriate.

As well as working in two dimensions, work with collage connections can be made to work in three dimensions. This is, in some instances, a part of collage, in that some sticking will involve adding texture to a flat surface and changing it from flat to more three-dimensional even if it is relatively shallow and close to the surface. Moving into making three-dimensional form using collage can be a logical next step to develop the technique.

One way of exploring this is for children to make a variety of collaged surfaces at the preparing and exploring stage of a unit of work – this could include any collage technique and may also go into rubbing and printmaking from collage textures. This material can then be used to create three-dimensional forms in various ways. Working with rigid sheets of card, forms can be made by cutting shapes and slotting them together. Working with flexible sheets, forms can be made by curving or wrapping them. Forms that hang suspended in the air like mobiles, hanging from sticks or rods, can also be made. Making any these forms can extend children towards thinking about how each side of their surface looks as well as the effect the qualities of materials have such as weight or transparency.

Making links to other curriculum areas

There is also scope to connect collage in art to learning within another subject area. Care should be taken when planning to do this. It is important for you to be clear about the art learning objectives and the learning objectives relating to the other subject (see Chapter 4).

Clearly the success of a link like this is dependent on the clarity of the planning and the ability to be flexible with use of time. It is important to consider the strength of the links and whether they support learning sufficiently within each subject area to make the additional organisation worthwhile.

Practical task

Making connections to another subject

Learning objective:

● to identify some connections between subjects that support learning in each one.

In this practical task you will consider the connections that can be made between a collage unit of work in art and a unit of work in another subject. The focus will be on being able to identify learning in art, in the other subject and how learning in each subject is enhanced by the connection being made.

What to do:

1. Read the brief description of the unit of work that connects art and English.
2. Identify learning in each subject in the pro forma below (and any other learning that may also occur).
3. Consider how learning is enhanced by the connections that are made.

The class is going to make up their own story based on *Too Much Talk* (Medearis and Vitale, 1995). The children explore the patterned language and repetitive structure of the story. They examine the illustrations which relate to the origins of the story in Ghana, West Africa. As a class they identify a new group of characters and a new sequence for their own story to follow, but retaining the African setting. The sequence is divided up so that smaller groups within the class can work on each part and these can later be joined together to make the whole story as a book and sequence of illustrations that can be shown on an IWB. The children all draw a version of the new main character in black pen and one is chosen that will be photocopied and used throughout the illustrations to provide continuity. A set of backgrounds are made for each group to use again to provide continuity throughout the story. The children have identified the patterns that frame each page and will be using this feature in their illustration. Each group produces one shared collage illustration to go with their section of the new story. These are scanned to display electronically and made into a shared story book to add to the book corner. The story is retold using the slides in a class assembly.

Learning in English	Learning in art	Any other learning?

Questions to consider

● *Learning in English*: There is potential for exploration of patterned and rhythmic language and deconstructing the structure of the story. The story is from Ghana so there is the potential to learn about traditional stories from another culture, perhaps identifying similarities and differences between other known stories. The strong pattern allows for a good model to use in making up the classes own retelling of an alternative story. This can allow for devising and writing new characters and a new sequence of events. Retelling the new story orally to an audience can allow children to develop their speaking skills.

- *Learning in art*: There is potential for identifying features in illustrations that children might go on to use in their own art – in this case: patterned borders, bright colours and strong patterns on clothes, and simple textured backgrounds. Children also create backgrounds using rubbing and ink washes. When making their collages they cut out, place and glue characters onto the backgrounds and add the new text they have written. They are also encouraged to add detail to increase interest when the illustrations are shown large on the IWB.

- *Other learning opportunities*: There is opportunity to develop positive group work as well as some use of ICT.

- *Enhancing learning*: You may have identified that learning was enhanced by this connection in that children could think about their story as a whole considering how illustrations can support and enrich a story. Often whilst working on the illustrations talk would be focused on the original story, the new version and the details of each. Going beyond writing a new version in their exercise books allowed them to create a satisfying and worthwhile book for their own library and share the story with an audience both through the book and the slides.

When making connections between collage in art and other curriculum areas it is important to keep a clear grasp on the learning in art or the activity or the art could become too illustrative of the other subject. An example of this might be collecting images of a variety of landscapes or weather in geography. If the images are collected, sorted and discussed to develop geographical knowledge, skills and understanding children are learning geography and the mere collection of the pictures does not necessarily contribute to their learning in art. If, however, children go on to make a collage landscape of their own based on an observed, researched or imaginary place they will be using materials to create something more personal, exploring colour, texture and space.

Conclusion

Collage is a versatile and varied area in which to create artwork. It builds on the enjoyment that younger children gain from choosing, cutting and sticking and can be developed into more sophisticated and thoughtful pieces of art by older children with more control over tools and materials and creative ideas. For some less confident children being able to choose, combine and manipulate 'ready-made' images can be supportive and engaging, allowing them to express their ideas and imagination.

As well as working within this technique collage techniques can enhance artwork in other media such as drawing, painting, printmaking or sculpture. There are strong links to other curriculum subjects and there is also scope for using ICT and moving into using digital media to create moving images by making simple animations.

Next steps

- Investigate your school library for examples of where illustrators use collage in their work.
- Find out how to make simple stop go animations – children can make collage backgrounds and characters to use in this process. Start by talking with the ICT co-ordinator.

References

Baker, J. (1987) *Where the forest meets the sea*. London: Walker Books.

Baker, J. (1991) *Window*. London: Random House.

Child, L. and Borland, P. (2005) *The Princess and the Pea*. London: Puffin.

Cox, S. and Watts, R. (eds) (2007) *Teaching Art and Design 3–11*. London: Continuum.

Medearis, A.S. and Vitale, S. (1995) *Too Much Talk*. London: Walker Books.

Further reading

Fenwick, L. (2009) 'Autobiographical montage project'. *STart*, Vol. 33, pp. 26–7.

Manie, A. (2008) *Collage in the Classroom*. London: A and C Black.

Dream Collages, p104 to p107 in:

Meager, N. (2006) *Creativity and Culture: Art Projects for Primary Schools*. Corsham: NSEAD.

Perkins, T. (2009) 'Cubism and still life'. *STart*, Vol. 33, pp. 28–9.

Wilford, A. (2010) 'Cubist collage'. *STart*, Vol. 35, pp. 10–11.

Web resources

The illustrations of Polly Borland for Lauren Child's 'The Princess and the Pea': *http://www.illustrationcupboard.com/artist.aspx?aId=199*

The illustrations of Jeannie Baker: *http://www.jeanniebaker.com/picture_books_index.htm*

An online interactive activity to explore Tony Cragg's work: *http://kids.tate.org.uk/create/make_a_collage.shtm*

Susan Stockwell's website: *http://www.susanstockwell.co.uk/archive.php*

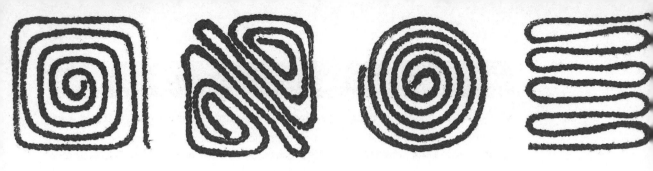

Chapter 10

Working in three dimensions

Introduction

Making art in three dimensions is a rewarding sensory and tactile experience for children. It is vital that children have opportunities to create art in three dimensions using a range of materials and techniques throughout their primary years. The experience itself is very different from that of working on a flat surface and can offer children who are less confident or less interested in drawing and painting a very different context within which to enjoy making art. In this chapter the following areas will be considered:

- Subject knowledge that underlies making
- Teaching children to use media to make in three dimensions

Opportunities for children to work in three dimensions in schools can sometimes be less frequent. Practical considerations such as space, time and cost of resources as well as lack of confidence or subject expertise on the part of teachers and teaching assistants can result in fewer units of work exploring and making art in three dimensions being planned. This can result not only in less experience of working in three dimensions but also encountering fewer processes because of the limited range available.

There are opportunities to connect some ways of working in three dimensions to learning in other aspects of art, such as collage and textiles. ICT can be used to support learning effectively especially when seeking to record temporary art work or the stages of development of a three-dimensional work. Inspiration can be found from learning in history, RE and geography.

There are connections between design technology and creating art in three dimensions. It is important to be aware of the differences between these subjects so that every three-dimensional experience is not focused on an outcome that is mainly within design technology. When working in three dimensions in art there may be less focus on making a useful finished object and more significance placed on making to satisfy a creative urge. In design technology the outcome will have a purpose or function.

Subject knowledge that underlies the teaching of making art in dimensions

Developing some subject knowledge about different ways of working in three dimensions will underpin successful planning, teaching and support. Some aspects that you may need to learn about are:

- tools and materials;
- visual elements that can be taught and developed effectively;
- vocabulary to use;
- media and techniques;
- the work of artists, craftspeople and designers.

You may find it useful to explore the definition of 'sculpture' and consider the range of materials that could be used.

Find out more

What is sculpture?

Explore the activity 'Sculpturama' on the Artisan Cam website. Find this listed under 'activities'. These resources can help you develop your subject knowledge and widen your understanding of sculpture and how it is made.

LINK

Explore the Tate Tools Module called 'sculpture and installation'. Reading, thinking about and responding to the ideas and subject knowledge presented in this module can support your own subject knowledge as well as give you ideas for sculptors' work to explore and starting points for making sculpture with your class.

LINK

Tools and materials

Storage of three-dimensional materials may pose more of a challenge than two-dimensional materials. You may find that some materials must be ordered in advance: using the long- or medium-term plan can help you identify when materials are required. Some materials can be collected from children's homes or local environments: again some planning ahead may be needed to ensure that you collect sufficient materials in time for the unit of work. Using materials from a local scrapstore can also be useful (see Chapter 9).

As well as the materials listed in Appendix 1 found natural materials can also be used to create sculpture. These include leaves, flowers, twigs, seed heads, grasses, shells, stones and many more. These can be collected by the children themselves and brought into school for a particular project or they may be collected on site and used immediately. Teaching children about collecting natural materials whilst showing care for the natural environment and habitats should be considered before setting this task.

ICT and digital media can support adults and children in recording the progress of three-dimensional work, recording it from different viewpoints and preserving it long after it has been taken home or removed. It can also be used as part of making environments and installations by projecting onto the IWB or a screen.

Practical task

Learning objective:

● to explore the qualities of malleable materials.

In this practical activity you will use malleable material to explore what you can do with it and how it can be used with children.

You will need:

● A fist sized amount of a malleable material such as salt dough, plasticine, clay or play dough. If you have more than one of these it could be useful to try out the activity with each and compare the different qualities.

What to do:

1. Roll your lump around to make a rounded sphere shape. Stick both thumbs into it to make a thumb pot shape. Move your thumbs around the edges making your pot larger and the sides thinner.

2. Roll your lump into some sausage shapes, rolling them thinner and thinner. Coil these around to make a cylinder shape on a round base.

3. Flatten your lump and roll it using a rolling pin or other cylindrical roller. Cut five square shapes from it and join them to make a cube with an open top.

4. Roll your lump out again into a round or square shape about 2 cm thick, make marks in it and press things into it to make marks and shapes. Reroll it and draw into it.

It can be a good idea to try each of these several times as you will get better at each and as you do this you can begin to identify teaching tips and suggestions to help children when you teach them these techniques.

LINK

Questions to consider

- *Thumb pot*: You may have found that it requires a fair amount of fine motor control to stick your thumbs in far enough to make a good hole and not so far that you go through to the bottom of the lump and out the other side. Continuing on to press just enough to enlarge the hole and make the sides of the form thinner can also be a challenge, especially for children.

- *Coil pot*: You may have found that making evenly sized coils got easier as you practised. Being able to pick them up and form them into a three-dimensional form also takes some care. It can be useful to have a form to guide you such as a box or roll of card.

- *Slab pot:* You may have found that rolling so that the material is of an even depth all over can be hard and picking each piece up to join as you make a form can test your fine motor control. Exploring the thickness of the material in relation to the size of piece to be cut and joined can help here.

- *Relief surface:* You may have found yourself experimenting with how deep you press into the surface of the material before going through it.

- *General questions:* If you were able to try these activities out with several of the materials you will have been able to consider the differences between them and the implications for teaching and learning. It is easier to manipulate and control some materials, whereas others can be harder to manipulate but tougher and able to withstand rougher treatment. You might also consider having some of these materials around for children to play with freely in order to develop their skills and practise especially in the lead up to a unit of work where children will be using them as part of their art work. When making the three-dimensional forms you were aiming to make them solid so that they could stand up securely – perhaps the thickness of the material, the base you used and how you joined the materials affected the solidity with which the forms stood.

In the task above you tried a few basic ways of using malleable materials to make three-dimensional forms. These can be used in combinations to make more ambitious forms: joining two thumb posts could make a spherical or egg shape which can be cut through to reveal the inside or have parts attached to make handles, legs or other features;

coil and slab pots can be made around any base shape. If you are going to teach these to children they must have the chance to practise and improve their skills before making their final piece of art.

Opportunities for teaching visual elements through working in three dimensions

The chart below makes suggestions in relation to each of the eight visual elements when using a range of materials: some of these are applicable to many materials and others are more focused on one particular material: these are indicated in brackets after each suggestion. When you are planning and teaching a unit of work that involves working in three dimensions it is important to identify one or two visual elements that you will develop with the children; it is likely that this will have been done at the long term planning stage. The elements that will be most readily explored will depend upon the materials you are using for the experiences that you plan.

Line	Tone
Mark making and drawing into the material with tools Using coils and strips of the material Using linear materials that can be shaped Using straight linear materials to create a framework (sticks)	Using lighter/darker or contrasting tone (buff/red clay) Using various tones of the material Decorating the form with tones of same/different colours
Colour	**Pattern**
Using various colours of the material Using glazes (clay) Painting on the material Using colours of paper, card, fabric over a framework or on a mould	Applying surface decoration on the material before or after construction Constructing the material in a patterned structure Placing materials/objects to create a pattern in space
Texture	**Shape**
Pressing into soft materials to create surface texture Choosing materials for their texture – contrasting or complementary	Creating 3D shapes (regular/irregular; solid/hollow; using frameworks; wrapping or draping;) Using 2D shapes to decorate the surface
Space	**Form**
Cutting away to reveal inside space, see through the form Placing several forms together Making forms which define/contain space Using space to arrange within – installation Changing how natural materials are distributed in a space Placing objects of made forms in order to change the way we see them	Building up forms from coils, slabs or hollowing out Constructing forms from sticks, withies Building up forms by using a mould Draping and wrapping forms to change them Placing 3D objects in an environment Creating an installation that can be entered and experienced

Form and space are the key visual elements that are intrinsic to working in three-dimensions. The potential for learning about and exploring these will depend on the materials and outcome that you are planning on: clay will provide a very different experience to that of using withies, for example. Children should encounter a variety of materials to explore these elements during the primary years. It is likely that other visual elements will be part of the experience especially when decoration is part of the creation of the outcome.

Key vocabulary

When you plan a unit of work using three-dimensional materials it is important to identify any words that will be used: these might be entirely new; familiar but used in a different context; or an opportunity to consolidate and re-enforce words. Vocabulary could be considered in relation to the visual elements that underlie the planned learning (see Chapter 2 for discussion of vocabulary relating to form and space) and also in relation to the materials being used and their properties or qualities.

Practical task

Learning objective:

- to explore the vocabulary relating to some three dimensional materials

In this practical task you will consider some of the most commonly used materials and identify some of the relevant vocabulary you might expect to plan for children to develop and use. You may wish to reread the section about visual elements in Chapter 2 before completing this exercise. Looking at a unit of work where you have used the materials or thinking back to activities you have supported or taught could also be helpful.

You will need:

- The pro forma below and any plans relating to working in three dimensions that are available.

What to do:

- Consider each material/activity and identify some key vocabulary that you think you would be able to introduce or consolidate. Note down the words into the sections: visual element, material, activity.

Material / activity	Vocabulary		
	Visual element	Material/qualities	Activity
1. A malleable material such as clay, play dough, salt dough or plasticine being used to make an animal.			

Material / activity	Vocabulary		
	Visual element	Material/qualities	Activity
2. Sheet materials being placed over a mould such as paper and paste around a jar to create a cylindrical shaped container.			
3. A collection of natural materials from the immediate environment such as stones and sticks being arranged on grass.			

Guidance notes

- In activity 1 it is likely that you have identified exploring the form that can be created by manipulating the clay. In addition to this children could also be exploring how to make regular and irregular shapes as well as adding texture or pattern to the surface of the clay. When talking about the qualities of the material younger children could be using words such as soft and squashy, whilst older children could be using words such as flexible or malleable to describe the way the materials can be manipulated. When using the material to make an animal they could focus on words related to the animal including describing its form and how this could be made by rolling, hollowing out and joining, as well as how it can be decorated by mark making to create textures or patterns or by smoothing the surface.

- In activity 2 it is likely that you have identified form where the child is creating a new form by applying paper and glue to the chosen container. Texture may also be discussed especially where the aim is to make a smooth surface to decorate later, when colour and pattern might also be relevant. When talking about the qualities of the materials, words such as slimy, wet, thick and slippery can be used to describe the paste. The contrast between the smooth, hard surface of the container might be described. The flexibility of the gluey paper can be explored as well as the changes that occur when the paste dries leaving a hard surface. Within this activity vocabulary relating to creating a smooth surface, overlapping strips and pieces of paper can be explored as well as words relating to any decoration that will be added later.

- In activity 3 it is likely that you have identified space as children arrange and rearrange their chosen items; as well as one or more of form, shape, colour and texture as children collect, evaluate and choose natural materials based on their visual and tactile qualities. When arranging their chosen materials space and pattern may also be important depending on what criteria they choose to base their arrangements on. Given the openness of this activity there may be a greater range of individual responses that each relate to different visual elements. Talking to children about their choices and arrangements will be crucial to understanding what has inspired and influenced their response and outcome. In addition positional vocabulary will be used to identify and describe where items are in relation to each other and how space has been used.

When working with three-dimensional materials there are many opportunities to develop a range of vocabulary in practical situations and these can be especially supportive for children learning English as an Additional Language and children with an IEP target relating to language development.

Media and processes

The media and processes you might use when exploring art made in three dimensions are varied and dependent on the material being used. As with any art technique or material it is vital that the adults teaching and supporting learning know enough about the material and how to use if to explore and make in art. This may appear more daunting because of the range of materials available and the factors such as the cost of resources, the need for specialist equipment or tools and the space required for storage of materials, work in progress and finished work. It is vital to overcome any anxieties and allow children to have these opportunities for learning rather than restrict them mainly to two-dimensional materials. There are some children who enjoy the making process, who achieve more and feel happier and are more confident in these areas than when they are holding a pencil or paintbrush.

The chart below suggests some techniques that children can be taught and how these might be explored in making finished outcomes.

Materials	Techniques	Ideas
Materials that can be manipulated and moulded (clay, plasticine, salt dough, play dough, Fimo, etc)	Rolling out to make a flat surface to work on Rolling out flat and constructing slabs into forms Hollowing out (thumb pot) Constructing from coils Shaping into forms (small scale)	Make clay tiles, shapes or hanging plaques Make cylinders, box shapes, buildings, wrap around card to make a hollow body for a creature Make pots, bowls, bodies of creatures, rounded hollow forms including spheres
Pouring and casting (plaster of Paris, papier-mâché)	Creating or finding a surface/mould to take a cast from Pouring into the mould Pressing papier-mâché onto the surface	Find interesting textures in the environment to take casts from Make a surface to mould from by collecting and sticking material onto a surface (2D/3D) Use a mould (bowl, plate, jar) as a basis for the shape
Linear materials (wire, sticks, straws, withies, rolled paper)	Bending, twisting, shaping wire Rolled newspaper tubes and cylinders joined to make forms Flexing withies and joining them into the chosen form with tape, string Placing and joining sticks and straws with wire or tape to hold their form	Make a figurative form (fish, leaf) and extend from there Make an abstract form exploring the shapes that can be made (curved/linear) Make a framework with an inside and outside or views through Make a curved framework from card strips to form the basis of a mask or face

(ctd)

Materials	Techniques	Ideas
Sheet materials (paper, paper lamination, modroc, fabric)	Drape over linear forms (wire, withies, sticks, rolled newpaper) Wrap around hollow forms (boxes) Stretch between (poles, sticks, fences, floor to ceiling) Create holes by tearing, cutting	Build on the ideas above Fully enclose or cover the shapes and forms Leave spaces to look through so both inside and outside can be seen or entered
Natural/manmade found materials	Collect and rearrange within the existing environment Place found or made objects together in groups	Make subtle alterations to the landscape by collecting and placing Collect and arrange manmade and familiar objects for a personal purpose or to suggest an idea or feeling

Exploring and making with the materials before you plan, teach and support is vital as this first-hand experience will allow you to identify how you can plan for learning, suggest ways of overcoming any challenges and plan effective and worthwhile experiences. In addition to this there are many resources available to support the development of your subject knowledge and confidence when using three-dimensional materials and some of the most readily accessible are online. One site to start with is called Artisan Cam. This website has some short video clips that explore different types of sculpture showing different stages of the process of using them to make sculpture: the provide useful background information tips as well as teaching ideas. Look under both sculpture and ceramics to explore clay and a range of other sculptural materials.

Another way of gaining some confidence and expertise is to take any opportunities available at local museums, galleries, parks or craft fairs. Workshops and open days are frequently held with artists and craftspeople demonstrating or talking about their work as well as providing opportunities for you to have a go and learn new techniques. There may also be members of staff, governors or people in your local community who carve wood, make pottery or work in other three-dimensional areas whose expertise you can call upon.

Artists, craftspeople and designers working in three dimensions

There are usually a few, sometimes many, examples of sculpture or three-dimensional art available to look at in the local environment. Public sculptures have been installed for different purposes over time and more recently this has become even more common. You may find a sculpture park nearby or a sculpture trail that has been set up temporarily or permanently. If there are several sculptures nearby you could create your own sculpture trail identifying some background information, questions and starting points to support learning in relation to each sculpture or, with older children, help them to do this. It is vital that children can see and explore original sculptures at first hand; given the sensory and tactile nature of sculpture as well as the significance of the scale of a sculpture and the space around it, looking at a photograph or image on a screen can rarely convey the qualities and impact effectively.

Case Study

A group of initial teacher training students are organised into threes and allocated a sculpture from the campus to use as a focus for talking about art and inspiring the making of art in the primary-age range. Before they consider their sculpture they discuss, as a group, the essential areas to include. They identify the following areas:

- Who made the sculpture? Information about the sculptor and his or her work.

- How was the sculpture made? The materials, tools and techniques used by the sculptor.

- What do you notice, think and feel about the sculpture? A personal response to the sculpture after looking at from all viewpoints, feeling and talking about it.

- How might this inspire your own making of sculpture? A connection to the children's own ideas and practical art work.

Having this framework allows the groups of students to work independently but develop a consistent approach to use as a sculpture trail. They are also challenged to include two levels so that their material can be used by younger and older children within the primary-age group. Although their trail is focused on some specific sculpture their learning and the approach can be applied to sculptures near their placement schools or first jobs.

When you are researching sculptures or sculptors that you can use to inspire and support learning you may need to know more about the types of material sculptors use; some of these would not available to use in school. The list below identifies some materials you might encounter when looking at sculptures outdoors and in galleries and museums:

- metal – bronze sculptures are often cast from a mould, or sometimes made from pieces of metal welded together. Other types of metal can also be used to make sculpture.

- Marble is a type of limestone rock that can be carved into a sculpture. Other types of stone can also be carved.

- wood can be carved into a sculpture and/or pieces of wood can joined.

- terracotta can be made into relief or sculptural forms and then fired without glazing.

- ivory from animals' tusks and teeth has in the past been carved to make sculpture. More recently attitudes towards the use of ivory have changed.

- concrete can be cast and/or carved.

- fibreglass can be used to cast into forms and then decorated. It is hardwearing and light.

Whilst it is unlikely that primary-aged children will make sculptures using these materials they can see them and learn about them when exploring sculpture and sculptors.

It can be interesting to give children a sense of how sculptors work. It is important to convey that sculptures do not spring to life fully formed but are the result of research, inspiration and hard often very physical work. When an artist makes a sculpture, especially if it is going to be large scale, they often make a maquette – a small scale model to show what the sculpture will be like, before the full-size sculpture is made, often by other specialists in the material and technique. Looking up Henry Moore's 'Maquette Studio' at Perry Green on the internet can allow children to have an insight into the work that goes on underlying the finished sculpture.

 LINK

Exploring Anish Kapoor's website to see pictures of his studio can convey the sheer size, scale and extent of his work.

LINK

If it is not possible to plan for children to meet and talk or work with a sculptor there are some very good short films of contemporary artists making sculpture on the Artisan Cam website. These include Antony Gormley, whose work tends to be inspired by the human form, and Mike Eden, a potter who makes and decorates unusual shaped forms in clay. 'Andy Goldsworthy' an artists whose work is based in and inspired by the natural environment, is also featured and watching these sequences will give you an insight into why and how this art is made. It is important for you to know and plan to teach children that there is more to the work of artists who work in this way than merely collecting and arranging natural materials. One sculptor whose works are environmental is Richard Long. Some of his art also uses words in a way that could allow you to make a meaningful link to English.

You can also consider the inspiration or purpose for the sculpture. Perhaps it was to commemorate a local or national figure, event or occupation; it may have been to provide a focal point or enhance a public space or it could have been to provoke or please viewers. People's feelings about a piece of sculpture in their locality change over time and it can be interesting to consider the range of responses a piece of public art can inspire.

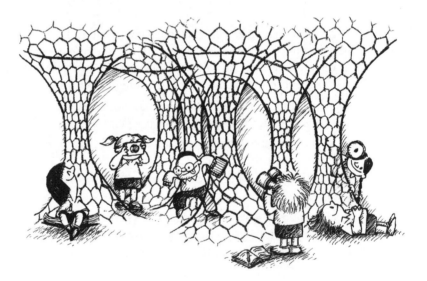

Over time it is important to introduce children to different types of sculpture made from a variety of materials and in different styles. Think about looking at both figurative and more abstract sculptures so that children can learn about the changes in approach to sculpture and the range of possibilities there are for making three-dimensional forms and using space. Sometimes a more abstract piece of sculpture will inspire more open discussion and speculation about the artists' intentions and the response from the viewer.

In addition to creating separate forms some artists work in three dimensions by making installations. An installation is the transformation of a space, often temporarily, in a particular location either inside or outside. Look at the work of Rebecca Chesney on the Artisan Cam website to find out more about an artist creating an outdoor maze – it is interesting to hear about her reasons for creating temporary work, choosing the materials she used and giving the work a title. Search also for Greyworld, a group of artists who create installations in urban spaces. On their website click on 'public art' and then scroll down to 'worldbench' to read about an installation that connects schools around the world.

Find out more

...about how artists make sculptures by exploring:

- 'sculptural techniques' on the V&A website where there is information about casting, carving, modelling and surface decoration;

LINK

- 'sculpture/construction' in the glossary of the Tate schools online resources part of the website;

LINK

- 'Greyworld' website.

LINK

Teaching sculpture and three dimensional work

The various materials that allow children to work in three-dimensional techniques present a unique opportunity to create. When planning for a successful learning experience there are some significant factors to consider:

- organisation of space and resources;
- use of tools and materials.

In addition there are opportunities to:

- work in relief and three dimensions;
- making connections to other aspects of art.

Organisation of space and resources

Three-dimensional art works may present challenges when you are organising space and resources in the primary classroom. This will depend on the size of the space available to you. It is important to consider how work in progress will be stored, how finished work will be shared and/or displayed and how time can be organised effectively.

When you are considering how to store incomplete artwork any special requirements of the material will be vital. Half-finished clay work, for example, will need to be stored in a damp airtight container so that it is still malleable enough to continue using. Other materials, especially fragile materials, may need a space where they will not be squashed or knocked over. Some materials will have characteristics that mean that they need to be used to make the work in one session without stopping and others allow work over several sessions with no detrimental effects.

Being flexible about your use of time can be helpful in addressing the considerations outline above. If you are planning to work with a material where the making experience will be most successful when accomplished in one session, but you usually have an art lesson only once a week, you might be able to bring forward the time from the following week so that the class has all morning or all afternoon to work continuously. Identifying the most effective use of time at the planning stage can help you allocate it to support learning throughout your unit – an equal amount of time each week may not be the most supportive for learning when working in three dimensions. When working with older children, building in short periods in which to stop, reflect and evaluate is also important to plan for. For some types of three-dimensional work working outside might be the best choice, or perhaps working offsite. The weather and the temporary nature of the outcomes will then need to be considered.

It is also important to plan ahead for how the finished outcomes will be shared, displayed and recorded. A different kind of space is needed to display three-dimensional art: small individual pieces can be arranged on shelves or cupboard tops at different heights. It can give a sense of completion if each child makes a label identifying the name, title and material used to display with their art, as in an art gallery. Large-scale, collaborative and installation art could be displayed temporarily inside or outside whilst children and parents look at it or more permanently if space of the appropriate kind is available. Recording the artwork perhaps by taking several photos from different angles or taking a short video moving all around the sculpture can record the finished work without having to store it indefinitely.

Use of tools and materials

Since children might have few and less regular opportunities to work in three-dimensions in art, it may take longer for them to recall the knowledge, skills and understanding from prior experience. Some materials and associated tools may only be used as one-offs or used very occasionally in the primary years especially, for example, if they are part of special project or work with an artist in residence.

At the planning stage it is important to identify any knowledge, skills and understanding that children need to build on in order to be successful in the new learning experiences that you are planning. It may be that prior experiences took place so long ago that it would be unrealistic to expect children to have retained them. Building in additional time to play with and freely explore the material and associated tools will be important to the effectiveness of your planning and the success of the children's learning. Observing children working with the materials as they use them freely will give you an insight into their prior knowledge and inform your planning, teaching and support in the rest of the unit. With older children you might identify some of the prerequisite skills and challenge children to try these out as a lead in to your planned new learning.

If possible within your classroom organisation, and the organisation of the curriculum, planning regular opportunities to play with and create with three-dimensional materials will allow children to maintain and develop their skills. Having play dough or plasticine available, for example, will support children's use of clay. Whilst a range of materials are often more readily and frequently available in Early Years classrooms and may continue into Key Stage 1 there are fewer opportunities for older children who have the fine motor skills to make more varied and intricate models, possibly leading to stop–go animation using IT.

Another aspect of working with the variety of materials that can be used to make three-dimensional art is the consideration you must give to health and safety. When using materials such as clay, plaster of Paris or withies, it is vital that all the adults working with the children, and the children themselves, use the associated tools and materials with care for their own and others' safety. It is good practice to note the steps you are taking on the plans and essential that all staff know about these when teaching or supporting children. Advice is often present on the packaging of materials as well as on the NSEAD website.

There are many starting points that can inspire the making of three-dimensional forms and the use of space in art and the long term planning should ensure that children encounter a variety of these. Productive and meaningful links can be made with other areas of the curriculum, such as looking at artefacts made in the past (history and RE), exploring and using the environment (geography), and using stories and poetry (English).

Work in relief and three dimensions

Relief

As well as creating artwork that is free standing and can be seen from all around, artwork can also be created in relief: texture or images that cut into or stick up from a flat surface. Making relief forms can be similar to and a development from some of the collage techniques discussed in the previous chapter. When a sculptor creates a relief this could be through adding to the flat surface to lift up parts of the surface or it could be by taking away from the flat surface to leave some parts higher depending on the material being used. Reliefs can be explorations of texture, decorative patterns, figurative designs telling a story or depicting a person or could be entirely abstract.

When adding to a flat surface children might be using collage bits and pieces, card and paper to create some raised elements before layering paper and paste over and pressing this in around the raised areas so that they are covered smoothly. A similar approach can be employed using sheets of modroc over a surface which has been prepared. Rolling out thin layers of salt dough or clay and cutting shapes from them and then placing them or fixing them to a flat surface can be another approach.

Case Study

A class of Y6 children have been making careful observations of the surface of shells, rocks and stones using magnifying glasses and microcopes. They have made drawings and collected close up photographs and have focused on the textures and patterns. It is clear from their sketches and notes that some surfaces exhibit more random features and others have more patterned elements. All the surfaces they take a closer look at are more interesting and varied than they first appear when investigated in depth.

Following their research each child makes a relief plaque based on the texture and pattern they have observed, aiming to expand and exaggerate the texture so it can felt more readily than when part of a very small object. The children are shown two rechniques for making their relief: using plaster and casting; and using paper lamination to cover the surface with flat sheets of tissue soaked in wall paper paste. They can choose which they want to use depending on the effect they would like to achieve.

> Children who have chosen to cast with plaster work on shallow card/plastic trays using thread and different thicknesses of string; seeds and pulses; paper and card; and other found and collected materials to create a raised surface. Children who have chosen paper lamination work on a thick card base that they have cut to the shape they choose.
>
> When the relief plaques are cast or covered and dry they are all varnished and mounted on a wall inside the school so that children and adults can enjoy the sensory experience of feeling them as well as looking at them.

In the case study above the emphasis is on creating a textural form in relief that can be touched as well as looked at. Each child has designed and made their relief shape and these have been combined in a display to make a collection. Another approach might have been to challenge children to work on a large-scale collaborative piece which would have required them to plan, explain and negotiate how to use the larger space.

Reliefs can also be figurative, perhaps representing single simple shapes (fish, leaves), a scene from a story, a real or imagined person, a creature or a building from observation or research. Tiles or shaped plaques can be created and holes cut through. When working with older pupils more control over tools and materials is likely to result in more detailed and complex result than when younger pupils are using this technique.

Organising a class, a year group or even the whole school to each make a small piece which becomes part of a greater whole can be a great way of creating something long lasting to display in the school. Alternatively, building in this kind of activity for each Year 6 class to do and add them to those made by previous Year 6s can be a pleasing commemorative activity to mark their time at the school. It is important to ensure that, although there may be a unifying theme such as technique, process, colour range or shape, there is still some opportunity for individual creative response.

Three-dimensions

Art that is created in relief can also be transformed into something more three-dimensional by changing it into something that can either be hung or stood up. Curling a rectangular relief around into a cylindrical form for example, or creating two pieces of identical size and shape then hanging them so viewers can look at each side. When this is part of the outcome it gives children the opportunity to consider what the viewer of the sculpture will see from a variety of viewpoints rather than just looking at the one view of the relief surface.

Case Study

Year 2 children have previously explored mark making into a malleable surface. They are familiar with using play dough and plasticiine and early in the unit of work they have been given the opprtunity to use wooden tools to make marks in the surface so they can practise the sorts of possible marks they might use when working with clay. They have also collected some found items from around the classroom that make interesting textures and patterns when pressed into the surface. The children have been taught how to use wooden guides and a roller to make a smooth surface of an even depth to make marks into.

In the middle of the unit of work the children have developed a design by working a rectangular piece of paper of the same size of clay that they will use for the finished piece. They can also pick up and reshape the paper into a cylinder so that they can have a look at the design in three dimensions as well as when working in relief. Their teacher has encouraged them to think about the marks made at the right and left edges of the rectangle so that the place where it curls round and joins might be disguised.

When the children make their rectangular reliefs some designs are random explorations of marks and textures; some are repeating patterns and some have figurative elements created from the combinations of marks and textures. Some children have deliberately planned for continuous marks that join when the relief is rolled into a cylinder and others are more interested in the free mark-making experience.

They are supported in changing their relief into a cylindrical shape using card shapes to give them stability at first. Help is also needed to make sure that the marks and textures do not get smoothed over or squashed during this process. Later the clay cylinders are fired and the children can consider the change from malleable material to hard surface.

If this unit of work was carried out with older children more could be expected of them in terms of designing a pattern or image that 'joins up' when the left and right edges are joined. As well as mark making and pressing into the clay surface they might also draw and cut additional thin layers of clay in shapes to attach to the surface. These activities would work with air drying clay which does not need firing but would be more fragile and have a somewhat different finished result when dry.

When we plan for children to make sculpture and other three-dimensional forms in art we must ensure that we teach the necessary techniques so that children can use these to create their own outcome. At the early stages of a unit of work some time must be spent on learning or developing the required skills. It may be possible to build on prior experience of the material and related techniques or these could be entirely new. Connections could perhaps be made to the experience of using materials, tools and techniques in design technology and science.

At these early stages it is important to demonstrate techniques and skills clearly and give children opportunities to try these out, practice and improve. Working on a smaller scale, in pairs or with more 'throwaway' materials can be useful as children will feel under less pressure to achieve their final outcome immediately.

Work on a larger scale

When working in three dimensions children should also have the opportunity to create three-dimensional forms in space not just on a small scale but in a range of scales and situations. Although small individual pieces can be combined to make a greater whole, such as when making tiles, making one very large sculpture or installation is an exciting experience with different learning opportunities. Planning for the large-scale experience to be temporary and perhaps outside, either on or off site, can be a useful way of addressing concerns about space in the classroom.

It may be that younger children have the opportunity to move and change forms in space more often than older pupils because they are likely to have access to role play indoors and outdoor play. In the outdoor context children will spontaneously make collections of natural materials such as leaves, flowers, seed heads and sticks, arranging them in space in random and decorative arrangements. Older children can be given this opportunity but with teaching and time to think and experiment can work with more intention and subtlety. It is important for developing learning that when this kind of activity is planned as part of the art curriculum that learning is extended beyond simply finding and placing, that it challenges children to articulate why they have made the choices they have made and how this relates to form, space and other visual elements such as shape, colour, texture and pattern. Using the video clips of artist who work in this way from the Artisan Cam website can support this.

LINK

A next step for older children can be to make installations leading to a bigger and more purposeful investigation of form, space and viewpoints. In the context of a unit of work this might include learning about what an installation is; researching outdoor/indoor installations and information about the artists who created them; making some mini-installations with junk materials, found objects and small world toys; and leading to designing a large-scale, collaborative and temporary installation in the school grounds. This can result in an event where other children and parents come and experience the installation before it is removed giving a sense of creating for an audience and getting feedback from them.

Case Study

Year 5 pupils base a temporary outdoor installation on the maze installation made by Rebecca Chesney (watch the videoclips about this on Artisan Cam). In Rebecca's work a temporary maze is created using translucent plastic and wooden frameworks.

The Year 5 pupils work in pairs outside around the school site using large sheets of plastic. They choose places to either hang or stretch the plastic and then cut shapes into the plastic so that part of what is behind is revealed. Before using the plastic they use large sheets of newspaper to experiment with what can be seen through and what is covered up. Some children place their sheet suspended over the ground between four sticks. Others consider the views through standing on either side of their sheet. The use of various size holes allows children to focus the viewer on an aspect of the environment they might otherwise have missed or have stopped looking at as it is so familiar.

When their installation is complete children photograph their own installation and write an explanation of it to record their reflections on the process and outcome. They share it with other children and parents where they can observe the reaction of an audience and talk with them about the choices they made, acting as curators of their exhibition. After this the installation is removed.

LINK

In this case study children work together and create a large-scale and temporary work that allows them to explore space and viewpoints as well as share their work with an audience. Another approach to scale might be to trick the viewer by making a relatively small form or maquette and placing model people or animals near it and photographing or filming it. When displayed on the IWB this can allow children get a sense of what their sculpture would look like when made on a large scale. Photographing or filming it against a photo of a local scene or the playground could also be fun.

Making connections to other aspects of art

When planning opportunities to work in three dimensions, connections can be made to other areas of learning in art. Painting can be used to decorate; drawing, painting and prints can be cut, folded and reformed into three-dimensional objects; collage can easily move into work in three dimensions depending on the materials chosen and how they are attached. In the task below the connections between using threads, fabric and textiles to make three dimensional forms are explored.

Practical task

Working in three-dimensions using threads, fabrics and textiles

Learning objective:

● to consider how to work in three dimensions in the context of another area of art.

In this practical task you will explore the connections between using threads, fabrics and textiles and working in three dimensions. This will give you the opportunity to think about how learning can be enhanced and developed: consider especially how children might explore and learn about the visual elements of form and shape as well as texture.

What to do:

● identify a suggestion for a learning outcome or experience to go in each of the boxes below.

	Working in three dimensions
Threading, tying	
Weaving	
Surface decoration on textiles (drawing, painting, printmaking, stitching)	
Sewing and stitching fabrics together	

Guidance notes

● *Threading/tying*: You might have considered making threadings on single or multiple strings that hang from the ceiling, a pole or a tree branch. This could include threading small pieces of fabric onto a long thread, suspending long strips of fabric that have had material sewn onto them or sewing around a fabric shape that is then hung. Suspending long strips could allow children to walk through their hangings and feel their different qualities.

● *Weaving*: You might have suggested weaving around a basket or inverted pyramid shape, weaving on flat panels that are then joined to make three-dimensional shapes (wigwam, cube) or weaving around a cylindrical shape.

● *Surface decoration (drawing, painting, printmaking, stitching)*: You might have thought about decorating fabric to drape over a framework, hang as a banner or suspend from the ceiling from all corners. This could be an opportunity to work in large scale to make hollow forms that can lead to the exploration of being inside and outside of a space.

● *Sewing and stitching fabrics together*: This could include making flat shapes to sew together and stuff. At its simplest this might be two identical shapes that are sewn around the edge and then stuffed. With older children this might be using more shapes together to make free standing or hanging stuffed forms such as balls, pyramids or cubes constructed from flat shapes.

In this practical task the idea of using threads, fabrics and textiles whilst also working in three dimensions was explored. This provides an opportunity to plan for children to explore the challenges of working in three dimensions – an area often less apparent in the primary art curriculum. Using form and space along with other visual and tactile elements in this context can allow children to build on, develop and apply their knowledge, skills and understanding.

Connect and extend

Read Victoria Pavlou's article ' Understanding young children's three-dimensional creative potential in art making' published in the *International Journal of Art and Design Education* in 2009 (Vol. 28, No. 2, pp. 139–50). Think about how the learning experiences of the five- and six-year-olds outlined could help you in your practice – especially when planning for older children.

Conclusion

Working in three dimensions in art is an exciting experience for children and as such must be included in any sequence of unit of work. It offers scope for creativity and sensory experience and may engage some children who are less attracted to working in two dimensions. Although it might pose challenges to us in relation to our subject knowledge and organisational skills the enjoyment and learning opportunities should give us the impetus to overcome these challenges and ensure that children have a varied and inspiring experience.

Next steps

Find out more about the sculptures available to you locally by:
- looking around your immediate school and local environment;
- researching on the internet.

Learn a new three-dimensional art technique by finding a local workshop or event.

Further reading

Black, K. (2005) 'Learning on a large scale'. *STart*, Vol. 16. pp. 16–17.

Clough, P. (2007) *Clay in the Primary School*. London: Bloomsbury.

Clough, P. (2007) *Sculptural Materials in the Classroom*. London: Bloomsbury.

Fenwick, L. (2008) 'Papier mâché: let your imagination run wild!' *STart*, Vol. 27, pp. 20–21.

Hall, K. (2004) 'The art of communication'. *STart*, Vol. 10. pp. 14–15.

Hucks, A. (2009) 'Angry expressionist cat sculptures'. *STart*, Vol. 32, pp. 10–11.

Kitto, M.C. (2005) 'Hands on in the classroom: fossils'. *STart*, Vol. 16, pp. 4–5.
Krumbach, M. (2007) *Clay Projects for Children*. London: Bloomsbury.

Utley, C and Magson, M. (2007) *Exploring Clay with Children*. London: Bloomsbury.

Web resource

V & A: Sculptural techniques: *http://www.vam.ac.uk/page/s/sculpture-techniques/*

Chapter 11

Threads, fabrics and textiles

Introduction

Working with textiles gives children the opportunity to explore familiar and unusual materials: both making and decorating them. They can learn to construct fabrics and textiles from materials such as wool, thread, string and other fibres or by joining and reforming existing fabrics to make new ones. Learning can also be focused on adding surface decoration in a variety of ways including some techniques children will be familiar with using on paper such as printing, painting and drawing as well as those specific to fabric decoration such as stitching, dyeing and appliqué. The textures of the materials used can be engaging for children as a sensory as well as a visual experience. In this chapter the following areas will be considered:

- Subject knowledge that underlies teaching
- Teaching children to make and decorate fabrics and textiles

Exploring this part of the art curriculum can be an opportunity to explore traditional craft techniques as well as more contemporary applications and combinations of these. There may be people connected with the school or in the local community who are practitioners of some crafts and techniques and can share their expertise. Textiles are familiar to children around the home and school and these can be appreciated anew by exploring them more closely.

There are connections between design technology and the making and decorating of fabrics and textiles in art. As discussed earlier in reference to working in three dimensions it is important to be aware of the differences between these subjects so that every one of these experiences is not solely focused on an outcome that is mainly within design technology. Links can be made to history when exploring examples of threads, fabrics and textiles from the past and how they were made; to geography when considering how people and cultures in other places have designed and made them; and their role in the context of worship in RE.

The subject knowledge that underlies teaching

Developing some subject knowledge about different ways of working with thread and constructing and decorating fabrics and textiles will underpin successful planning, teaching and support of learning in this area of art. Some aspects that you may need to learn about are:

- tools and materials;
- visual elements that can be explored and taught;
- vocabulary to use;
- media and processes;
- the work of artists, craftspeople and designers.

Tools and materials

Some of the issues related to storage and expertise discussed in relation to working with three dimensions are also relevant to working with threads, fabrics and textiles. The availability of materials will play a part in the choices that can be offered to children and the satisfaction that they can gain from using just the right texture, colour or pattern for their work. If you are lucky enough to have access to more specialist sets of materials and equipment, such as those for felt making, batik or screen printing, it is likely that these will be kept together and used as a set – screens and squeegees for screen printing or *tjanting* tools and wax for batik for example. You may be able to learn how to use these and incorporate them as part of the curriculum, when working with an artist, craftsperson or designer or as part of out-of-school learning opportunities.

Practical task

Learning objective:

- to explore stitches and sewing.

In this practical task you will try out some sewing of your own, considering the challenges of teaching children to use sewing in art and how to overcome these.

You will need:

- A needle, some thread (several colours if possible), some fabric to sew onto, some buttons, beads and pasta.

What to do:

1. Try out some different stitches on the fabric. You might try running stitches of varying lengths; stitches that overlap; straight stitches in groups and any stitches you know or remember such as cross stitch, back stitch etc. If you were using stitching with children what would you need to anticipate and plan for?

2. Try attaching items to the fabric such as a button, a piece of pasta and a bead. If children were attaching to fabric using sewing how could you help them?

LINK

Questions to consider

- *Stitching*: Some of the points that you may have identified are starting off the sewing; not pulling stitches too tight so that the fabric bunches up; getting the stitches where you plan for them to be; and looping the thread around the edge of the material from underside to topside.

- *Attaching items to fabric*: Some of the points that you may have identified are being able to attach the item exactly where you want it and getting it to sit on the fabric securely.

- *Supporting children*: How you do this will relate to their prior experience, their fine motor control and the task they are working on. When sewing it can be useful to begin with bigger needles, thicker thread and fabric with holes or an open weave that is easy to sew through. It can also be useful to practice on plastic or card with holes punched in it (these can be bought or made). Allowing children to experiment and devise their own approach as well as showing them how to place stitches to make patterns if appropriate can help them decide what to do. Starting and finishing the sewing might be times when adult help is especially needed. When attaching items taping them in place with masking tape so they can be sewn on without moving can be useful.

Sewing can easily fall into design technology as well as art and can sometimes not be taught or developed fully in either subject. Considering when children learn to sew and apply and develop their sewing skills in both these subjects is important in order to avoid repetition or omission.

Teaching visual elements through making and decorating fabrics and textiles

The chart below makes suggestions in relation to each of the eight visual elements when using a range of media and processes: some of these are focused on one medium or process in particular and are indicated in brackets after each suggestion; others can be explored across a range. When you are planning and teaching a unit of work it is important to identify one or two visual elements that you will develop with the children; it is likely that this will have been done at the long term planning stage. The elements that will be most readily explored will depend upon factors such as the materials that you are using and the starting point and the learning outcome that you plan.

Line	Tone
Exploring using lines to make patterns, pictures and shapes (weaving, stitching) Constructing linear patterns (weaving) Using line in drawing/painting on textiles	Using tones of the same colour/different colours in combination (weaving, painting, printing, sewing, appliqué) Exploring the effect of tones when dyeing and printing (moving from lighter to darker, contrasts)
Colour	**Pattern**
Changing the colour of fabric using dyes Choosing and using coloured fabrics and thread (weaving, appliqué, embroidery and stitching) Using crayons, paint and printing inks on textiles	Choosing and using existing patterns on fabrics (appliqué, patchwork) Making pattern whilst making new textiles (weaving) Making new patterns to decorate the surface of textiles (dyeing, printing, stitching, appliqué)
Texture	**Shape**
Choosing and using the tactile qualities of threads and fabrics when making or decorating textiles Exploring contrasts between textures of materials Choosing and using texture to create a feely fabric picture/pattern	Decorating fabric with shapes (pattern/pictorial) Exploring tessellation and geometrical shapes (patchwork) Exploring repeating pattern using shapes (borders, stitching, printmaking on fabric)
Space	**Form**
Considering several viewpoints when making forms (front and back of a hanging, inside and outside of a draped form) Exploring how textiles can be used to delineate and make new spaces Considering movement in space (hanging threading, banners, flags)	Creating and using textiles in three dimensions (weaving around a 3D shape, decorating fabric that will be draped to make a form, joining fabrics to make a patchwork) Creating new forms from thread (weaving, knitting)

Texture is a key visual element when working with threads, fabrics and textiles. Exploring and using the tactile qualities of the materials can encourage children to consider the choices we make with our clothes and in our homes as well as in craft and art. Encouraging children to touch materials, choose them on the basis of how they feel and use texture to evoke feelings on the part of others who see and feel their work adds an extra dimension to their learning. Visual qualities such as pattern, colour and shape are also integral to many making experiences in this area.

Other visual elements will also be relevant depending on the media, process and outcome of the learning experience. Form may be important if the children are perhaps using weaving to create a three-dimensional form or a fabric that will be draped or stuffed whereas line may be important if a flat weaving is made using lines of thread, wool and string or line stitch is used to create a picture or pattern as part of appliqué or embroidery.

Key vocabulary

There are many opportunities to learn, apply and extend vocabulary when working with threads, fabrics and textiles, either making or decorating them. These may include naming fabrics, tools, equipment and processes as well as discussing relevant visual elements such as texture, colour and pattern and describing the properties and qualities of materials. When you plan a unit of work based around exploring, making or decorating textiles it is important to identify any words that will be used; these might be new, familiar or involve extending and refining the children's understanding of them. Although many of the materials used when making and decorating textiles can be familiar to children they often use generic terms to refer to them rather than being able to use specific names for particular types, designs and forms.

Firstly, it is important to consider the general terms: fabric, textiles, cloth and material. These can sometimes be used interchangeably though in this context their precise meanings could be explored. Fabric is a more generic term with many different types falling into it including those made from weaving, knitting and felting and other processes. Textiles are specifically those fabrics made from weaving or knitting thread together. Cloth and material are often used as synonyms.

Many fabrics are constructed from fibres, yarn or threads. These can be divided into natural fibres from plants (cotton, jute, etc.); from animals (silk from silkworms, wool from sheep, goats, etc.) and synthetic fibres (nylon, polyester, rayon, etc.). The thread will be spun and often dyed before use to make textiles or could be decorated later. Other fabrics are made from non-woven methods where the fibres are overlaid, entangled and then joined using thermal, adhesive or mechanical bonding. Examples of this are felting and creating synthetic fabrics with specific properties such as being waterproof (laminated fabrics). These can be made from recycled materials or be used once and recycled themselves.

Another aspect of vocabulary to consider is the naming of different types of fabric. Although children may be familiar with a variety of fabrics, what they are used for and their texture the specific names of many different types might not be part of their day-to-day vocabulary. Fabrics made from plants such as cotton, jute, and flax range from delicate materials such as gauze and voile to strong materials such as twill and denim. This group also includes canvas, corduroy, drill, gauze, gingham, jersey, muslin, lawn, linen, organdie, satin, seersucker, terrycloth, velour and velvet. Fabric can be made from silk spun by silk worms or wool from sheep, goats and rabbits. Those made from silk could include brocade, chiffon, crepe, damask, georgette, organdie, taffeta, tulle and velvet; those made from wool might include cashmere, chenille, felt, flannel, mohair, tartan and tweed.

Since the late nineteenth century scientists have developed a range of synthetic fibres from which to make fabrics. These have been developed as replacements for natural materials or to have specific properties such as lightness, durability, strength or resistance to water and include nylon, lycra, polyester, rayon and vinyl. Some fabrics can made from a combination of both synthetic and natural materials or might be a manufactured version of what used to be a natural fabric.

As you plan and work with children on particular processes there will be useful vocabulary to teach them in relation to the tools and equipment that they are using. An example of this is in weaving when they will need to know that the framework we weave on is called a loom; that the loom has two sets of threads – the warp threads that remain in place and the weft threads that are passed back and forth. Identifying these at the planning stage will allow you to introduce and model them as children learn and apply in the context.

Case Study

As an activity in the early stages of a unit of work where Year 1 children will be choosing and using different fabrics a teacher collects 10 cm square pieces of fabrics and textiles, some of which the children are likely to be familiar with through their clothing, soft toys and homes, along with some more unfamiliar ones. She includes fur, hessian, net, silk, knitted wool, denim, jersey, felt, fleece, towelling, chenille, vinyl and velvet in the collection.

As an introductory activity each piece is put inside a bag so that each child can put their hand in and feel the fabric but not see it, and each bag is numbered. They are asked to feel the fabrics and think about words that could describe the texture to each other and to their TA and teacher. Their suggestions are recorded on paper by the adults and the words are pinned to each bag.

Intially the adults prompt children with comments and questions such as 'I wonder if this will be scratchy or smooth'; 'Does this feel warm to you?'; 'This reminds me of my jumper'; and 'I can feel some holes.' Their comments and questions are planned to suggest words children might go on to use themselves to describe and make connections with their own clothes and experience of fabrics.

Later the words attached to each bag are read, predictions are made about which fabric it could be and what it might be used for before revealing the fabric itself from the bag. Later in the week the children are given bags with words pinned on and asked to feel and choose fabric that match the words to go in the bags. This gives the teacher the opportunity to extend descriptive vocabulary by using some words that children were unsure or of unfamilair with in the earlier activity.

These activities will underpin later work in art where they will choose and use fabrics for their sensory qualities as much as for their colours and patterns.

In this case study young children are challenged to use and develop their descriptive vocabulary as well as naming fabrics and making connections to what they are used for in some instances. This activity could have been simplified by having matching pieces and asking children to feel them unseen and match this to what they can see. It could have been developed by challenging children to sort and order them according to textural qualities such as smooth to rough or close to more open weave.

An interesting aspect of language and vocabulary in the context of threads, fabrics and textiles is the number of words and phrases from this area that are used in day to day talk. Kapp (2010) suggests that this is an indication of the integration of making fabrics into our culture. We talk of weaving spells, stories, plots, bobbing and weaving, and weaving in and out; we use proverbs like 'every cloud has a silver lining' and 'a stitch in time saves nine'. Exploring words and phrases in our language and where they have come from is a part of what older children learn as part of the English curriculum when they explore word origins.

Media and processes

There are many processes and techniques using threads, fabrics and textiles that can be explored and taught to primary-aged children. The chart below summarises some of those most commonly used in schools along with basic information about each and an example from the classroom. Although an example is given for each there many other ways of exploring each process or technique that you can try out based on your own ideas and the interests of the children teach.

Technique	Definition	Example
Using threads to wrap, knot, tie, plait, knit, crochet	Textiles can be made by combining threads in a variety of ways: both unstructured (wrapping, tying, knotting) and more structured using tools and specific stitches and patterns (knitting and crochet).	Children choose from a range of found and recycled items and thread and tie them onto a single thread at random or in a pattern.

(ctd)

Technique	Definition	Example
Weaving	A way of constructing fabric using a framework (loom) threaded with threads that remain in place (warp) and thread that is passed back and forth and in and out (weft). Weaving can be done by hand or by machine.	Children make a simple loom from twigs tied together and threaded with warp threads of gardening twine. They weave with weft threads of natural colours including wool, string and dried grasses.
Patchwork and quilting	Fabrics can also be made by joining smaller pieces together as a patchwork. Traditionally patchwork tends to made from geometrical shapes that tessellate. This is part of quilt making where the patch-work is sewn onto a backing with padding between. Quilts and other items can be made from patchwork. Padding could lead into stuffing when making 3D fabric items.	Children explore fabrics and choose one that evokes a memory. They each make a patch with a pocket into which they slide a short piece of writing describing the memory. An adult machine sews the patches together to make a class memory quilt.
Appliqué	Appliqué means 'to put on' and is the technique of cutting and joining pieces of fabric onto a base piece of fabric to deco-rate it. These might form a picture, a pat-tern or be more abstract. When the fabric shapes are cut to reveal what is below this is called 'reverse appliqué'. Appliqué may be used along with stitching and embroi-dery as well as stitching to attach other decorative items as above.	Children make an appliqué of the first letter of their name, decorating it with stitching and attaching beads, sequins and buttons.
Dyeing	Textiles can be dyed as whole pieces; tied to keep dye from colouring the whole sur-face (tie-dying) or painted with wax or paste to provide a resist to the dye (batik). Dyes have been made from natural materials (plants, insects, minerals) or more recently have been manmade, using chemicals. This has changed the range of colours available.	Children experiment with dye-ing a large piece of cotton several times, adding more tying each time they dye, moving from yellow, to orange to red.
Drawing, painting, printmaking	There are many other ways of decorat-ing fabric many of which involve applying familiar techniques onto fabric rather than paper. These include drawing directly onto it using fabric crayons or pens; drawing on paper and transferring the design by ironing; painting onto it using fabric paint or ready mix paint mixed into a fabric medium and printing onto it using block printing, screen printing and stencilling.	Older children are taught both stencilling and blocking out techniques to use when mak-ing a pattern on fabric. They apply these techniques to making a fish.
Sewing, stitching, embroidery	Sewing can be used to join fabric or add decoration to fabric by stitching in differ-ent ways or by using stitches to attach beads, buttons, sequins, mirrors or other decorative materials. Using stitches such as running stitch, cross stitch, chain stitch, back stitch and many others can be used as well as stitching more freely to add decorative detail to fabric.	Children use simple stitches to decorate the print of the fish they each made above. These are arranged by the children (and sewn on by an adult) on a large piece of fab-ric made using tie dyeing in blues and greens.

In addition techniques such as screen printing, tapestry, felt-making, macramé and spinning thread from wool before using it to weave might be introduced depending on the resources and expertise available to you.

Find out more

Explore the 'Talking Textiles' activity on the Manchester Children's University website. This can help you find out more about what fabrics and textiles are, how they are made and how they are decorated, as well as exploring some textiles from different times and places.

This interactive activity could also be used by older children to research textiles and textile making or shared with the class on the IWB.

LINK

The work of artists, craftspeople and designers

Examples of original textiles to explore may be more readily accessible to you because of their use for both decorative and functional purposes all around us, for clothes, toys and soft furnishings amongst others. It is important to make choices so that children encounter a range of processes, techniques and purposes throughout their primary years. Taking into consideration those examples available to use locally, which may be from a variety of cultures present in your community as well as those made further away in other countries, can be a good starting point. Exploring those made in the past as well as those made by contemporary artists, craftspeople and designers should also be represented.

As with any aspect of art, craft and design it is important to know about and use those examples available in the local community. This might include those available to look at in local places of worship, museums and galleries, stately homes, theatres and civic buildings as well as those related to children's own families and cultures. This might give you access to traditional crafts from this country as well those from other cultures around the world but now present in your locality. Your own knowledge of what is available locally and would support learning is important here. There may also be people using these processes whose expertise can be drawn upon.

Giving some thought to fabrics produced in other cultures and places around the world will also enhance the experiences that you give to children. Whilst it may be more difficult to find original examples that you can use in the classroom or visit easily there is a lot of material available online that can support research and learning. Look for examples from Africa and India on the Victoria and Albert Museum website as well as searching for images using a search engine. Examples of crafts using threads and textiles from the developing world are sold in Oxfam shops as part of their support for Fair Trade in developing countries. You might also consider linking your choices to learning in geography, design technology or RE where there are interesting and inspiring examples that will support learning in art as well as the linked subject.

Case Study

Year 6 have been introduced to Sujuni embrodiery. This is a technique from Bihar in north-east India. The large-scale fabric work involves creating shapes with a running stitch outline on a plain coloured background, often slighty padded underneath and filling the shape with small, straight running stitiches in a different colour. It is used in north-east India where the large fabrics are traditionally made by groups of women working together on the same piece and is given to family members. These usually depict the natural environment and daily life.

The class have seen a very large example in their local museum based on a rural Indian landscape and including fish, birds, animals, rivers, trees and other images from the natural world. It was hanging on a wall and easy for the class to sit in front of and observe. They first looked at the figurative images, identifying and listing what they can see. They consider the layout of the individual images in relation to each other, the scale and the overall effect of the whole fabric.

They then take a closer look at how the textile has been made: the outline of each image has been sewn around, and the inside has been filled with straight running stiches filling the outline completely. The colour of the fabric below, the embroidery thread used for the outline and for the inside of the image is considered. They also think about how a group of people working together could organise the making of such a large piece of art.

LINK

In the case study above children have explored a specific traditional Indian craft in terms of the overall imagery and the technique used to make it. This was chosen by their teacher because it is available locally to look at as well as giving children the opportunity to consider textile art from another country and culture. There is much potential for using this experience to inspire artwork as well as speaking and listening and research about the context of the place, culture and tradition.

Another aspect that can be explored is work from the past. This can include fabrics with historical significance and those that give the children evidence and insights about life in the past; interesting links with the history curriculum can be made here. One example could be looking at samplers. These began as a way of learning embroidery stitches, an 'exampler' and became part of childhood where children (primarily girls) practised sewing skills focused on letters and biblical and moral sayings. There are some links to more recent cross stitch on mesh designs still prevalent in the 1950s. Another example to research is that of military quilts that were made by soldiers in the nineteenth century. These tend to feature strong geometrical patterns and were made by soldiers as part of their recuperation after injury. The links and overlaps between art, craft and design can be explored by learning more about the work of William Morris and the Arts and Crafts movement.

As well as fabrics made in the past it is important to remember that there are many living artists, craftspeople and designers making work using threads, textiles and fabrics. It would be wrong to accidentally convey, by the choices we make, that this area is largely focused on small-scale domestic work made by women. Explore the work of John Jones, who makes 'story coats' stitched with images inspired from stories; Alice Kettle, whose large-scale stitched work uses colour and line; and Salley Mavor and Janet Bolton, who make images and illustrations for stories from fabrics. Look at the 'knit the city' website to find out more about contemporary use of knitting in the form of 'guerrilla knitting'.

LINK

Find out more

Explore fabrics from around the world and from the past on the Victoria and Albert Museum website.

LINK

Explore the connections between people and plants on the 'Plant Cultures' part of the Kew Gardens website. Find out more about making fabrics by weaving and using natural dyes.

LINK

Explore how living artists use weaving and textile techniques on the artisancam website.

LINK

Teaching children to make and decorate textiles

There are many and varied learning opportunities involved in exploring and using threads, textiles and fabrics. When planning for a successful learning experience there are some significant factors to consider:

- developing skills;
- using tools and materials.

In addition there are opportunities to:

- work individually or collaboratively;
- make links to other aspects of the art curriculum;
- make links to other curriculum areas.

These will be explored more fully later in this chapter.

Developing skills

Some processes that involve making and decorating fabrics may be completely new to children, whilst others may be familiar from their experiences of using similar tools and techniques on paper. When planning it is important to identify the skills that are necessary for children to have in order to learn and make in the unit of work. This will allow you to build in opportunities to support children in developing and improving their skills so that they make progress and are satisfied with what they create. Thinking about including some activities that allow children to recall and practice their skills before working on their main outcome can be both supportive and inclusive.

Practical task

Planning for development of skills

Learning objective:

- to identify some key skills required for some techniques using threads, fabrics and textiles.

In this practical task you will identify the skills required in order to weave, sew and stencil. This will support your planning and teaching.

What to do:

- Think about each of the processes listed and identify what the required skills are. Think about how children's learning could be supported in each of them. You may wish to consider children of a particular age or children generally.

Process	Skills	Supporting learning
Weaving		
Stencilling		

Guidance notes

- *Weaving*: When considering the skills involved in weaving you may have identified being able to take the weft thread under and over the warp threads from one side to the other, turning around and coming back the other way this time going over and under the warp threads. This requires good fine motor control and being able to make and sustain a repeating pattern. In addition not pulling the weft thread too tight or leaving it too loose is necessary. In order to support children with weaving you might plan experiences where they are weaving on a small scale: using single threads rather than going back and forth; using thick threads such as ribbon or strips of fabric that are easier to hold and manipulate; having warp threads that are strong and well spaced; weaving around a spiral; or attaching the thread to a piece of card or needle that is easier to hold. You might also make the process bigger and easier to see and experience by weaving with skipping ropes. Have children holding the warp threads at each end and a child threading the weft thread in and out by physically passing over and under, and then going back and doing the same to see the pattern that emerges on a large scale. You might also allow children to practice by making paper weavings, although this can be a challenge as paper is so easy to tear.

- *Stencilling*: When considering the skills involved in stencilling you may have identified being able to cut clear and simple shapes and place them on the fabric in order to press fabric paint over the edges, understanding that the area covered will remain unchanged. Dabbing right up to and over the edges of the stencil but not allowing colour to leak underneath is also important to making a clear edge. To support children beginning to understand and use this process you might provide precut stencils for them to use to practice on in order to explore and refine their skills – keeping the stencil still is important; sticking it down so it does not move is a good idea. When devising a stencil allowing children to make and try out prototypes, perhaps printing these on paper will help them arrive at effective and pleasing shapes and combinations of shapes. When working on fabric cutting the stencil from sticky back plastic and then sticking this on the fabric is another way of overcoming the frustration of the stencil moving around.

When you are planning a unit of work focused on threads, textiles and fabrics identifying and building upon children's prior knowledge skills and understanding is vital and all the more so because there may be long gaps between one experience and the next. As when planning work in three dimensions planning some free exploration and practice using the materials, tools and skills that will underpin your unit of work can support the children's confidence. As with some other aspects of art building in opportunities for exploration at the preparation stage will support a more considered outcome. You can draw upon existing knowledge, skills and understanding from other art processes (drawing, painting, printmaking) and other subjects (design technology) so that the children are not beginning anew each time. Identifying and using these links is a valuable aspect of long term planning.

Case Study

Before they go on a placement a group of PGCE students work in small groups to learn about and then plan a unit of work using an art process of their choice. A group of four students work together to experiment with fabric painting with a view to planning and teaching a unit of work based around fabric painting to some Year 2 classes where they are on placements.

The students identify what they have to find out about the children's prior experience and their current knowledge, skills and understanding so that they can plan to pitch their unit at an appropriate level. They list some questions that they aim to answer on a preliminary visit. These include:

- What have the children already learned about painting?

- What tools they are familiar with using? (sizes, types of brushes, sponge paddles)

- What scales have they worked on before? (small, medium, large)

- Which visual elemements have they explored through painting before?

- What has inspired their painting or work with fabrics before?

From a practical point of view the students consider the availability of materials and tools at the schools and the space available to work in and store work in progress. In terms of planning the students talk with the class teachers about the medium-planning expectations, any meaningful cross-curricular links that can be made and any other constraints or aims for the half term as well as the individual needs of children in the class.

On their return from initial vists to their placement schools they find that across the Year 2 classes there is some variation in prior experience and aims for medium-term planning. Each student modifies the original shared plan to take account of these factors.

In the case study above the students had to take a range of issues into consideration as part of the planning process, partly but not entirely because they do not know the children and the long term plan as well as a class teacher might. When answering these questions it will be important that both planning new experiences and building on prior knowledge are taken into consideration. Having learned about the practicalities of fabric painting they are able to each plan and teach it in a way that will best inspire and promote learning in their particular class. Working together with colleagues is a supportive approach especially as you learn and develop as a teacher of art; conversations about teaching and learning will help you explore possibilities and share ideas as well as anticipate any challenges and work out how to be prepared for them.

Find out more

Explore the interactive activity 'Stitch it up' on the Artisan Cam website.

LINK

Think about what the children you work with could learn from it. How could it support learning in a unit of work?

Using tools and materials

Some of the processes or techniques that can be explored and taught in the classroom will require you to introduce new tools and materials and teach children how to use these effectively in their artwork. The chart below suggests some techniques that children can be taught and how these might be explored in making finished outcomes.

Process	Techniques	Ideas in context
Threading, tying, wrapping	Wrapping around Tying onto Threading in and out	Choosing colours of wool to wrap around a cylinder to make graduated or contrasting stripes. Collecting and tying cut paper shapes onto a horizontal pole to hang down at different lengths and blow in the wind Choosing colours of wool and ribbon to thread in and out of a piece of card with holes punched around the edges.
Weaving	Weaving single weft threads Weaving a continuous thread Using a premade loom or framework Making own loom or framework	Making a small piece of weaving using single strands of thick wool and ribbon. Making a larger-scale piece of weaving using several continuous threads of tones of the same colour going from paler to deeper Weaving on a framework made from a card or plastic container, threaded with warp threads by an adult – choice of size and shape. Choosing a shallow box or plastic tray to thread with warp threads and weave on. Constructing a framework to weave on by tying sticks or twigs together or choosing a branch with a gap that can be threaded with warp threads to weave on
Patchwork	Single patches, combinations of Tessellation of geometrical shapes Borders	Making a patchwork of 12 squares Making a larger-scale collaborative patchwork exploring tessellation and symmetry Adding a decorative border around the above
Appliqué	Layers of fabric Cutting to allow fabrics to show through Adding stitched decoration	Developing the above by cutting holes to reveal the fabric below Adding additional decoration using stitching
Using dyes	Tie dye	Using elastic bands and string to tie up cotton before dyeing it once or several times

Process	Techniques	Ideas in context
Surface decoration – drawing/ painting / printmaking	Drawing Painting Printing (block printing, screen printing, stencilling)	Drawing with fabric crayons on textiles Painting with fabric paint Printing with found objects, press print tiles or card tiles on fabric Stencilling using simple cut shapes
Sewing, stitching, embroidery	Stitching freely Using stitches (cross stitch, running stitch) Using stitches to attach decoration (sequins, buttons, mirrors, etc.)	Adding stitched detail and decoration to some of the outcomes described above. Sewing onto binca or more closely woven fabric using free stitching or named stitches

There are many starting points that can inspire the making of outcomes using threads, fabric and textiles. Long term planning should ensure that children encounter a variety of these throughout their primary years. Some starting points may be linked to learning in other subjects. Children should also be able to revisit the same media or process several times so that knowledge, skills and understanding can be built up and extended over time in response to different starting points.

Work individually or collaboratively

When you are planning to work with threads, fabrics and textiles it is likely that you will consider children making individual pieces, individual pieces that will be joined to make a larger whole or working together to make a collaborative piece perhaps on a larger scale. Across the primary years children should have the opportunity to work in all of these ways. It is important to allow children the freedom and opportunity to make choices that working individually offers as well as the chance to co-operate and be part of a larger whole that working collaboratively provides.

When working entirely individually it is likely that the children will also be making on a smaller scale so that their outcome is manageable in terms of the size and time available. They might also be given more choice of the materials and processes they use in order to meet the learning outcomes or choice can be created by giving them several options or complete freedom in the colours or starting points that they use.

Case Study

A Year 5 class are going to making individual small fabric paintings with additional decoration using stitching based around designs they have made using painting software on the computer. Before beginning this unit of work they were told about how the artist Gerhard Richter would focus close up on small areas of his paintings and use this as a means of creating a new painting. They use viewfinders and zoom in on areas of painting they have found online and use these as the basis for their initial work.

Working on the computer screen first has given the children the opportunity to experiment with their ideas extensively before deciding what they will transfer to their piece of fabric. Being able to save several drafts and make and undo changes has allowed them to explore more than they might usually have done.

Later they experiment with painting their chosen design on paper to help them consider the practicalities of painting – whether some colours can be painted over others, what size brushes to use and whether to paint freehand or sketch a faint outline on the fabric before painting. After painting on the fabric the children decorate their work further using stitching and sewing beads and sequins into the design.

When the work is complete the progress from computer design, painted prototype and completed fabric allows children to identify the decisions they made at each stage of the process and evaluate their work.

In the case study above children work as individuals around the same starting point, using the same materials and processes. They can make choices over their design, the colours they use and any additional decoration added later. Building in these choices results in a variety of finished outcomes as children's creative decisions along the way result in their work becoming more personal.

Individual pieces of work by a class or year group of children can be planned and made with the aim of joining them together to make a much larger finished outcome. In order to create a sense of unity a theme, a limited range of colours or a coherent way of joining might be planned from the outset so that the finished pieces work together as a completed whole. When working in this way each child can still identify their own work in the larger piece.

Planning to make a genuinely collaborative large-scale outcome will allow children to opportunity to talk about their ideas, sharing and justifying them and eventually agreeing on an approach that satisfies everyone. This can give them a meaningful opportunity to discuss their art and co-operate in order to meet an outcome. As an adult it is important to consider the points at which children will make choices and how you will support them in coming to an agreement that allows all to be satisfied, as well as helping them divide up the tasks and record each individual's contribution to the whole. In this context it is important that children are not guided so completely that they are merely following instructions to produce an outcome that is largely directed by an adult's vision.

Case Study

Children in a Year 3 and 4 class plan a large collaborative weaving based on the colours they see around them in autumn. Although the children in this class have experience of weaving on a small scale as individuals they have not had the opportunity to work together and on a large scale before.

The children are taken on a walk to experience the colours of autumn first hand as well as collecting reminders and taking photos. They then talk and plan together, sharing their ideas and coming to a class decision that will guide the weaving. Several approaches are suggested including two that are settled on as most popular: firstly, moving from green, through yellow to orange and finally to red from top to bottom gradually; and, secondly, using contrasting colours so that the drama of the colours is emphasised. Plans are modified to allow two weavings to be made so that the two main ideas emerging from discussion can be developed.

Plans are made showing the overall design for each weaving and materials such as string, wool, ribbons and strips of plastic are collected and organised so that it is easy for children to weave following the designs. Progress is evaluated regularly and photos taken to record the development from beginning to completion. Having the ongoing weavings around the classroom and working on them when possible allows discussion of their progress to be part of classroom life. Some children seek out materials to bring in from home to contribute.

In the case study above it will be difficult to identify the contributions of individuals when the weavings are finished; the collaboration at each stage is part of the unit of work. During this project it would be useful for children to keep a diary of their contributions and thoughts about their own participation supported by photos and drawings. This would allow them to reflect on their individual role within the shared outcome. This project could also have been adapted so that each child made and contributed an individual leaf to a larger banner or hanging; choice could be given in the media used to allow for personal response and creativity.

Making links to other aspects of the art curriculum

Opportunities for making connections to drawing, painting and printmaking have been considered earlier in this chapter. Some of the processes discussed earlier can be used when working in three dimensions. This can allow learning to take place that is centred on using the tactile qualities of threads, fabrics and textiles as well as tackling some of the challenges of manipulating space and form. Indeed this may be a way of allowing children to draw upon earlier learning from several areas of art, pulling them together to make artwork that combines knowledge, skills and understanding across the art curriculum.

Working with form using threads and textiles could include making three-dimensional forms by making several two-dimensional forms and joining them such as when children make faces or panels that will be sewn together and stuffed. This could at its most simple be two identical shapes, each decorated and sewn around the edges then stuffed or it could challenge children to consider using more than two faces that will fit together to allow the finished form to be freestanding (with a flat base perhaps or by weighting down).

Working with space could include using weaving and textiles to create new spaces such as cylinders, wigwams and cubes by draping over and from frameworks. This can allow children to consider the inside and outside of what they make. Weaving and fabrics can also be used to explore changing and enhancing existing spaces using mobiles, hangings and banners.

Find out more

Find Naomi Renouf's article 'Recycled textile art' in *STart* (2008, Vol. 31, No. 27).

Explore how children made three dimensional structures to weave onto using recycled materials such as strips of cotton and other fabrics, threads, lace and plastics.

Making links to other curriculum areas

Interesting and meaningful links can be made to other curriculum subjects where learning in each subject can be enhanced and complementary. It is important to avoid the needs of one subject overwhelming the other: using illustration as art where it is really a means of recording is a danger here.

In English and literacy connections can be made with stories where making fabrics, items made of fabric and fabric techniques themselves play a role. Spinning and weaving feature in some Greek myths including that of Arachne and Athena and in fairy tales such as 'Sleeping Beauty' and 'Rumpeltstiltskin'. Fabrics and fabric techniques are used to illustrate stories such as those by Salley Mavor or Janet Bolton. Making an appliqué that brings to life a scene from a known story or is part of a new story that the maker will go on to write could be a link between reading and writing and art.

In mathematics there is scope to explore patternmaking and tessellation in two dimensions and the use of shaped panels to construct three-dimensional textile objects. Children may have considered the properties of materials such as strength, density, transparency, resistance to water and many more in science and then designed functional items using these properties in design technology. They may have explored how fabrics are constructed by looking closely at them, taking them apart and considering the tools and equipment involved in making them either by hand or by manufacturing processes. This knowledge and understanding can be used to underpin work in art related to the visual and sensory impact of the making and decorating, rather than the purpose and function.

There is much scope for making connections between history, geography and RE when choosing examples made by artists, craftspeople and designers. This might include looking at and talking about what can be learned about the culture, geography, history and worship of an area or people from looking at their textile art. It could also focus on learning a new technique exemplified by work from another time, place or religion and applying it themselves in another context or in response to a different starting point.

Connect and extend

Read the article 'Sensitising children to ecological issues through textile eco-design' by Taieb, AH., Hammami, M., Msahli, S. and Sakli, F. in 2010 in the *International Journal of Art and Design Education* (Vol. 29, No. 3, pp. 313–20.

Think about your choice of materials and what we do with them in the classroom can give children the opportunity to explore sustainable development and environmental issues.

Conclusion

Giving children regular opportunities to explore threads, fabrics and textiles both looking at the work of others and making their own is an engaging and interesting part of the art curriculum. Opportunities to build on prior knowledge from other areas of art, applying it in new contexts so children can extend their skills and understanding can be planned. Often the art created using threads, fabrics and textiles is easy to display (as banners, hangings, drapes) and can enhance the school environment as sharing ideas and outcomes with viewers.

Next steps

- Look around your home and school environment for examples of threads, fabrics and textiles to use as examples.
- Find out if anyone in your local community makes art with textiles: felt-making, knitting, appliqué, quilting, etc.
- Start collecting resources that children can use in their art work

Reference

Kapp, E. (2010) 'Warp + weft: language and literature'. *STart*. Vol. 37, poster.

Further reading

Finley, K. (2010) 'Our town quilt project'. *STart*, Vol. 34, pp. 18–19.

Mainstone, T. (2003) 'Simply to dye for'. *STart*, Vol. 1, pp. 4–5.

Renouf, N. (2008) 'Abstract collage and stripy seascapes'. *STart*, Vol. 31, pp. 15–18.

Richards, A. and Wood, D. (2006) 'Making it work: making, meanings and materials'. *STart*, Vol. 20, pp. 16–17.

Woods, K. (2008) *Creative Textiles Projects for Children*. London: Bloomsbury.

Woods, K. (2011) *Creative Textile Art: Techniques and Projects*. London: A & C Black.

Web resources

Gerhard Richter: *http://www.gerhard-richter.com/*

Victoria and Albert Museum: *http://www.vam.ac.uk/*

Going further

There is so much to learn about art and teaching art to children: this book should be seen as a basic place to start. Throughout this book indications of specific next steps have been made at the end of each chapter. As you complete your training as a teacher, move into teaching and develop your subject knowledge and pedagogical understanding you will continue to learn in response to your own reflections on your practice and your evaluations of the needs and interests of the children you teach. Below are some suggestions of how you can continue to develop your knowledge and interest.

Be observant when you are in schools whether as a visitor, on placement or as a member of staff. There is so much to learn from the ideas of other teachers and the learning experiences they plan for their children. Just walking around an unfamiliar school can serve as an injection of new ideas and different ways of approaching learning. Make sure that you take notes (or photos, with permission) of things that catch your eye.

Be prepared to learn about unfamiliar art processes and materials and seek help from your colleagues to develop your skills, knowledge and confidence. If you have an interest or skill in an area of art, craft or design share this with your peers, colleagues and children. Seek out workshops, courses and online study to help you follow interests or fill gaps in your knowledge.

Look out for local art exhibitions and art in galleries, museums, parks and historic houses. As well as expanding your own knowledge of art this may lead you to possible visits for the children you teach, useful learning resources and contacts with artists and curators. Some exhibitions also have activities and workshops for adults and/or children to participate in. Pay attention to stories in the media about high profile exhibitions of the work of significant artists.

If you are concerned about your own ability to draw and teach drawing seek out local classes and workshops so that you can learn and build your confidence as a teacher. Join the Campaign for Drawing and look for 'Come Draw With Me' events. Work your way through Meg Fabian's drawing activities in *Drawing is a Class Act* (2005: Brilliant Publications) or sign up for an online course through the Access Art website.

Join the National Society for Education in Art and Design. This will help you keep up to date with issues of art education, give you access to interesting teaching ideas and people with expertise and ideas.

Get your school involved with art-based events in your local area or join in national events as a school. Think about putting on a school exhibition or supporting and encouraging children to participate in local exhibitions and share their work with sudiences.

Make connections with people involved in art in the local area – artists, craftspeople and designers; curators and gallery staff; and art students at college and university. Get to know parents and governors and find out about their interest and expertise in art.

Above all enjoy teaching art and make sure that the children you work with enjoy and learn in art lessons.

Appendix 1

Vocabulary to use when discussing visual elements

Colour

- Names of colours (both identifying and descriptive)
- Technical vocabulary – primary, secondary, complementary, hue, tint, shade
- Words to describe the quality of the colour – bright, vibrant, intense, dull, pale, pastel, neutral
- Comparative vocabulary to describe and compare the tone of the colour – light, lighter, lightest, dark, darker, darkest
- Words to describe how colours affect each other – matching, clashing, contrasting
- Words to describe the 'feel' created by colour – hot, warm, cool, cold

Tone

- Tone, tonal, contrast, light source, shade, shadow, gradual, distinct, reflection
- Black, grey, white
- Words to compare tones – light, lighter, lighter than, lightest, dark, darker, darker than, darkest (these can be attached to colour words)

Line

- Line, linear, outline
- Words to describe continuous lines – straight, curved, flowing, zig-zag, wiggly, smooth, spiral, sweeping, looping, continuous, angular, rythmic, boundary, corner, turn, joined, overlapping
- Words to describe the quality of line – thick, wide, broad, narrow, thin, light, dark, soft, hard
- Words to describe marks and broken lines – dot, dash, point, spot, broken, short
- Words to describe the position/relationship of lines – diagonal, horizontal, vertical, parallel
- Words to name and desrcibe shapes when outlines are made with lines (see next)

Pattern

- Words to describe pattern – random, regular, irregular, decorative, rotation, transformation, translation, tessellation, linear, spiral, repeating, symmetrical, line symmetry, reflective symmetry, line of symmetry, axis of symmetry, geometric, natural, manmade, simple, complex, interlocking, overlapping
- Words to identify parts of pattern – border, motif, grid, surface
- Words to describe the design of specific patterns – plaid, polka dot, stripes, gingham, basket weave, etc.
- Words used to describe specific patterns from different times and cultures – rangoli, Celtic, Greek
- Words to identify two dimensional shapes used to make patterns, see next.

Texture

- Feel, touch, surface quality, tactile
- Words to describe textures – coarse, rough, bumpy, scratchy, smooth, silky, slimy, squashy, hairy, furry, feathery, wet, dry, soft, hard, cold, cool, warm, hot

Shape

- Words to name two-dimensional geometric shapes – circle, circular, semi-circle, triangle, square, rhombus, rectangle, pentagon, hexagon, heptagon, octagon, polygon, qualrilateral, kite, paralellogram, trapezium
- Words to describe types of shape – geometrical, symmetrical, asymmetrical, simple, complex, regular, irregular, flat, negative, regular, irregular
- Words to describe qualities of shapes, edge, side, corner, outline, filled, surface,
- Words to describe relationships between shapes – tessellating, overlapping, intersecting, touching, background

Form

- Words to describe three-dimensional geometrical shapes – cube, cuboid, pyramid, sphere, hemisphere, spherical, cone, cylinder, prism, tetrahedron, polyhedron, octahedron, dodecahedron
- Words to describe viewpoints of forms – inside, outside, through, next to, beyond, beside, behind, in front, above, below
- Words to describe how forms are made – join, stick, twist, tie, squash, bend, fix, fasten, arrange
- Words to talk about form – solid, hollow, surface, viewpoint, scale, volume, weight, mass, rigid, framework

Space:

- Words to describe viewpoints, positions and relationships in space – near, far, next to, beside, under, below, above, inside, outside
- Words to describe the quality of space – enclosed, airy, claustrophobic, high, low, open, large, small, narrow, wide, dark, light, busy, full, empty, crowded, quiet, noisy, peaceful, still
- Words to describe space in a flat composition – background, foreground, perspective, distance, depth, middle

Appendix 2

There are a range of tools, resources and materials that are necessary for teaching the art curriculum effectively. It is important that you know what these are and how they can be used to support learning. The checklists below can be used as a basis for reviewing resources in relation to ICT and digital media, drawing, painting, printmaking, collage, working in three dimensions and textiles. Each checklist is followed by guidance notes where some of the issues related to the listed resources are discussed.

Practical task

Exploring the resources and materials at your school

Learning objective:
- to find out more about the tools and resources available for use in school

You will need:
- The pro formas below. This could be a paper copy photocopied from this book or downloaded and printed out from the website or could be completed electronically.

What to do:
- Use this checklist to look around the classroom and any central storage for art resources in the school. If possible talk with a class teacher or the school's art coordinator about the available resources.

Chapter 5 ICT and digital resources

Look for	Location	Notes/questions to follow up
Hardware		
PCs, laptops, tablets		
Digital cameras/flip cameras		
Visualiser		
Digital microscope		

Look for	Location	Notes/questions to follow up
Photocopier		
Scanner		
Printers		
Interactive whiteboard (IWB)		
Software		
Focused on learning in art		
Apps		
Internet resources		
For children		
For teachers		
School website / VLE		

Points to consider

Hardware

- Location and access to hardware – It is useful for you to find out what sort of hardware you have access to and how it is organised in the school. This could be by accessing large sets through an ICT suite, laptop trolley, set of cameras, etc, at specified times with the whole class. It could also or alternatively be by having sustained access to some key pieces through their allocation to classrooms. You will need to consider these ways of organising access in relation to teaching and learning in art so that you can build in ICT as an ongoing and supportive tool within lessons and creating art with digital media as the key outcome in an art unit of work.

- Using resources effectively – As with any resource it is vital that you are familiar with how to use it effectively in the classroom. Seeking help with unfamiliar technology or specific types that you have not used before must be a priority so that you can support learning effectively. Many computers, cameras, copiers, etc, have features in common and can be worked out with some trial and error but this must take place as part of your preparation. Think also about identifying any technical support available in the school.

Software/apps

- Identify the software and apps available that will support learning in art. This should include software that allows children to make marks, paint or draw onscreen using a mouse or touch pad or using their fingers directly on a screen. These may include an increasing number of tools depending on the age of the children using them. Software related to animation and video may also be available. Apps to support specific aspects of learning or related to the work of artists or the artwork or exhibitions in museums and galleries.

Internet resources

- For you as a teacher – Keep a list of useful websites by saving them to a folder in your favourites or keeping a Word document to which you add links under headings. This book is supported by links available online and these provide a good place to start. Find and join groups of teachers via social networking sites available through NSEAD or Access Art so that you can keep up to date and share ideas with your colleagues.

- For use with children – Follow the school's policy and guidance about how the internet is used with children. Be aware that some schools block some online resources that as an adult you might be used to having ready access to – it is important to find this out so that you are not surprised by it at the last minute.

- School website/VLE – find out about the way the school uses its website and VLE so that you can also use it share children's work – photos of outcomes, as well as the process of making, lend themselves to sharing with parents as an audience. Sharing links to local art activities and resources can help children pursue an interest in art beyond the classroom and use what their local community has to offer.

Chapter 6 Resources used in drawing

Look for	Location	Notes / questions to follow up
Graded drawing pencils 4H 2H H HB B 2B 4B 6B		
Charcoal and white chalk		
Coloured chalks		
Fine line black pens		
Pens of a range of thicknesses e.g. fine/ broad/brush/marker		
Oil pastels		
Soft pastels		
Biros/ballpoint pens		
Wax crayons		
Coloured pencils		

Look for	Location	Notes / questions to follow up
Watercolour pencils		
Charcoal/pastel pencils		
Sticks/stones		
Overhead projector pens		
Cartridge paper		
Sugar paper		
Newsprint		
Tissue/tracing paper		
Sand		
Clay/play dough/plasticene		
Cornflour		
Plastic/OHT/Perspex		
Viewfinders		
Rubbers (soft, putty)		
Fixative (for adult use)		

Points to consider

Graded drawing pencils

Drawing pencils are graded with numbers and letters. H pencils are harder and make a lighter mark, with 9H the hardest. B pencils are softer and make a darker mark, with 9B the softest. HB pencils are in the middle and commonly used for a range of general classroom purposes. A selection of B pencils should be available for children to use in art lessons – 4B is a good pencil to start with, although you will want older children to experience a greater range including 2B and 6B. They can be bought in boxes of twelve and will last a long time if cared for. These pencils should be stored separately and never mixed up with the pencils used in the class for general work. Children can be taught to identify their art pencils and look after them appropriately.

Black pens (fine, broad, brush, marker), felt pens and biros

Pens make a different sort of mark than pencils and children should have the opportunity to use pens of different qualities and thicknesses to draw with. Classroom felt pens often come in fine and broad as well as brush tip, and marker pens tend to be bigger to hold and can have rounded or straight tips: all of these make different marks. Most pens are now washable from hands and clothes, so even the youngest children can use them. Using black pen is also useful if you wish to copy, enlarge or reduce children's drawings on a photocopier.

Pastels

There are several different kinds of pastel available. Soft pastels have a chalky quality and can be blended although the colours are more vibrant than chalks. Oil pastels have an oily feel and again can be blended and have very rich and vivid colours. Pastels tend to come in sets of a range of colours and some can also be bought in skin tones or tones from white through greys to black.

Wax crayons

Most classrooms have wax crayons and these can be used in art especially for making rubbings and using with Brusho or ink washes to make wax resist. When using wax crayons for rubbing you need thick chunky crayons with the paper wrapper taken off so they can be held comfortably and rubbed sideways. Wax crayons can be bought in a large range of colours and are relatively cheap.

Coloured pencils

You may have coloured pencils that are used in day-to-day classroom activities. For art you might use these or you might have sets that have a larger range of colours, are softer or have other qualities. Coloured pencils are now available as water soluble, pastel and charcoal. These types could be considered to support children who are ether more comfortable with gripping and manipulating pencils than pastels or charcoal. Charcoal in particular can be quite fragile and may break when gripped hard.

Drawing surfaces

It is important to have a range of surfaces available to draw on. Cartridge paper in large sheets that you can cut to the size that you want is most useful. Paper in pastel tones such as buff and grey is also useful as you can use white, a range of tones and black on these. Paper that has been donated to schools if often too shiny and slippery to use with many drawing tools although it can be a satisfactory surface for drawing with some types of pens.

Viewfinders

A viewfinder is a piece of card with a hole cut in the middle. The size and shape of the hole depends on what the viewfinder will be used for. Making your own viewfinders fit for the purpose you intend to use them for is often more flexible in terms of size and shape and cheaper than buying a standard product. A viewfinder can be used to help children identify areas to concentrate on before they begin to draw. It can prevent them from becoming overwhelmed about where to start and how much to draw.

Rubbers

Your school may have a policy about the use of rubbers. In art you may discourage the use of rubbers in order to preserve the children's work. If this is your approach you should have some suggestions at the ready for when children feel that they have made a mistake.

This will be discussed more fully later in the chapter. Soft putty rubbers can be useful for blending softer drawing materials.

Fixative

If you are using chalk, charcoal and soft pastels with children these can be easily smudged and rubbed. When the work is finished it should be 'fixed' using a spray fixative or hair-spray. In terms of health and safety an adult should spray the drawings and this should take place in a well ventilated area or outside.

Chapter 7 Resources used in painting

Look for	Location	Notes/questions to follow up
Types of paint		
Powder paint		
Powder paint with added…		
Ready mix paint		
Cromar paint/metallic/pearlescent		
Tempera blocks		
Watercolours		
Acrylics		
Brusho (washable)		
Drawing inks (waterproof)		
Tools for painting with		
Paint shapers		
Sponge paddles		
Plastic tools/palette knives		
Bristle brushes (short/long handled)		
Hair brushes		
Tooth brushes		
Sticks/found and junk items		

(ctd)

Look for	Location	Notes/questions to follow up
Other useful equipment		
Drying rack		
Pegs on a line		
Easels		
Drawing boards		
Pots with lids and stoppers		
Palettes (flat/6 dips)		
Spoons		
Pipettes		
Disposable pots/trays, etc.,		

Guidance notes

Types of paint

There are many types of paint available to use in the classroom. Schools tend to rely on some for general use and others for special projects. The qualities and properties of these will be explored more fully later in this chapter.

Paintbrushes

There are two main types of paintbrushes: those with stiff, coarse bristles and those with softer natural or synthetic hair.

Stiff bristle brushes	Soft hair brushes
Made from bristle, hogshair or synthetic materials	Made from softer hair or synthetic materials
Comes in different sizes and round and flat shapes	Come in different sizes
Used for thicker paint, may leave brush strokes	Used for thinner paint, applying washes, can be shaped into a point for finer marks and more detail

Paintbrushes are expensive tools and must be cared for in order to make them last. They should be cleaned after each use, never left to soak or stood with the hairs/bristles facing downwards in a pot. It is important that we teach children to choose and use the right type of paintbrush for the type of paint and the sort of marks required in their artwork. It is therefore important that teachers and teaching assistants can choose the appropriate brush for the art they are planning and build in opportunities to investigate

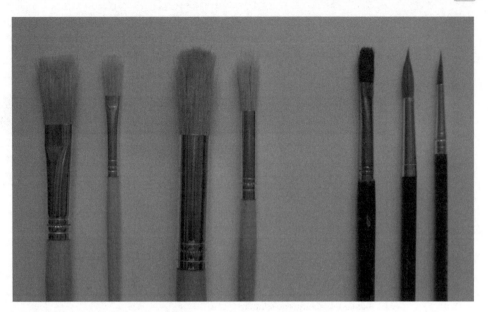

Figure A2.1 Types of paint brushes

the brushes and the effects that can be achieved with them. Paintbrushes can be bought with both short and long handles and some consideration should be given to which will suit the manipulative skills of the children using them.

Other painting tools

There are other tools that can be used for painting. Recently 'colour shapers' or 'paint shapers' have begun to be used in schools. These are short-handled tools with shaped rubber ends that can be used to apply paint and make marks in it. Sponge paddles of varying widths are also available and useful for applying large areas of colour or washes. Plastic palette knives also allow children to experiment with applying thick paint in a different way – strips of very thick card can also be used for this. Found and collected items such as toothbrushes and sticks can add variety to the range of possible marks that children can make.

Drying racks/line and pegs

It is essential to plan ahead to where finished or incomplete paintings can be left to dry safely. Some schools may have drying racks bought for the purpose. These can be a series of plastic mesh leaves with or without springs. A good habit to get into is to teach children to fill the drying rack from the bottom upwards. Drying racks without springs to keep the leaves up can be made more effective by taking out every other leaf. Drying racks with large gaps in the mesh can be covered with card or paper so that smaller pieces of work do not fall through and stick together. Lines and pegs can be useful if the paint is not thin and prone to running. Alternatively you may need to use the floor or flat surfaces and be ready to move the paintings as soon as they are dry and can be stacked.

Pots/lids/stoppers/pipettes/spoons

Items to support painting can be bought from catalogues. If children have mixed colours that they want to use again or if you have diluted ink or Brusho for washes these can be stored and reused if used in a pot with a lid and stopper or decanted into a plastic bottle.

Similar items can be collected and stored so they are available and the advantage of 'junk' items such as plastic pots and trays is that they can be thrown away after use, which can save time when cleaning up after activities.

Chapter 8 Resources used for making prints

Look for	Location	Notes/questions to follow up
Flat trays		
Hard rollers (63 mm, 101 mm, 152 mm, 200 mm)		
Sponge rollers (various sizes/textures)		
Plastic ink spreaders/spatulas		
Stamps		
Found natural and manmade objects/materials		
Sponge shapes/numbers/letters		
Polystyrene tiles (often called pressprint/polyprint/easyprint)		
Printing ink (tubs/tubes)		
Plastic/perspex tiles		
Lino cutting tools/lino tiles		
Screen printing equipment		
Marbling ink/pipettes, tray		
Plasticine		
Textured wallpapers		

Guidance notes

Flat trays

It is essential that the surfaces of the trays that you use for rolling out ink are kept flat and smooth. If, for example, glue or paint are allowed to make the surface bumpy this will impede the roller and cause an uneven layer of colour when printing. Always make sure trays are cleaned thoroughly and if possible keep some for printmaking only.

Printing ink

For most types of printmaking it is more successful to use printing ink rather than paint. Printing ink is thicker and stickier and will allow children to produce a clearer print. It can be bought from educational suppliers in tubs or large tubes. It is water soluble and will wash out of clothes. For some types of printmaking such as screen printing specialist ink is required.

Polystyrene tiles

Many primary schools use fine polystyrene tiles bought from educational suppliers or art catalogues. Common commercial names for this are pressprint, polyprint and quickprint. Although this material can be expensive it is very versatile and a safe and accessible alternative to lino for primary school children.

Found and collected materials

A great variety of found and collected materials can be used in printmaking. These include natural materials such as leaves, grasses, stems and pressed flowers and manmade items such as pieces of construction kit, wooden bricks, containers and items of packaging. In addition textured wallpaper, from DIY suppliers, fabric with a textured surface and any paper or card with a surface texture can be used in printmaking. You may find it useful to keep a collection of these materials to use.

Bought printmaking items

Educational catalogues and art suppliers now sell a range of items to use in printmaking. These include numbers, letters and shapes formed from sponge and pre-made stamps. These can be useful to use with children in exploring, developing and improving processes and techniques but can impede creativity if they are the only printmaking experience children encounter.

It is also important to bear in mind that the surface children print on – the colour and texture of the paper – will contribute to the overall effect of the work. Trying out prints on a variety of papers and other surfaces should be considered when planning.

Chapter 9 Resources used to make collage

Look for	Location	Notes / questions to follow up
Tools		
Scissors (left/right handed)		
Scissors (with pattern cutting blades)		
Larger, sharper scissors (for adult use)		
Pinking shears (for adult use)		

(ctd)

Look for	Location	Notes / questions to follow up
Craft knives (for later KS2 and adult use)		
Cutting mats/pads of newspaper to cut on		
Paper trimmer (for later KS2 and adult use)		
Glue spreaders		
Brushes to apply glue with		
Sticking/attaching		
PVA glue		
Wallpaper paste		
Glue sticks		
Double sided sticky tape		
Blu-tac		
Spraymount (for adult use)		
Laminator (for adult use)		
Materials		
Papers of different types		
Card of different types		
Magazines and catalogues		
Thread, string, wool		
Natural materials		
Pasta, rice, seeds		
Recycled/collected materials		
Papers created by children for use in collage – printed, marbled, etc.		
Surfaces to glue on – papers, cards, plastics, wood, etc.		
Buttons, sequins		
Labels/packets/wrapping		
Photos/text		

Guidance notes

Cutting tools

Most primary classrooms are equipped with appropriate scissors for cutting paper for both right- and left-handed children. A set of scissors that have blades designed to cut in various patterns add to the range of edges children can easily make – these will generally only cut paper. It may be necessary for adults to cut some materials for children so it will be useful to have good quality adult scissors available. In later Key Stage 2 children may use craft knives in DT and art and, if so, these and cutting mats can be used in both subjects. If not, or with younger children, an adult may use the craft knife where necessary. The paper trimmer is also a tool that adults will use in preparation but in some schools children in later Key Stage 2 might be taught to use. The use of these sharper tools should follow school health and safety policies. It should also be noted that when working with paper tearing can create unexpected edges that could be more interesting than cut edges.

Sticking and attaching

Typically PVA (white glue) will be available for all sorts of sticking in the primary classroom. When using PVA in art it has several qualities that can add to the outcome – PVA can be used as it comes out of the tub or diluted with water to make it easier to paint on or over surfaces. When it dries it will both clear and shiny and this can add to the finish of the collage both in terms of sealing small items into the surface and enhancing the overall appearance. Children often have access to glue sticks for routine sticking of paper and these may also be useful when making paper collages. Being able to put down and lift up and replace is a useful quality of this type of glue. Spraymount can also be useful for this but should be applied to surface in a ventilated area by an adult. Wallpaper paste can also be useful for some sorts of sticking, especially when covering large surfaces with paper or creating three-dimensional surfaces through papier mâché. Double-sided sticky tape can also be used effectively especially when the materials to be stuck on are unlikely to stay in the arrangement chosen – string, for example. Glue spreaders can be used to apply glue to smaller surfaces and where control is needed. Brushes of different sizes can also be used, perhaps to apply glue to large surfaces. Care must be taken to wash brushes thoroughly after they have been used to apply glue, or some brushes should be reserved for gluing only. As with cutting tools, health and safety policies should be followed when using glues with in school.

Materials to use

There are so many materials that can be used to make collage that compiling an exhaustive list is almost impossible. One of the advantages of making collage is the opportunity for using materials that are readily accessible in school or in the local environment. Children and their families can be involved in collecting the items and materials to be used. Many areas have access to scrap stores – organisations that collect unwanted materials of all kinds that can be used by playgroups, nurseries and schools. Usually an annual subscription and then a fee for each visit is required to use the facility. Your nearest scrapstore can be found with some research online. One of the challenges for this aspect of collage is storage – primary schools will vary in how this is approached and it is important to find out what is readily available and what you must plan in advance to collect for your unit of work: perhaps as early as the previous term or half term.

Chapter 10 Resources used to make art in three dimensions

Look for	Location	Notes / questions to follow up
Materials that can be manipulated and moulded		
Clay (natural)		
Air drying clay (manmade)		
Plasticine		
Salt dough (home-made)		
Fimo		
Play dough (bought or home-made)		
Sand (damp/wet)		
Materials that can be poured and used with moulds or casts		
Plaster of Paris		
Papier-mâché		
Linear materials		
Wire		
String, thread		
Withies		
Art straws/plastic straws		
Sticks, twigs		
Pipe cleaners		
Sheet materials		
Boxes, cards, papers of different types including newspaper, tissue paper, cartridge paper, sugar paper, magazines, etc.		
Paper lamination		
Plastic – bags, sheets, corrugated plastic, packaging		

Look for	Location	Notes / questions to follow up
Modroc/plaster bandage		
Tools and equipment for		
Cutting: scissors, craft knives, paper cutter, wire cutters (for use by older children and adults)		
Shaping: clay tools – wooden or wire, wooden roller and guides, items to press into a malleable surface; items to mould onto, garlic press		
Joining: tape, staples, glue, string and thread,		

Guidance notes

Malleable materials that can be manipulated and moulded

There a number of materials that can be squashed and shaped by hand or by using tools to make sculpture, ranging from home made (salt dough and various recipes for play dough) to bought (clay, fimo). Many of these could be used and reused as well as made into a finished outcome. Clay (a natural material that needs to be fired in a kiln) is different to air drying clay in that the latter has different tactile qualities. The latter is fibrous and does not require firing: to make this material hard 'hardeners' must be bought and applied.

Materials that can be poured and used with moulds or casts

Materials that can be pressed onto an existing mould (dish, plate, balloon, etc.) to hold their shape whilst under construction can be useful when making a shape that would be hard to create from nothing. Some malleable materials can also be used with casts.

Linear materials

Some materials are linear in nature: some in manageable lengths when bought or collected and some that require cutting to different lengths for use to make art work. Some of these, such as wire, can be shaped and will keep their shape, while others, such as withies, need to be held in place by tying or using tape.

Sheet materials

Flat, sheet materials can be draped and wrapped to transform objects or frameworks into three-dimensional sculptures. Modroc can be used when wet to wrap and cover frameworks or objects and will set so that the new form created can then be added to and decorated.

Tools and equipment for cutting, shaping and joining materials

These will vary depending which materials are being cut, shaped or joined. As with all other aspects of art having the appropriate tools and equipment available is important and will vary according to the age of the children and the particular unit of work.

Chapter 11 Resources used to make art from threads, fabrics and textiles

1. Making fabrics and textiles		
Look for	Location	Notes/questions to follow up
Materials to use:		
Wools		
Threads		
Strings		
Tools to use:		
Knitting needles		
Crochet hooks		
Frameworks / cards / looms to use for weaving		
Needles / bodkins (variety of)		

Guidance notes

Wool, threads, string

When planning to weave, knit or crochet your choice of thread will be guided by what is available, what can be found or collected and the teaching and learning experience itself. Investigating what is available through joining a local scrap store and appealing to parents and the local community can be a good idea, supplemented by buying some more special materials where required. Look out for interesting textures and colours as well as a variety of thicknesses and those made from both manmade and natural materials. Think also about found and recycled materials that can be used as thread such as ribbon, raffia, strips of plastic, etc.

Tools – knitting needles/crochet hooks

If teaching children to knit it is advisable to start them off with thick (4 mm) short, plastic needles as these are easier to manipulate.

Tools – needles/bodkins

Starting with flexible plastic needles with large holes through which to thread, or plastic bodkins can be supportive when children begin. Alternatively a piece of thick card with thread anchored to it and wrapped around can be useful to weave or thread in and out with.

Tools – weaving cards/frameworks/looms

Weaving can be structured by making or buying these. Making your own or helping children to make their own frameworks on which to weave can allow for more choice and flexibility of size and shape.

2. Surface decoration		
Look for	Location	Notes/questions to follow up
Dyes (cold water)		
Fabric paint		
Fabric crayons/pens		
Fabrics of various types and qualities		
Binca, plastic canvas		
Threads/wools/strings		
Decorative items to add – sequins, beads, buttons, feathers, etc.		
Tools		
Needles (different types)		
Scissors		
Embroidery hoops		

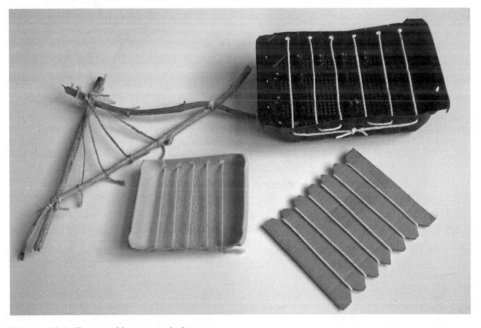

Figure A2.2 Types of homemade loom

Guidance notes

Dyes

Fabric can be dyed using Brusho (discussed in Chapter 6, Painting) and other cold water dyes.

Fabric crayons/pens/paint

Materials familiar from drawing and painting on paper can be bought as versions that can be used on fabric. Berol fabric medium can be used with Berol paints to allow them to be used on fabric more easily. Some of these can be fixed by ironing.

Textiles and fabrics

A variety that can be decorated and changed; the choices you make will be guided by the technique or process that you are teaching. Plain, light coloured cotton is perhaps easiest to draw, paint and print on whereas cloth with a more open weave or holes can be useful for sewing, especially with younger children. Collecting and using a very wide range of fabrics and textiles taking in consideration not only colour and pattern but also texture allows children to explore and use the sensory as well as visual qualities in their making.

Tools – needles

Starting with flexible plastic needles with large holes through which to thread can be supportive when children begin to join fabrics and sew materials together. Later using sharper, metal needles will be essential. Identifying the appropriate type of needle for the manipulative skills of the children is important.

Tools – scissors

Fabric can be very difficult to cut especially with the scissors children use. It may be more practical for children to mark out lines and shapes and allow an adult to cut with sharper scissors.

Tools – embroidery hoops

When stitching with older children using embroidery hoops to keep the fabric stretched can be helpful.

In addition to these tools and materials specific techniques such as batik, felt-making and screen printing might form part of this aspect of art. It is likely that the tools and materials to use in these activities would be kept together in sets for use in specific projects. Learning about any of these so that you can use them in teaching would be a next step and would enhance your subject knowledge.

Index